Praise for *The D Word*

"Kate Anthony's approach to the discussion of divorce is both compassionately informative and beautifully permission-giving. If you are considering what life might look like outside of your marriage, *The D Word* will help you make decisions with clarity and integrity. I will be relying on this book as a resource in my work for years to come."

—ALEXANDRA H. SOLOMON, PhD, licensed clinical psychologist, faculty at Northwestern University, bestselling author of *Love Every Day*, and host of the podcast *Reimagining Love*

"When it comes to making one of life's most difficult decisions, there is no one better to guide you toward absolute divorce clarity and understanding than Kate Anthony. Her powerful words combined with her killer insight, strategy, and wit, make this the ultimate guide to determining whether or not to leave your marriage—and more importantly, how to do it safely."

—MICHELLE DEMPSEY-MULTACK, host *Moms Moving On* podcast

"Read this book if the future seems uncertain and the present feels intolerable. Kate Anthony understands the factors that keep women in bad marriages and knows how to help women decide whether their marriages can be saved. Like a really smart best friend who has been there, she opens women's minds to their many options and helps readers build a life they love, whether they decide to say or go."

—ZAWN VILLINES, *Liberating Motherhood*

"One of the most heart-wrenching junctures for a woman is the end of her marriage. The questions and the unknowns that accompany such a huge life change can feel paralyzing. While this journey can feel isolating, you are not alone. Kate Anthony will hold your hand through the darkness and provide you with the answers you are longing for. This book will serve as a trusted companion to anyone considering divorce or in the process of a divorce."

—TINA SWITHIN, author of *Divorcing a Narcissist*, founder of One Mom's Battle and the High Conflict Divorce Coach Certification Program

"Kate was the trailblazer. Well before many recognized the imperative, Kate was educating and empowering her audiences on how being treated well in relationships should be a given, not the exception. This book is a guide for that trail, where Kate is out in front holding the torch."

—DR. CHRISTINE MARIE COCCHIOLA, DSW, LCSW, coercive control advocate, educator, researcher, and survivor, creator of The Protective Parenting Program

"The decision to stay in or leave a marriage is often accompanied by shame, fear, and self-doubt. In this compassionate and engaging book, Kate Anthony provides much needed guidance for the journey. Readers will not only discover they aren't alone, they will also gain practical and actionable tools to help clarify the foggy and confusing road of "do I stay or do I go."

—BRITT FRANK, LCSW, SEP, licensed psychotherapist and author of *The Science of Stuck*

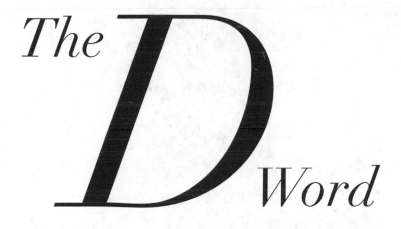

The D *Word*

MAKING THE ULTIMATE DECISION
ABOUT YOUR MARRIAGE

KATE ANTHONY

CITADEL PRESS
Kensington Publishing Corp.
www.kensingtonbooks.com

CITADEL PRESS BOOKS are published by

Kensington Publishing Corp.
119 West 40th Street
New York, NY 10018

All Kensington titles, imprints, and distributed lines are available at special quantity discounts for bulk purchases for sales promotions, premiums, fundraising, educational, or institutional use.

Special book excerpts or customized printings can also be created to fit specific needs. For details, write or phone the office of the Kensington sales manager: Kensington Publishing Corp., 119 West 40th Street, New York, NY 10018, attn: Sales Department; phone 1-800-221-2647.

ISBN: 978-0-8065-4235-5
First trade paperback printing: January 2024

ISBN: 978-0-8065-4236-2 (e-book)

10 9 8 7 6 5 4 3 2 1

Printed in the United States of America

For Emmett,
You are my reason for doing all that I do.
I love you the most, forever and ever.
xoxo Mom

And for women everywhere,
You, my love, deserve to be happy.
xoxo Kate

Contents

Introduction

WHEN I WAS IN THE DEPTHS OF despair struggling to decide whether or not to leave my marriage, I consulted a good friend. I wanted a burning bush; I wanted someone, or something, to tell me clearly, *It's time to go*, or *Stay, and you'll get through this*. Because at the end of the day we want to know if whatever struggle we're going through is actually worth it. We want a guarantee that if we stick it out, it will have been for something or conversely, that if we leave, what awaits on the other side will be better than... *this*. There's a distinct line in the sand, and we just want to know if we should cross it.

So, I asked my friend Mark. We were in group couples therapy together. (Yes, that's a thing; it's like couples therapy, but with other couples. In our group, we practiced something called Imago Therapy, in which we identified our emotional triggers, figured out what childhood wounds they stemmed from, and asked our partners to make specific changes to their behavior that would, theoretically, help us heal those wounds. It was all very controlled and ultimately it saved everyone's marriage—except mine.) I turned to Mark because he was in his second marriage and had been through a divorce before. He was one of the only people I knew, besides my parents, who'd gotten divorced, and since we were in group couples therapy together, he had a pretty intimate knowledge of my marriage.

Against our therapists' advice, our group had gotten pretty close outside of therapy, and every Saturday after our three-hour-long group session, we'd have a potluck at one of the couples' houses. At these dinners we'd abandon the intensity of the afternoon's work in favor of laughter, food, and wine. The husbands even started a band called, of course, The Wounded Children. Our kids (of those of us who had them) were all exactly a year apart (newborn, one, and two when we began), so they grew up together under the utterly bizarre circumstance of their parents bonding over marital strife and, ironically, childhood wounding. These potluck dinners were the perfect pressure-release after deep, hard work, and it allowed us to avoid going straight home and stewing in our own relation*shit* post-therapy.

As much fun as we had with our cohort, I always knew my husband and I were in deeper trouble than the others. While many couples would talk about how it made them feel when their spouse didn't change the toilet paper roll (which, by the way, was a much more layered dynamic than you may think), my husband and I would talk about how the way he criticized me dredged up my feelings of having been emotionally abandoned as a child. And this was still just scratching the surface of what was really going on.

In addition to this group form of couples therapy, my husband and I were in individual couples therapy with one of the therapists who ran our group. I was also in my own therapy with another therapist, as was my husband. And we were both in 12-Step programs. There was a lot of work happening—and a lot of money being spent—to try to save this marriage, but it only seemed to be getting worse. (It's important to acknowledge here that we were privileged enough to be able to afford such work. Many are not. In addition, there are many cultural barriers that might bar couples from being able to engage in this kind of work, all of which I will address in later chapters.)

I truly didn't know what to do. I was drowning in misery, but I believed our Imago therapists when they said that anything could be solved with Imago Therapy, so I kept trying. I believed one of our therapists, who was a children's specialist, when she told us it was better for children to be raised by two unhappy parents than for the parents to separate. I believed that every relationship is 100/100, not 50/50, so if I gave it 100 percent, I could eventually fix this.

But despite all this work, I was still miserable, and I really needed someone to tell me: *Should I stay or should I go?*

And so, at one of those dinners after therapy, I gathered up the courage to ask Mark. He was smart and kind and introspective and curious and so damn gentle. If anyone could tell me what to do, it would be him. I took him aside, looked at him with wild desperation and asked, "How do you know when it's time to leave?"

He looked at me firmly, but kindly, and said, "When you know, you'll know."

In case you're wondering, this was not the burning bush I was after. I'd been churning this question for two years and here's this guy telling me *You'll know when you know?* The whole point was that I *didn't know!*

I was pissed. But more than that, I was terrified. I'd done all of this work, and I *still* didn't know? WTF was wrong with me? I was moving through my life, marriage, motherhood, in a numb dream, vacantly staring into closets, sinks full of dishes, grocery store aisles... This was who I was now; I was a Stepford Wife: seemingly having it all together, but somehow not quite there. I made it all look good on the outside, but inside I was slowly dying. My self-esteem was crushed. I had everything I thought I ever wanted, and yet I was more miserable than I'd ever been in my life.

And it was during one of these vacant staring sessions a few months later, as I was standing in my closet, impassively staring at the jumble of clothes, that it hit me—like a frying pan upside my head—and suddenly I was more awake than I had been for years. Because suddenly I *knew*. I knew that I had to leave my marriage. And not just to save myself from mindlessly meandering through my days, getting lost in closets and grocery-store aisles. I had to do it for my son.

We're told over and over again that we have to stay for our kids, that children from *broken homes* (a term I loathe) do less well in school, are damaged, and grow up to have poor coping and relationship skills; they become drug addicts and alcoholics. So we try. And then we try harder. We bend ourselves into pretzels trying to make this square peg fit in that round hole come hell or high water, because if we don't our children will suffer, and we will have *failed*. At marriage, at parenting, at life.

But in that moment in my closet, I saw clearly that my partnership with my husband was inherently flawed. That we were, and always had been, mismatched. That what we were modeling to our son wasn't what I wanted him to grow up to have for himself. That while I was projecting the perfect life with the perfect house, the perfect child, and picture-perfect moments, what I really had was a marriage devoid of truth, love, mutual respect, and substance. And that the longer I remained in such a marriage, the more devoid of truth, self-love, self-respect, and substance I became. That while I had this vision of myself as being strong and powerful, I was actually locked in a deeply codependent relationship dynamic, and I knew that the only way my young, innocent child had any chance at creating a happy, healthy, lasting, loving relationship in the future was for my husband and I to end our marriage. *Now*.

In that moment, I knew that my husband and I brought out the worst in each other, and that staying in our marriage was keeping us from finding people we actually *liked*, with whom we could create meaningful, trusting bonds, and that if we could find that (outside of each other), our son would have a chance at finding that for himself down the line. And I knew that if we stayed together, he stood absolutely zero chance of that.

After a few more months of last-ditch-effort work, on Christmas Eve of 2008, I finally blurted out those dreaded words: *I want a divorce*. (Dear Reader, this is the absolute worst time to make this announcement; it makes for a really uncomfortable Christmas. If, by the end of this book, this is your decision as well, I'll have told you how to do this better than I did.)

I'd always thought that if I was just a better communicator, if I was just smarter, skinnier, taller, prettier, funnier, took more responsibility, lowered my voice, raised my boobs, shrunk my hips, did more crafts, cooked better, had more interesting hobbies, then I'd be able to make my marriage work. Turns out, some marriages are simply unworkable, and no amount of Stepford-izing myself or my marriage was going to get us to happily-ever-after.

Despite the fact that Mark's words, *When you know, you'll know*, eventually proved true for me, as time went on, I knew there had to be a better way for the millions of women who struggle with this question every day. This book is my antidote to *When you know, you'll know*. This book is a guide to your personal truth and clarity.

This book is for the reader who's in the depths of despair, going through the most painful transition of her life. She's paralyzed with fear and desperate for answers. This book is for the reader who is simply questioning her marriage and wondering if there's perhaps something better out there—or if this is all marriage really is.

- She wants to know if the grass really is greener on the other side.
- She wants to know how she ended up in a marriage that makes her this unhappy in the first place—and how to avoid doing so again.
- She wants to know that if she leaves, she's not going to screw up her kids and that she'll be ok in the end.

This book will answer all of these questions, and many more.

This book is primarily written for cisgender, heterosexual women married to cisgender, heterosexual men because those are the relationships that are most deeply impacted by the systemic structures that most affect relationships today. That being said, I have worked with a number of lesbian women over the years who resonate with my work and whose marriages also reflect these systemic biases. These women will also benefit from this book. And while I've mostly used ungendered language, there are sections in which my language is more gendered because the circumstances are also more clearly defined by gender. In addition, I talk mostly about marriage because that's the most common place these issues crop up, but women who are not married will also benefit from this book.

This book will lead you to a place of clarity, from which you can make a truly informed and empowered decision. But here's the thing, my love: I need you to be ready for that. In order for you to get the most out of this book, you need to be ready for answers.

For many of us, sitting in the in-between is preferable to getting to a place of clarity. In her book *Untamed* (Dial Press, 2020), Glennon Doyle calls this the choice between an "uncomfortable truth and a comfortable lie."

You know you can't continue on like this, but for many, the idea of finding out that they have to fully commit to their marriage, or fully commit to *leaving* their marriage means they no longer get to sit on a fence they've made their home. They no longer get to *not know*.

In her book, *Too Good to Leave, Too Bad to Stay* (Plum, 1997), Mira Kirshenbaum talks about how her mother sat on that fence for forty years, and how painful it was to watch her never choose happiness either way. I see this often with clients, and even some close friends. This book asks you to get off the fence and choose. But more than that, it gives you the tools to do so.

So, the first thing I want you to do is to ask yourself if you're truly ready for answers.

I've been helping women get these answers for over a decade. Thousands of women have gone through my programs and worked with me privately as a coach, and they have all gotten the answers they were seeking. Not always the answers they wanted—but always the answers they needed. Are you ready to find yours?

This book will challenge you. You will feel confronted, and even angry at some points. If you have the feeling of wanting to throw the book across the room, while also holding it close to your heart, I've hit a nerve and this book is absolutely for you.

You may have a lot of feelings that you don't understand as you navigate these pages, and you may wonder if they're "normal." In my years of working as a coach, running programs for women, and running an active and engaged Facebook community for thousands of women, I can't tell you how many times I've heard women ask, *Is this normal?* But I think what they're really asking is, *Is the way I'm processing and experiencing [x] valid?* and *Am I alone?* My response is always the same: *Yes. Your feelings are valid. Your experience is valid. You, my love, are valid, and you are not alone.*

And so, I say to you, whatever you experience while reading this book is completely valid, and there are thousands like you—and the most important thing you can do is to have *grace and compassion* for yourself as you move through it. Give yourself breaks. Pat yourself on the back for learning something new about yourself; please don't use it as a weapon to beat yourself up.

I want you to really prepare for how you will be with yourself when things get hard. Perhaps you'll promise yourself a walk to clear your head, or a call to your best friend or therapist. This is what real self-care looks like. It's not just mani-pedis and massages. It's honoring yourself when things are hard, and taking care of your emotional well-being, always. Similarly, how do you want to honor yourself when you have a breakthrough or set (and hold!) a new boundary? Maybe you'll buy yourself that cute skirt you've wanted for a while or treat yourself to some fro-yo with all the toppings! Do something fun that feels like a treat. You deserve it.

Fill out this form to make these promises to yourself:

I, _____, promise to honor myself and my process as I move through this book.

When things get hard I will: _____

_____

When I have a breakthrough, or find myself setting new boundaries, I will: _____

_____

Signed: _____ Date: _____

It's important to note that doing this work may unearth some hidden trauma, so you might want to have a *good* coach or therapist in your corner to help you process things that come up. A good therapist should have advanced training in Internal Family Systems (IFS), the work of John Gottman, Emotionally Focused Therapy (EFT), or some other modality that addresses your particular concerns. If you're unable to afford therapy, if there are no good or available therapists in your area, if you're not ready for therapy, if there are cultural or other barriers that make therapy unavailable, or if you just don't want to go to therapy, that's fine too. Just please be good to yourself throughout this time. (The section on Self-Care has some great tips.)

I strongly recommend that you have a journal on hand as you work through this book. There are a number of exercises for which you'll need one, and there may be several things that come up while you read that journaling may help you process.

Before we get to the meat of this book, I want to answer one of the most pressing questions, and probably the biggest elephant in any room in which contemplating divorce is circulating.

Should You Stay in Your Marriage for Your Kids?

From the day you became a mother, every decision in your life has been filtered through the lens of "what's best for my kids," and no decision has been put through that filter more than this one. You may have avoided looking more deeply at your marriage up until now because you've heard a million times that divorce screws up kids. And you've determined that if divorce screws up kids, then you'll just have to suffer. You'll do anything to protect them, so you should stay, no matter how bad it is for you. And my guess is that you didn't buy this book because things are great.

Let's take a moment to unravel this oft-stated myth about children and divorce and look at the science. In 2000, psychologist Judith Wallerstein wrote *The Unexpected Legacy of Divorce: A 25 Year Landmark Study* (Hyperion 2001). In it she and her colleagues presented detailed case studies suggesting that most children of divorce grow up to become adults with an array of social and psychological problems, including depression, relationship issues, and, often, drug and alcohol abuse. Needless to say, these findings terrified a lot of people into staying in unhappy marriages for the sake of their children. With this data, it made perfect sense to sacrifice personal happiness for the mental health and safety of our children. In fact, this book was what informed my couples therapist when she insisted that I stay in my unhappy marriage.

Later studies showed that the research Wallerstein and her colleagues did was not accurate, and her theories, though widely accepted and still quoted, have been debunked. Wallerstein had no control group, and she only interviewed sixty families from one county in California, many of whom were in disastrous marriages rife with domestic violence, economic insecurity, and other circumstances that would lead any child, whether their parents were divorced or not, to have lasting emotional issues.

In the years since Wallerstein's study came out, there have been other, more controlled, studies done that show the impact of divorce on kids in a different light. According to one study done in 2002 by E. Mavis Hetherington, a psychologist from the University of Virginia, and published in *Scientific American*, while many children are negatively impacted by divorce in the short-term, most of the negative effects diminish by the end of the second year, and only a small handful of children suffer longer-term. Paul R. Amato, a sociologist at Penn State, did comparative studies of children several years after divorce, comparing children of married parents with those who experienced divorce at various ages. This study appeared in the same 2002 *Scientific American* article and followed children into their teen years and assessed academic performance, emotional and behavior problems, delinquency, self-concept, and social relationships. The studies found very little difference on all measures between the two control groups, suggesting that children from intact homes do not fare better in the long run than those from divorced homes. In other words, your kids will be affected in the short-term, because of course they will, but, given the right support systems (like therapy and parents who put their children's needs first), they can—and will—ultimately get through it relatively unscathed.

In my own research, I've learned that there are two sets of kids who fare the worst in terms of mental health and ability to engage in healthy relationships as adults. The first are those whose parents remained in volatile, toxic, or high-conflict marriages, and the second are those who were dragged through bitter divorces in which they were used as pawns and put in the middle of a nasty fight. Two sets of children fare the best: children whose parents remain together in healthy marriages and those whose parents divorce amicably, putting their children at the center (not in the middle) of all their decisions. Both of these sets of kids tend to grow up to be healthy, well-adjusted adults. In other words, divorce itself isn't the culprit. Toxic relationships, whether in marriage or divorce, are the problem.

The truth is that almost all divorces could be cooperatively mediated if only the litigation system didn't prey upon our pain. Before going into mediation with my husband, I consulted a divorce attorney to better understand my legal rights, especially when it came to spousal and child support. Since mediators are neutral by definition and don't give legal advice, I needed to know what to even ask for once we got into mediation.

In many states in the US, two factors are considered when calculating child support: one is income differential, and the other is percentage of custody. Because of this, the first thing this attorney wanted me to do was to accuse my husband of being an unfit parent (which he in no way was) so that I could gain full custody of our son and therefore get more child support (which I never said I wanted). If I accused my husband of

being an unfit parent we'd surely end up in protracted litigation as he fought to defend himself. And then my attorney
would make a killing using my son as a pawn in this fabri-
cated fight.

I walked out of that attorney's office with a basic understanding of what I was legally entitled to, and a horrible taste
in my mouth about where this man wanted to take my divorce.
But more than anything, I knew that had I been slightly more
vulnerable, slightly more angry, and slightly more vindictive, I
could easily have been persuaded to put my son in the middle
of a nasty battle.

As I've been working in this field for the last ten years, I've
heard numerous stories like this. One attorney I work with recounted a story of being on a panel at a divorce conference
with a mediator and two litigators. The attorney asked one of
the litigators, "How do you know when to stop litigating?"

The litigator replied, "When the money runs out."

In other words, no matter how many possible solutions
may have presented themselves along the way, the litigator
would continue to litigate until they could no longer be paid.
Once the well ran dry, they'd find a solution— likely one that
had presented itself months (and thousands of dollars) earlier—and settle. But until then, the litigators would add fuel to
an already emotional fire, fanning the flames of anger and revenge, and putting innocent children squarely in the middle
of the divorce process—all for their own financial gain.

Famed celebrity divorce attorney Laura Wasser told a story
on my podcast of a case in which she and her opposing counsel had almost come to an agreement in court when suddenly
her opposing counsel brought up a totally unnecessary point
which put a stop to the case they were about to settle. When

Laura saw her opposing counsel in the hallway after court, she asked her what the hell happened. The opposing counsel replied, "I haven't even made my retainer yet!" And so, a nasty litigation raged on. And who suffered the most? The kids.

So, does divorce screw up kids? No. Being used as a pawn in an unnecessary fight, being used as a weapon to exact revenge, being told that one of their parents (one-half of them) is a piece of shit, or otherwise bad-mouthing someone they deeply love—*that* will have a devastating effect on your kids. Having an amicable split, in which personal responsibility is at the core, in which blame and shame are kept at bay, in which forgiveness and collaboration are the priority, all with the intent of putting your children at the center of every decision you make, will not screw up your kids. In fact, that will show them how to manage conflict and loss in healthy, mature ways, which is probably one of the most valuable lessons anyone can teach their children.

If, by the end of this book, you choose to leave your marriage you'll have enough information and insight to be able to do so in the most amicable and healthy way possible.

But what if you have a totally vindictive husband who's swearing up and down that he's going to make this as difficult for you as possible? What if you live with an emotional and psychological abuser who will never agree to mediate a divorce and who assures you they'll destroy you and take your kids in the process? Well then, I'd say you're in a volatile and toxic marriage rife with power and control issues and you probably need to leave—*for your kids*. (I'd also tell you to check the laws in your state because those threats usually hold no weight whatsoever and are simply used to scare you into submission. More on this later.)

It's commonly believed by victims of abuse that they need to stay in their volatile marriages in order to protect their kids from the toxicity of the other parent, and that's almost always false. Children who are raised in highly volatile households can suffer from PTSD and other emotional scars. Their imprinting around relationships can be permanently damaged, and they'll be more likely to continue the cycle of unhealthy relationships for another generation.

Some women worry that if they divorce, their abusive partner would have unsupervised custody of the children. They reason that it is better to stay in the relationship so that they can protect their kids from being alone with an abuser. However, in a 2018 interview I conducted with clinical psychologist Dr. Linda Bortell, who specializes in working with such children, she said that staying with an emotionally abusive narcissist so you can be there to run interference is not a healthy solution for kids. Dr. Bortell says that even if your kids have to be alone with the abuser half the week, they'll be completely *away* the other half, whereas they'll be with the abuser 100 percent of the time if you stay. If you stay, you're unintentionally cosigning the behavior, teaching your kids that this is okay; if you leave, you can create a loving, safe environment for them to grow up in, even if it's only 50 percent of the time, and they'll have *that* as a guidepost and a model for their futures. Studies have shown this to be enough to have a positive impact on children.

Fiona co-parents with a malignant narcissist. Her daughter is eight, and because she's created such a loving, stable, and sane home for her daughter at her house, the child is already able to articulate how different it is at Daddy's house. Because Fiona has created safety for her daughter, her daughter is able to see and verbalize when she feels unsafe. Her daughter can only see her dad's darkness in contrast to her mother's light. Had Fiona stayed in that highly volatile and abusive marriage, her daughter would never know loving kindness existed; she'd simply be swimming in darkness—and she'd grow up to recreate it in her adult relationships. Fiona put a stop to that by leaving her husband. She's supportive and validates her daughter's feelings without bad-mouthing her father (which, in his case, can be really difficult), and four years post-divorce, her daughter is thriving—as is Fiona, who recently remarried and is in a healthy, loving, kind, and fulfilling marriage with a man who adores her daughter. Fiona has worked super hard to keep her new home and relationship a positive example for her daughter, and it's made all the difference for both of them.

This is what I call *keeping your side of the street squeaky clean.* What does that mean for you?

It means that no matter what the other person does, you act with integrity. It means that no matter how hard someone is working to push your buttons, you work harder to keep your cool—and when you lose it (and you will), you clean it up, even if it means saying *I'm sorry* to someone you hate. It means that you act in such a way that when your kids grow up, they'll look back and see the truth, regardless of what the other parent is telling you (or them) now. It means that you act in line with your personal values in such a way that when you lay your head on your pillow at night, you don't regret your words or your actions. The more you can do this, the more your kids will understand and appreciate it as they grow up. No matter how messy the other side of the street is, if your kids always have a safe and soft place to land with you, it will have a lasting impact on the rest of their lives.

Now, are there situations when leaving your marriage might be dangerous for you and your kids? Yes, absolutely. If you or your children are in *any* physical danger, you must call your local domestic violence shelter immediately to seek help. Seventy-five percent of women who are murdered by their batterers are killed when they leave. This doesn't mean that you should stay, but it means you must seek professional help to get you and your children out safely. Call the National Domestic Violence Hotline at 1–800–799–7233 for more help. (More on the different types of abuse and how to get help in later chapters.)

Should you stay in your marriage for your kids? No. You should stay if your marriage is healthy and communicative and collaborative and loving and kind. But if it's toxic and abusive, staying will do them more harm than good.

But what if it's not toxic? What if you're just not happy?

Permission

When you think about leaving your marriage you may feel like you're doing something *wrong*. You may feel like reading this book is subversive. And in some ways, it is. First of all, you're probably doing it behind your partner's back, so there's bound to be some shame or guilt associated with this journey. But most of all, I believe that women looking deeply at their marriages and making strong and empowered choices for themselves *is* a subversive act. It is a radical act of rebellion for a woman to want to find happiness in her life, and to put her own happiness first.

Women spend most of their lives waiting for men to make choices for them. We wait for men to ask us on dates, to ask us to marry them, and so much more. The number of things we ask the men in our lives permission for is staggering, whether it's overt, covert, or simply unconscious.

As women, and especially as moms, we're conditioned to put everyone else's needs before our own. Traditionally, we are the nurturers and caretakers, and we've been putting our needs, ourselves, our hearts, and our spirits on the back burner for a long time. We wear this as a badge of honor, but we all secretly know that it's an oppressive weight around our necks that we can barely hold up for another second.

A client once told me that she'd learned to walk on eggshells around her husband because she was afraid of how he might react. She was afraid of what he'd think, do, or say. She wasn't in any danger, but she'd learned to tailor her habits so as not to upset him. She said she was afraid of rocking the boat. After some discussion, I said, "If you're afraid of rocking the boat, it's probably not your boat."

How many of us have been adrift in someone else's boat? How many of us have been tailoring our habits and activities so as not to upset someone else?

- Having sex we don't want to have, just to keep the peace?
- Losing or gaining weight for someone else's approval?
- Getting boob jobs we may not want?
- Modulating our voices so as not to offend?
- Cleaning up other people's messes?
- Keeping quiet so we don't crack the delicate eggshells we're walking on?

All so we don't rock someone else's boat.

We've given away pieces of ourselves, inch by inch, pound by pound. We've given someone else our power—be it our mothers, our fathers, our husbands, our bosses. Often, all of the above. And we stay in marriages that make us deeply unhappy—all so we don't rock someone else's boat.

But what if this was your boat?

What if, just for today, you grabbed the oars and rowed in the direction you wanted to go? What if, just for today, you owned every piece of wood, every ounce of water dripping off the oars, every rock and creak of the vessel in which you exist? Would you do anything differently?

If the answer is *yes*, then you may be in someone else's boat. And the truth, my love, is that you are allowed to build your own boat. Your happiness, your future, your fulfillment as a woman, as a human, as a mother depends upon it.

Interestingly, when my client learned to build and navigate her own boat, she was actually able to save her marriage. Building your own boat doesn't always mean ending your marriage. It could actually be the key to saving it. By creating your own *Self*, apart from your marriage, by cultivating your own passions, hobbies, and identity, you could heal many of the rifts that now present themselves. I'll show you how in Chapter One.

And here's something else I need you to know: *You are allowed to change.*

You are allowed to change the rules of the game, no matter how long you've been playing it.

You are allowed to ask your partner to help you change the game you're playing if it no longer works for you. Part of the human condition is growth and change, and just as you'd want that for your kids, you get to have it for yourself. The real question is whether or not you have a partner who's open enough to support and join you in that growth and not feel threatened by it.

In a healthy marriage, a partner will be exuberant in their response to your desire to change and grow because they, too, want you to be happy.

If you still feel scared to give yourself permission to do this work, to explore your own happiness, to row your own boat, then let me grant it to you. You, my love, deserve to be happy. As radical a concept as that may feel, it is entirely true.

Now let's go find out what that happiness is.

CHAPTER 1

Is It Them or Is It Me?

Answering the Eternal Question

W HAT, REALLY, IS HAPPINESS?

Philosophers, theologians, and laypeople alike have been trying to answer this question for millennia, and there are as many answers as there are people asking the question.

I believe happiness is made up of three main components:

1. Having positive emotional experiences, such as falling in love, looking at your sleeping baby, laughing yourself silly with your best friend, or taking a walk in nature and being present to the sounds, smells, and sights.

2. Having a deep sense of meaning and purpose, such as work that makes a difference to others, volunteer-

ing and being of service, a commitment to social justice, living in alignment with your values, or a
connection with a higher power.
3. Having deep self-knowledge. In order to be happy,
we must have solid self-esteem. The primary ingre-
dient of self-esteem is self-knowledge.

Because we live in a material world, many of us believe that
happiness is something that happens *to* us, or comes from outside of ourselves. If we get the job we want, make the salary
we've worked so hard for, lose five, ten, or fifty pounds, get the
ring, the house, the car, the husband, and the baby, then surely
we'll be happy. We compare our insides to other people's out-
sides. We scroll through Instagram and see what other people
have and use that as a measure for who we *are*. We all know, in-
tellectually, that happiness is an inside job, yet we continue to
seek it outside of ourselves because it seems easier, and that's
what our society tells us to do. In fact, the entire multibillion-
dollar advertising industry depends upon us buying things
they tell us will make us happy.

There are, of course, things outside of ourselves that can bring
us happiness, but these are mostly social structures—nearly all
of which, unfortunately, are missing in the United States. According to *The World Happiness Report* put out annually by the
United Nations, in 2022 the happiest nations in the world were
Finland, Denmark, Norway, Sweden, and Iceland, all of which
have social safety nets built into their economies, low rates of
corruption, and a deep sense of community in which people
take care of one another—all noticeably absent in the US.

Social and financial stability are key to happiness, but they
are not *the keys* to happiness. In other words, it's almost impos-

sible to be happy when you have bills you can't pay piling up and an eviction notice on your fridge. But having economic security doesn't guarantee happiness. I've been so broke I couldn't pay my bills, and I've been wealthy and stable with a nice house and a luxury car. I was also raised in extreme economic instability, and I can tell you with absolute certainty that having financial security is far less stressful. But was I *happy* when I had money? No. I was in a miserable marriage and had no sense of self. I had very few positive emotional experiences—in fact, most of my life was filled with negative ones—and I certainly had no sense of meaning or purpose in my life outside of being a wife and mother, which wasn't enough for me, personally.

There are two things I often hear from clients regarding their personal happiness. One is that everything else in their life is great; it's their relationship that's making them miserable. The other is that their partner tells them that they're a miserable person and that's why they're unhappy in their marriage. It's entirely possible that you're reading this book exactly because of this conundrum: are you miserable because of your marriage, or are you just a miserable person? *Is it you or is it them?* But if your partner is telling you that you are miserable, placing the blame for all your relationship problems on your shoulders, or disparaging you in any other way, you might be miserable because you're in an emotionally abusive relationship and you are being *gaslit*—a form of psychological manipulation commonly used by abusers. And just as one can't experience true happiness with the stress and pressure of being socially and financially marginalized, one also cannot experience true happiness while being abused. If you have any sense that you may be being abused, please be sure to read Chapter Five, "Am I Being Abused?"

However, asking about the source of your unhappiness is an important question, and this book will help you uncover the answer. We're going to be looking at your levels of happiness in different areas of your life, as well as uncovering *who you are* in some rich and complex ways. After all, how can you know if you should stay in or leave your marriage if you're not deeply connected to your own sense of being, your sense of Self?

Who Am I?

So often when we're trying to make this life-altering and diffi-cult decision, the focus naturally goes onto the other person. *What are they doing to hurt me? Are they really that bad? Are they a narcissist? Are they abusive?* We take a magnifying glass to the other person, trying to dissect if what they're doing/who they are rises to a level at which separation or divorce is *acceptable—* otherwise we'll be making an enormous mistake.

And while those are important questions, which I'll discuss later in this book, the *first* question we should be asking is, *How does this relationship make me feel?* which, on the surface of it, seems a simple enough question. The trouble we run into is that so many of us who have been unhappy in our marriages for any length of time *don't know* how we feel (which is why I was asking Mark for a clear answer) or we feel more than one thing at the same time. (*I love him! I'm so unhappy!* Or *I hate him! I don't want to lose my family!*) or, as I've said, we know how we feel, but we don't know *why (Is it them or is it me?).*

It's because of this that the very first thing I do with my clients is help them shift their focus back onto themselves. *What do* you *want? What would make* you *happy? How does this relationship make* you *feel? Ignoring all societal expectations, ignoring the expectations of others in your family, first and foremost, what do* you *want?*

At its very essence, I'm asking my clients to connect with Self. *Self* is distinct from self in that it is the most authentic and true part of us. While self is made up of our identity and who we want people to believe we are, Self is who we actually are, deep inside. Self is that part of us that will often break through the self and yearn for something... more. In *Untamed*, Glennon Doyle tells the story of Tabitha the cheetah who, despite having lived her entire life in captivity, looks longingly into the distance as if she knows she's meant to be out there running free. Every fiber of her being yearns for the open plains, even though she's never actually seen them. That story is, in essence, about Self.

Somewhere along the way most of us lose that connection to Self, learning to ignore the yearning voice from within. We're raised in families that ask us to play a role that we don't feel comfortable in, but, afraid to rock the delicate family boat, we comply. Often, we get the message early on that our parents' love is deeply tied to playing particular roles. Perhaps it's playing the Good Girl, getting perfect grades, or excelling in sports—even if we don't like them. Societal expectations of women play a part in this as well. When we express our feelings, we're called *emotional*, or worse, *hysterical*. There's a narrow lane in which women must operate in order to be accepted, so we adapt to meet those expectations, suppressing parts of ourselves that don't conform.

Every time we suppress our authentic Self and put on another layer of self, or outward-facing identity, the stronger that identity becomes, and the weaker and more hidden our

Self becomes. When we experience trauma, especially complex trauma, in which trauma occurs over a long period of time (such as in cases of child neglect or abuse), we become disconnected from Self as an act of preservation. If I'm being starved, I disconnect from my feelings of hunger so that I don't feel the pain of starvation. If I'm being emotionally abused or neglected, I don't even know my Self exists, because the very people who were meant to help me develop it were absent. But, as with Tabitha, there is always that part of us that *knows*, which is why the very first step in this journey must be to reestablish a connection with Self.

We start with intuition.

Women's Intuition

Scientific research recently proved what many of us already know: Women have more finely tuned intuition than men. We have a better ability to decode and empathize with nonverbal cues such as facial expression or body language; we're better able to correctly identify emotions from photographs of only eyes; and, when comparing MRI scans, women's brains tend to have more neural connections, making us more efficient and skilled at reading social cues. (Men are better at logic and problem-solving.)

In many ways, this is an evolutionary necessity that the propagation of the species depends upon. Since infants are unable to use words to tell us what they need, much of their survival depends upon mothers reading their babies' nonverbal cues (or screams) to assess what's needed in any given moment.

There are also cultural aspects that govern our ability to read nonverbal cues, such as the historical expectation that women be seen and not heard, which forced us to become much more observant and sensitive to our surroundings.

Women's powerful sense of intuition has been seen as a threat for centuries, so much so that entire systems have been created to try to distract from (or discredit) our inner sense of knowing. Powerful, intuitive women were cast as witches and burned at the stake in Salem in 1692. The sixty-billion-dollar diet-industrial complex is based on making sure women don't maintain connection with their own bodies, telling us to ignore our own inner knowing of what our bodies need in favor of fad diets, shakes, mega-supplements, and more. This disruption causes many of us to feel cut off from our emotions and our bodies, disconnected from our environments, and doubtful of our own experiences. And that, of course, is the point. Women's inability to connect with ourselves keeps us compliant, removing our source of free will. In essence, it removes our ability to *choose*. This manifests in many ways, from laws governing women's bodies to our confusion about ending our marriages.

When I work with my clients, the very first thing I have them do is a guided visualization to help ground them in their intuition. I call this the Inner Guide Visualization and you can find a link to it on my website (kateanthony.com/book-resources). Inner Guide work is the foundation of all my client work because whenever women get stuck or jumbled in their thoughts or say they don't know what to do, I simply ask, "What does your Inner Guide want you to know about this?" and, because they've spent months honing this connection, they almost always have instant clarity.

Now, it's not always as simple as this, but once you've met and connected deeply with your Inner Guide it becomes relatively easy to reconnect with her again and again. And the more you do so, the stronger and more powerful your connection to her will be, and, in time, to your Self (because ultimately, she is you).

This is basic neuroscience. When we repeat an action over and over again, we end up creating new neural pathways in the brain. These neural pathways become habits. I like to think of neural pathways like ropes. If you lay one piece of fiber from point A to point B you've successfully connected the two points, but the connection may not be very strong. But if you continue to lay fiber upon fiber from point A to point B over and over again, eventually you'll have a really strong rope. This is why it takes between twenty-one and thirty days to create a new habit. If you do something once and never again, it's an action. But if you do it over and over and over again, eventually your brain simply works on autopilot, eliminating the effort of conscious choice from the equation, and follows the established neural pathway. That's a habit.

It's been said that for every negative thought or experience we have, the brain requires at least three positive thoughts or experiences to override it. Which means we need a connection with our Inner Guide that's at least three times stronger than the one we have with our myriad inner critics, and we need to establish that connection repeatedly in order for it to become automatic. Once you've met your Inner Guide, it's crucial for you to keep up that relationship with her so her voice doesn't get drowned out by your Inner Critic. I recommend you do at least one of the following exercises before moving on to the next section.

Exercises for Connecting with Your Inner Guide

Do the Inner Guide Visualization on my website at kateanthony.com/book-resources. If you don't have access to the internet right now, or if you're not a visualization person, here are some other exercises for you:

OPTION ONE:

1. Take out your journal and write down a question you want answered. It could be as simple as, *What do I need to know?* If you want to go deeper, ask a more complex question, like, *What do I need to know about my marriage?* Or, *Am I making a mistake?*

2. Now close your eyes and take three, deep, grounding breaths. Take more if it takes you longer to get grounded. Grounding should feel like you are present with yourself. You may notice outside noises and distractions, but you aren't pulled away by them. You should feel calm and centered. Breathe in and out, noticing your surroundings. Hear the birds chirping, or your air conditioner cranking. Simply breathe and be in this moment.

3. When you feel completely relaxed and grounded, ask your question, and then simply listen.

4. Notice the first voice you hear. Not the one that follows that negates everything the first voice said. The *first* one. Write down what it says to you.

5. (Optional) If you hear a second voice that conflicts with the first, write a conversation between the two

of them. This second is your Inner Critic. This conversation could read something like this:

> **YOU:** What do I need to know?
>
> **INNER GUIDE:** You're going to be just fine. Stay the course.
>
> **CRITIC:** Are you though? You haven't worked in six years, you have no money, how are you going to be fine?
>
> **INNER GUIDE:** That's right. There are a lot of roadblocks ahead. Fortunately, no decisions need to be made today. This is all exploration. We have work to do, for sure, but in the end, it will all be okay.

Continue to allow the critic to voice all its concerns. Thank it for its input. Continue to allow the Inner Guide to handle the conversation. (More on managing your Inner Critic in the next section.)

OPTION TWO:

1. Take out your journal and write your question, as above.
2. Freeform write what comes to your head and hand. Allow for a stream of consciousness. Write for ten to fifteen minutes, without taking your pen from the page, without thinking; just write.

OPTION THREE:

1. As you move through your day, notice your gut responses to things.

2. Follow through on your impulses. If you have an instinct to change seats on the subway or bus, do it. If you feel that someone isn't being truthful, ask them. If you get a good feeling about someone at the grocery store, smile and say, "Hi!"
3. Write down and notice any feelings you have about this. Was it hard? Was it fun? Were you right? Journal about this experience.

Your Inner Critic

You may have noticed that your Inner Guide was your ultimate champion. She was probably really loving and soothing, and told you things like, *Just keep going,* or *Be gentle to yourself.* And for a moment, you may have felt a calm come over you, a sense of serenity, clarity, and peace.

And then you may have noticed another voice ~~creep~~ barge in that maybe wasn't so nice. You may have noticed that as soon as you started to feel slightly empowered by your Inner Guide, another voice (or ten) cropped up to disrupt your peace.

If, right about now, you're saying, *What voice is she talking about? I don't have a voice like that. This is dumb,* it's *that* voice. This is the voice that whispers in your ear that you're a shitty mom, that you're selfish for even contemplating getting divorced, that you're not worthy of love . . . you know, *that* voice. That, my love, is your Inner Critic, and usually, as soon as you make a plan toward greater growth or change in your life (such as getting to know your Inner Guide, whose deepest desire is to see you expand and grow), the Inner Critic will crop up with all sorts of reasons that your plan won't work. Maybe it tells you that it's foolish, too risky, or unwise. It's possible that your Inner Critic is telling you that this book is dumb. (I'm not offended.)

You may start to feel like a crazy person with a committee arguing back and forth in your head, like you have a devil on one shoulder and an angel on the other. But you may also start to feel like you have no idea which is the devil and which is the angel. The voices may start to get confused and blurry and all you want to do is crawl under a blanket and be done with all of this.

Congrats. Your Inner Critic just won.

Now, you may be one of those people who swears they don't hear this voice in their head, who is 100 percent sure they don't really have an Inner Critic. Well, unless you're a verified unicorn, I'm sorry to say, you do. Sometimes our Inner Critics can be like a tape that's been running in the background for years, but because it's always running, we don't consciously notice it.

In case you don't hear specific voices in your head, here are some classic signs that your Inner Critic is alive and well:

- A feeling that things are black or white, good or bad
- You feel confused or cloudy, like you have brain-fog
- You want to run and hide
- You have a negative self-image
- You believe other people's negative assessments of you
- Things feel unnecessarily complicated
- You've been circling the same problem over and over and over and over...

If you relate to any of this, you, my love, have an Inner Critic, just like the rest of us. (Sorry to say, you're not a unicorn after all.)

The job of the Inner Critic is to maintain the status quo, so as soon as you begin any kind of change, your Inner Critic will get super loud—and if it's not loud, it'll be powerful. Reading this book is likely giving your Inner Critic a bit of a panic attack. Your Inner Critic does not want you to change. Period.

But why? Why would we have a part of us that doesn't want us to grow? Oddly, our Inner Critics are usually put in place to protect us. If you look deeply at your Inner Critic, you might start to notice a small piece of truth in what it's saying. We call that the 2 percent truth. For example, let's take this question you're wrestling with right now: leaving your marriage. Your Inner Guide might be championing you along like crazy, telling you you're worthy of happiness, that something better is out there for you, that your kids deserve to have healthy relationship models, all of which is completely true. But your Inner Critic suddenly kicks up and says things like, *You're selfish! How will you support yourself and your kids on your salary? I mean, is it really that bad? He's a good provider!! You're going to be alone forever! Maybe he's right and you are just a miserable person!* And while much of that may not be remotely true, if you accept that maybe 2 percent of it *might* be true, then what information might be useful?

Obviously, there are things to consider when taking a giant leap like leaving your marriage—and it's certainly not something to go into blindly. It could be that your Inner Critic wants to be sure you've considered all the angles. *Will* you be able to support yourself? *Have* you done enough work on yourself to figure out what's yours and what's theirs? Think of your Inner

Critic as a scared part of yourself with *really* bad communication skills that's *really* afraid of change and that might also have some valid points to consider.

When you look at it this way, you can see that the Inner Critic is just trying to protect you. It's going to keep on chattering until it gets your attention. Often, just acknowledging it, turning toward it, saying, "I hear you," can be enough to tame the beast. Once you've set the drama aside, heard what your Inner Critic has to say, and considered the 2 percent truth it might be bringing to the table, you might be able to have a conversation with your Inner Critic thanking it for its time and care, and assuring it that you've got this handled, or that you will take into account these important details it's bringing to the surface

Now, not all critics are there just to protect you. If you've been abused in your marriage, in your childhood, or in both, you've likely been *programmed* with some pretty critical voices. If you feel that you can never do anything right because that's the message you've been given (overtly or covertly), then you will likely have an Inner Critic that's really strong in this regard. In this case, your Inner Guide is your best asset, and strengthening your connection to her will be all the more important—along with trauma therapy, such as Eye Movement Desensitization and Reprocessing (EMDR), Internal Family Systems (IFS), or Cognitive Behavioral Therapy (CBT).

Identifying where you've heard this voice before is also very helpful in separating the Inner Critic from yourself. When you realize that the voice you hear echoes your mother/father/husband, and that those people have abused or mistreated you, it will be easier for you to discard its messaging and return to the loving voice of your Inner Guide.

This will be ongoing work. You may be able to sit down and identify your Inner Critic(s) in one sitting, or you may need to wait for a Critic to present itself in order to begin to work with it. However it works for you isn't wrong, no matter what your Critic is telling you right now. And remember, those suckers can be crafty, so they're going to come up with a whole lot of reasons why you shouldn't do the work to uncover them. When that happens, take a deep, cleansing breath, turn to your Inner Guide, and ask her to lead you to the truth.

Before you get too excited, let me disavow you of any notion that you can ever get rid of your Inner Critic. Your Inner Critic will always be with you. However, you can *manage* your Inner Critic, and sometimes doing so can even be fun!

Exercises for Working with your Inner Critic

Here are five ways to manage your Inner Critic (based on the CoActive Training Institute's coach training certification program):

1. **Listen to it.** Our Inner Critic can be like an audiotape constantly playing in the background; after a while we don't even notice that it's there. It's kind of like an air conditioner that's been humming all night that you only notice when it turns off. The best way to manage the Inner Critic voice is to actually turn toward it and hear every last terrifying word. Only when we know our enemy can we combat it. So, get familiar with it. Until you're able to hear it—all of it—you won't know how to work with it.

2. Amplify it: What's the meanest version of what the voices are saying to you? What's the absolute worst? Is it saying, *You're not good enough/smart enough/thin enough/funny enough,* or is it really saying, *You're an unlovable piece of shit?* Amplification can sometimes allow us to see just how ridiculous our Inner Critic is, and this can help to diminish its hold on us. Again, we can't combat it until we really know it, so even leaning in to the nastiest version of your Inner Critic can give us helpful insight.

3. Get curious about it: What might your Inner Critic be trying to protect you from? What 2 percent truth might be shrouded in its nastiness? Might it be trying to give you a shot of reality that you might want (or need) to consider?

4. Personify it: Give your Inner Critic a shape and form. It might be human, and it might take the shape and form of someone you actually know (often a parent). Or it might be completely abstract. Former clients of mine have described their Inner Critics as cartoon characters, a big fluffy (and ultimately not very scary) monster, and an actual giant piece of shit. Giving your Inner Critic a shape and form allows you to converse with it, or see it for what it really is, thus diminishing its power. When we get to know our Inner Critics, we're better able to say, "Hey, thanks for sharing. I get you're trying to help me out here, but how about you hang out in the corner and play with this ball of yarn while I take this super-important meeting, and we'll reconvene when I get done."

5. Overpower it: Just as present in each of us as our Inner Critic is our Inner Guide. When you feel the Inner Critic getting loud, take some deep, cleansing, grounding breaths, and ask for your Inner Guide to step in and guide you through the darkness. Ask her to do combat with your Inner Critic. Sit back and relax and know that at the end of the day, deep inside yourself, you really do know what's true and what's a big bunch of lies your Inner Critic wants you to believe.

See if you can start to hear some of the Negative Nellies that may have taken up residence in your head. Answer these questions for each Inner Critic you can identify, using your journal. Repeat as often as necessary:

- What is this Inner Critic saying to you?
- What does it sound like/look like/feel like (for example, it sounds nurturing, but it's really mean; it's a hovering blob of green slime; it feels cold and sticky)?
- Where might you have heard this voice before? (Mom? Spouse? Teacher? Childhood friend?)
- If there was a grain of truth to be found in the message from your Inner Critic, what would it be?

CHAPTER 2

I Don't Even Know Who I Am Anymore

Connecting with Self Through Values,
Boundaries, and the Art of Self-Care

I<small>N ORDER TO MAKE A TRULY</small> well-informed decision about whether to stay or go, we need to have a deeply rooted sense of Self, and be operating from a healthy, stable place. We began that work in Chapter One. There are additional building blocks to creating this sense of Self, which this chapter walks you through in depth. We start with values.

Values are our internal barometer that tell us when we're on the right path, and when we're not. When we live a life aligned with our values, we feel that we have that *purpose* I talked about as being one of the key ingredients of happiness. When we're living in alignment with our values, we feel confident and secure. And when we are misaligned with our personal values, we often experience stagnation, depression, anxiety, and sometimes even physical aches and pains. When we honor our values on a regular and consistent basis, life is good and fulfilling. Important decisions are easier to make (such as the one you're facing now). It's important to figure out your core values when trying to decide whether to stay in or leave your marriage because values are an essential component of Self, but also because misaligned values can point to two people who probably shouldn't be together.

I had a client, Fran, who uncovered in our work together that she had a strong value around personal development and growth. I guess this was obvious; after all, she was working with a coach. But she discovered it was more core to her essence than she'd realized until that moment. However, she also realized that she was married to a man who didn't believe in therapy or any kind of personal development work. Whenever she brought a marital issue to his attention, his response was, "You knew who I was when you married me. I haven't changed in twenty years!"

Besides the fact that that's just not a way to be in partnership with another human being, their very basic core values didn't align. If you take the judgment out of it and simply look at the facts, you have one person who values growth and change and another who values staying the same. It's hard to make a marriage work between two people that misaligned.

Another client, Sarah, lived in the Deep South. When she came to me, she told me that one of her biggest issues with her husband was the fact that he did almost zero work in the house and left all care for their children to her. Sarah was the breadwinner in her marriage, and her husband played golf almost every afternoon while he was supposedly building a business. Sarah was exhausted and resentful, understandably so. As we embarked on our work together, Sarah discovered that she had a very strong value around social justice and equality, and she realized her husband was a misogynist, a homophobe, and a racist. He would often make really uncomfortable racist and homophobic jokes at her work parties, which made Sarah want to sink into a hole. Part of his refusal to help in the house or with the children was based on outdated, misogynistic ideas of a woman's *place* in the home, and likely his resentment that she was more successful than he was.

Again, taking the judgment out of it, Sarah and her husband's values were misaligned. It didn't matter if he ever did the dishes or made the kids' lunch. She couldn't live with someone whose values were so diametrically opposed to her own, nor could she continue to raise her children in such an environment. While Sarah couldn't control what her husband did in his household in the future, she could create an inclusive environment in her new home, giving her children an alternate perspective from which they could choose later in their lives.

The process of clarifying values can be hard. People often intellectualize the process or choose values off a list that they think other people will approve of, or will make them look good. It's far more interesting and accurate, however, to look into your life and uncover the values that are already present.

For example, my ex-husband obsesses over fairness. When I met him, he was a stickler for splitting bills evenly, literally nickel-and-diming his good friends (dude tried to go Dutch on our first date). His fairness is universal though, not just self-serving. Because of the crash of the housing market, when we divorced in 2009 our house was $250,000 under water. He was keeping the house, and the accountant who was helping us with the financial aspect of our divorce explained that I'd have to give him $125,000 for the pleasure of leaving my house (the money to be deducted from my equity in his pension and other assets). Because of his fairness gene, my ex said, "That makes no sense. The house will recoup its value in time. Let's just take the house off the top and split everything else." He kept the house and I got to keep my full equity in his pension. My ex-husband *values* justice and fairness. It's a core part of who he is—so much so that we call him "Justice Man."

As you work with your values, don't worry if you can't find one word that you feel expresses a value. An experience, an essence, or a metaphor might be more meaningful. I have a client who used to go roller-skating in blue sparkly leggings, and we identified her need for adventurous fun as her "Blue Sparkly Leggings" value. I have a value around getting really emotionally messy and dirty, walking through fire and coming out clean on the other side. I call this my "Mud-Bath" value.

Many of my clients have said that working with values was a game-changer in understanding what felt so *off* in their marriages, or in helping them reconnect (for example, recognizing that they were aligned at their cores, but perhaps had some basic communication issues to unpack). I hope you find the same.

Exercises for Uncovering Your Personal Values

These exercises are based on the CoActive Training Institute's coach training certification program. Since values show up over time in our lives, it's unlikely that you'll be able to capture them all in one sitting. It may take several months to come up with a somewhat complete list of values, but this will give you a good starting point, and may even provide some clarity right off the bat.

- **Brainstorm:** Take a few minutes to brainstorm a list of values you feel you stand for in your life. If you can't come up with any, fear not, there is help in the following steps to guide you.
- **Find your peak experience:** Think of a time when you felt truly, deeply at peace. Perhaps it was a fleeting moment in time, perhaps it lasted a week, or an entire summer. No matter its duration, this is your moment. It's the first one that popped into your head; don't second-guess it. In this moment, there was a sense of effortlessness, harmony, and congruence with the world around you. You may not have had all the things you wish you had, but what you had was a deep sense of aliveness. You were living your life *on purpose*. Once you have found your moment in time, close your eyes and breathe into the memory of the experience. Ask yourself these questions and write out your answers in your journal:
  - What was the feeling of that experience?
  - How did you feel in your body? Your mind? Your heart?
  - How do you feel now, just thinking about it?
  - What specifically were you doing that made you feel so alive? (For example, were you doing a job you loved? Were you meditating every day? Were you experiencing a certain level of support from someone in your life?)

- Knowing that you owned this experience, that it is yours, and therefore portable to this time and place, what would you import to the here and now? What elements can you put into action today?
- What values can you see were present in your life during this moment in time?
- **When we talk about values, most people tend to go for the obvious ones like integrity, honesty, etc., which is a great starting point.** But what do those words mean to you specifically? Write down the first word, then follow it with some other words that might connect more deeply to you. Don't be afraid to use random words that may mean nothing to someone else, but everything to you.
- **Think about a time you were most upset, angry, or frustrated:** What were the feelings associated with that experience? Often this points to a value that's being stepped on, or suppressed. For example, if a particular experience left you feeling trapped, backed into a corner, or held hostage, you might have a value around freedom and choice.
- **Beyond the physical requirements of food, shelter, and community, what do you need in your life in order to be fulfilled?** Do you need a form of creative self-expression? Do you need adventure and excitement in your life? Do you need partnership and collaboration? Do you need to be surrounded by nature? What are the values you absolutely must honor—or part of you dies? It may be that that you have trouble connecting with this because you feel this part

of you has already died. Fear not! Skip this for now and come back to it as you feel the tendrils of your inner Self begin to stir.

- **What are you obsessive about?** What is it that other people often say about you, or you often say about yourself? What do people tease you about that drives them crazy? Perhaps: *You are so controlling! All you think about is your students. You want all the attention.* These statements might point toward a value of personal power/leadership, of learning/growth, and of recognition/acknowledgment. These are values that have mutated into obsessions. Don't worry about the mutation for now; just write down the specific value that they point toward (sometimes just understanding that these obsessions are values-driven can ease their obsessive qualities).

Remember, this is an ongoing exploration, so keep this work handy and refer to these lists when you feel stuck, out of whack, or need to make a big decision in your life.

Boundaries

In her book *Facing Codependence* (Harper & Row, 2003), Pia Mellody describes boundaries as "invisible and symbolic *force fields* that have three purposes: (1) to keep people from coming into our space and abusing us, (2) to keep us from going into the space of others and abusing them, and (3) to give each of us a way to embody our sense of *who we are.*"

Mellody further describes boundaries as having two distinct parts: external, which protects physical and sexual boundaries, and internal, which protects thinking, feeling, and behavior. These internal and external boundaries apply both to how we protect ourselves, and how we protect others. For example, having clear external boundaries doesn't just protect us from the unwanted touch of others, but also prevents us from touching others inappropriately or not respecting their personal space.

Internal boundaries can be the most complicated to grasp because in essence they're asserting that the way you think, feel, and behave are completely separate from the thinking, feeling, and behavior of others. This puts the kibosh on the idea that someone else can *make you feel* a certain way, or that you can, in turn, make someone else feel or act the way you want them to. This doesn't mean that other people's behavior won't hurt us or have any impact on us whatsoever; it just means that we are responsible for how we allow their behavior to make us think, feel, or behave.

For example, if your husband cheats on you, of course it will hurt, and you're entitled to all the feelings about it. But you still have control over how you allow his actions to impact the way you feel or think about yourself (or him) and behave. You can choose to feel that you're an unworthy, unlovable, hideous oaf, or you can choose to be very clear that his behavior has absolutely nothing to do with you whatsoever. He cheats because he's a cheater, not because there's something deficient in you. This puts a clear boundary between his actions and the way you think and feel about yourself, and will cause you to behave appropriately. Perhaps you might call in a therapist who specializes in healing from infidelity, or, if he's unwilling to take responsibility, you may choose to leave. But if you have damaged internal boundaries, you may instead go on a severe, restrictive weight-loss program, take up pole-dancing, or some other activity that you believe will make you desirable enough to keep him from straying. Or you'll yell and rage and scream, thinking you can shame him into changing his behavior. This, in turn, violates *his* internal boundaries, because it assumes that you can control how *he* feels, thinks, or behaves.

Boundaries, by definition, are about knowing where the lines are between ourselves and others. When we have clear boundaries, we are more able to, as Pia Mellody says, *embody who we truly are*. When we have poor boundaries, we allow others to define who we are for us, and our Self is either lost or never properly develops. Having healthy boundaries also includes knowing who to let in, and when. If our boundaries are too rigid, we risk becoming isolated and incapable of intimacy.

Boundaries are particularly difficult for women because we've been socialized to believe that we shouldn't have any, and that our sense of Self *should* be defined by others. Our identities are culturally linked to how men see us: we are only pretty if men look at us, we are only smart if men hire us. In addition, we're conditioned to put everyone's needs before our own, and that if we do set healthy boundaries, we're *a bitch* or otherwise unpalatable. But when we lack boundaries, we not only lose our identity, but we tend to become extremely resentful of the people around us. When the pressure becomes too much, we explode, often creating more rigid boundaries than might otherwise be healthy. There's a slogan in 12-Step recovery that says, "Detach with love, not with an ax." Boundaries, when set properly, are, at their core, an act of love. Unless you're dealing with a narcissist or a psychopath, people generally don't want to violate your boundaries, and they certainly don't want to be exploded upon (a violation of their boundaries). Letting them know where your boundaries are is not only kind to you, but also to them.

It's important to have a solid sense of our internal boundaries so we don't blame others for boundaries we're violating within ourselves. For example, if I really need ten minutes of quiet when I get home from work before interacting with my family, that's my internal boundary. But if I never communicate this to my family, I may be really grumpy when I get home and they're climbing all over me and wanting to talk about my day the minute I walk in the door. Out of frustration, I might then behave in ways that don't align with my values, and in turn violate their boundaries. Over time, this can create an enormous wedge between my family and me. It's my job to know myself well enough to understand that my family isn't doing anything wrong by wanting to interact with me the minute I get home, and that in order to feel refreshed I need ten minutes of alone time before I can join the fray. It's then my job to clearly communicate this to my family so they understand my boundary and don't violate it in the future. Further, it's my job to continue to hold the boundary if in fact they do.

I like to think of boundaries like this: Imagine you have a house in the middle of the forest with a vegetable garden in which you grow precious food that sustains you year-round. You know that living in a forest there are bound to be various forms of wildlife that will be attracted to your garden and eat your veggies. Because of this, you would likely build a fence around your property strong enough and high enough to keep bears and deer out. Perhaps you leave it open a bit at the bottom so that bunnies can get through, because you like them and they help keep your grass tame. And you'd probably have a gate so your friends can come in and out. But around your vegetables, you might have a more enclosed fence so the bunnies don't eat your carrots. Now, it would be a form of insanity to expect the deer or bears or bunnies to know not to cross into your property, and even more insane to expect them to build your fences for you. When we don't take responsibility for setting our own boundaries, and blame other people for crossing them, that's exactly what we're doing.

In this metaphor there are varied levels of fencing for different animals, depending on what boundaries are needed. Setting boundaries with humans is no different. There are people we let deeper into our lives, and those we keep out. Knowing your Self well enough to be able to discern at what level each person is allowed in is key.

Sometimes we have to set boundaries with people we don't want to have to set them with. There are people we wish we could be close to, but with whom it's simply not emotionally safe. And, of course, these are the very people who are most likely to push our boundaries. For my client, Alex, it was her mother. I once remarked to her, "You set a boundary and your mom sees it as a goal post." Because of this, Alex had to work extra hard to build a fortified wall around her life to keep her mother at a healthy distance. This meant not telling her things that many daughters would tell their mothers, and it meant grieving the fact that she didn't have the kind of mother she so desperately wanted (one of the reasons Alex kept removing her boundaries with her mom to begin with). After many years of setting and resetting both internal *and* external boundaries with her mother, Alex became much more comfortable in their relationship—not because her mother had changed at all, but because Alex had.

One clue as to where boundaries are needed in your life is to notice when you start to feel resentment building. Resentments usually come from feeling like you're being taken advantage of or not appreciated. It's often a sign that you're pushing yourself either beyond your own limits because you feel guilty for setting a boundary, or because someone else is imposing their expectations, views, or values onto you. In either case, it's up to you to determine where that line is and to enforce it.

The more you get to know your Self—what you want, where you get stopped, where your inner power and strengths lie, what you're good at, who you really are at your core—the easier it will be to set and hold your boundaries. It's only when we're unclear about who we truly are that we feel the need to be all things to all people. That's why the work in this book is laid out in the order it is. This is a *process*.

Once you've been able to identify some needed boundaries, the next step in the process is to communicate your boundaries to those around you. Some people will get it right away and be respectful. Others, like Alex's mother, will need years of reminding. The most important thing to know about setting boundaries is that no matter how many times you have to say no to a particular person, you can always do so respectfully and kindly.

When you set new boundaries, you're radically shifting who you are in the world, and it might take those around you some time to catch up. We're all pieces in a giant puzzle called *Life*. When we begin to change the shape of our puzzle piece, the pieces around us either have to conform or pop out; and invariably there's a period of strain before one or the other happens. It's in this period of strain that you have to be the most diligent, holding your new shape and your boundaries most firmly. When you cease playing a particular role in your various relationships, it means that other people have to stop playing their roles too. If you stop being the perpetual care-taker, all the people that you've been taking care of aren't going to be very happy, and they'll probably push back. Eventually they'll have to shift into taking care of themselves, or they'll pop out of your life, which would be a shame, but would cer-tainly clarify who they really were to you.

One of the biggest boundaries I ever set was when I told my husband I wanted a divorce. I'd been trying to set boundaries with him for a decade, telling him that the way he treated me wasn't acceptable. But the problem was that he never changed his behavior, and by staying in the marriage, I was continuing to accept what I kept saying was unacceptable. The strongest boundary was to change *my* behavior and leave. He stopped treating me poorly after that because I was no longer available (literally or figuratively) to receive it.

The magic of that was that once I'd set that boundary, it overflowed into other areas of my life. The toxic friendships I had with people who treated me similarly gradually slipped out of my life. Once I'd set the hardest and most firm boundary, all the others felt a lot easier.

You may not want to start with the hardest one first, so start with the smaller ones. What small resentments do you have, and with whom? Make a list, and then see where your bound-aries might be porous or nonexistent. Then get to work building that fence around your garden, making sure to leave room for those you deem safe to let come in.

Why Self-Care Is So Important

It's no secret that women are overwhelmed, exhausted, over-worked, and underpaid. We're made to feel responsible for so much, from taking care of the house, meal planning, and food shopping to remembering birthdays, anniversaries, appointments, gift buying, school trips, school volunteer work, and so much more. For mothers it can feel exponentially worse, as a majority of childcare also falls on our shoulders. And when we express our overwhelm, we're usually told that we need to engage in *radical self-care*, and to *put your own oxygen mask on first*!

I'd hazard to guess that few of us know what that actually means. For the last many decades women have been told that self care is about getting massages and mani-pedis, or flying off to Cabo for the weekend. All of which are great, if you can afford them, but are they really *self-care*? Do they have any lasting impact beyond the time you're there? What's the metaphorical oxygen mask, *really*? Is it a bubble bath or a plane ticket?

What if self-care was about so much more than that? What if, instead of feeling like your life-force was being siphoned out of you all day every day, you felt as if energy was flowing into you? Might you be better suited to make the big decisions in your life (like, say, about your marriage) if you weren't exhausted by all the other decisions you have to make just to keep everyone else's lives afloat?

Decision fatigue is the idea that after making a lot of decisions, your ability to make more decisions lessens over time, so that by the end of a day, for example, you're unable to make any more decisions, and will often revert to the simplest choice. When most of the household and child labor falls onto you day in and day out, it leaves very little energy for greater discernment in the aspects of your life that arguably need the most attention. You're treading water, trying to stay afloat, without addressing the fact that your life preserver is full of holes.

We need to focus on patching up those holes so that you have the ability to sit back on the life preserver and breathe. In the quiet space of emotional reserves lies your ability to make the biggest decision facing you now.

So how do we patch the holes? We set boundaries with the people and systems that are feeding off of us for their very existence. We take the focus off taking care of and nurturing everyone else and put it onto nurturing ourselves. (How many doctor's appointments do we make for everyone else before we realize we haven't made any for ourselves?) We say no more often than we say yes—and we don't have to give reasons or excuses. And we don't pick up any volunteer hours at school.

When I interviewed thinker, teacher, activist, and coach, Kelly Diels, for my podcast and programs, she talked about women's volunteer work in schools as an example of systemic parasitism. Most schools rely on parent volunteers to function, and a majority of those volunteers are women. In 2022, Kyle Stokes, a reporter at my local NPR station, LAist, did an exposé called "Here's How Much Money L.A. Parents Are Fundraising for Schools and What it Buys." The series was about the public school system here in Los Angeles and how individual schools' operating budgets are often reliant upon parent fundraising initiatives to pay the salaries of teachers or administrators whose jobs are essential to the running of a school, such as an assistant principal, or a math teacher. These salaries are not built into the district's operating budget. Even the second largest school district in the nation relies on women's unpaid labor to pay the salaries of essential workers!

So, is self-care taking a bubble bath and getting a massage? Sure, maybe. But might it be more impactful instead to opt out of systems that rely on our unpaid labor, whether inside the home, or in the school system? I think so.

Other ways to engage in self-care can be more basic and foundational. Learning to identify feelings can be a radical act of self-care. When I was at the beginning of my healing journey, I worked with a sponsor in a 12-Step program who would ask me each morning how I felt. I'd always answer, "Good." "Good isn't a feeling," she'd say. And then I'd stare into space unsure what I was supposed to say. I was so deeply out of touch with my Self that I didn't even know how I *felt*.

My client, Sofi, recalled a time in her childhood when she was on vacation with her mother. She told her mother she was cold and wanted to go back to the hotel to get a jacket. "It's not cold," her mother declared. In this exchange Sofi's mother not only invalidated Sofi's feelings, but she also taught Sofi that her experience of the world was wrong. Sofi learned to disconnect from her Self as an act of preservation; knowing she couldn't trust even her feeling of *cold*, Sofi grew up having a very hard time identifying almost any feeling at all.

My experience was similar. My sponsor suggested that I needed to see a therapist so I could begin to get in touch with my feelings before she would be able to help me on my journey toward recovery. In my first session with that therapist, she handed me a list of feelings. She explained to me that while I was able to identify some "hard" feelings, such as anger, what we wanted to get to were the softer feelings that lived below the surface, such as fear, grief, or sadness. Over time, I became better able to identify more complex feelings, such as anxiety, disappointment, relief, humiliation, loneliness, abandonment, delight, and remorse.

Learning to identify my feelings became an incredible tool of self-care for me. Once I was able to name a feeling, I was more able to connect to it, and once I could connect to my feelings, I could better connect to Self. It was then that I could learn to ask for what I needed in a non-reactionary and more vulnerable way. It was through identifying my feelings that I was able to set boundaries with people I needed to. Without knowing I felt anxious around someone, for example, I couldn't create structures to protect myself from their impact on me.

At the end of the day, self-care is about so much more than we've been made to believe. And also, it can be so much simpler. Set boundaries, connect with Self, and take care of the basics.

Then, if you want to get a massage, take a bubble bath, or go to Cabo, have at it. You'll enjoy it so much more.

In this part of the book, we've done a lot to uncover more about who you are. I hope you're starting to feel some self-knowledge and self-esteem starting to emerge. Be sure to do all the exercises, because they will guide you there. When you feel secure and confident in your own Self, it will be far easier for you to answer the nagging question, *Should I stay or should I go?*

Exercises for Engaging in Self-Care:

PHYSICAL HEALTH:

- Make appointments for your regular
  - Dental cleaning

- Physical (including bloodwork)
- Pap smear
- Mammogram
- Colonoscopy
- Skin exam (dermatologist)
- Eye exam

- Take a close look at some of your unhealthier habits. Do you drink too much? Consider Dry January, or quit altogether. *This Naked Mind: Control Alcohol, Find Freedom, Discover Happiness & Change Your Life* (Avery 2015) by Annie Grace is a great book to teach you about the actual effects of alcohol on your body *and* mental health. This is the book that helped me get sober in 2018.
- Exercise daily. If you are a gym person, great. If not, exercising at home is readily available these days (*Thanks, Covid*).
- Walk at least 30 minutes a day, outside in nature, if possible (Bonus: this boosts endorphins and increases your mental health as well).
- Get enough sleep. Go to bed early, turn your phone or other devices off, and try to get seven to eight hours.

MENTAL HEALTH:

- Learn a new language or brush up on an old one. Duolingo is a great tool!
- Journal each morning for fifteen minutes.
- Write a gratitude list at the end of every day.

- Limit social media. Take the Facebook app off your phone and commit to only using it on your desktop/laptop.

SPIRITUAL HEALTH:

- Every morning, before getting out of bed, take three deep breaths. Include some affirmations or mantras, such as "I am capable," "I know who I am and I am enough." (A full list of affirmations can be found in the book resources on my website: kateanthony.com/book-resources)
- Meditate for ten to fifteen minutes (or even five!) before starting your day. There are a ton of great apps out there to help with this.
- Do a ten- to twenty-minute yoga routine. *Yoga with Adriene* is free on YouTube and she's great!
- If you're religious, commit to daily prayer. Find a religious community that accepts you at this stage of your life with no judgment or shame.

EMOTIONAL HEALTH:

- Find a good therapist. Check out my podcast episode, "How to Find a Good Therapist" with Katie Thompson, LPC, about how to do just that.
- To help ease anxiety, inhale slowly through your nose on a count of four, hold at the top of the breath for seven, and exhale out the mouth slowly for eight. Repeat five times.

- Get an animal! Pets are known to increase happiness in humans (as long as you can properly care for it).
- Be social. Plan a girl's night out or any kind of social interaction with people you love (and who love you!) at least once a month.
- Say no to things that feel like a burden to you. Try this phrase on: *No is a complete sentence.*
- Ask for help when you need it!

FINANCIAL HEALTH:

- Follow The Broke Black Girl on Instagram (@thebrokeblackgirl) and get on her mailing list to receive amazing financial tips for starting over. She's a divorced mom and she gets it.
- Bari Tessler is a financial therapist and a great resource for financial healing. You can find her at www.baritessler.com.
- Follow Naseema McElroy on Instagram (@financiallyintentional) and learn how she paid off $1 million in debt, gained financial independence, and increased her credit score—and how you can too!
- Get down and dirty with your money. If you don't have access to your accounts, get your own passwords (if your name is on the account, they'll have to give you your own login). Make sure you have a clear understanding of the financial picture of your household.

- Start a small savings account just for yourself. Set up an automatic deposit to go into it each week or month. This can be as little as $5.
- Track your spending for seven days and see what "frivolous expenses" you can cut out.
- Check on all your automatic subscriptions. You can download an app like Truebill and look on your phone to see if there are any subscription apps you're paying for but don't realize.
- Pay your taxes on time and file quarterly taxes on time if appropriate. If you're behind on your taxes, call the IRS and make arrangements.

CHAPTER 3

Why Are Women So Unhappy in Their Marriages?

How Marriage Exhausts Women and Benefits Men

I HEAR TIME AND AGAIN, "HE'S A good guy, I just don't feel it anymore," or "He's a good guy; he just has anger issues," or "He's *fine*... why can't I just be happy?"

When I dig more deeply into these relationships there's almost always more going on than meets the eye. Often, he's really *not* a good guy at all; in fact, many of these men are actually abusive. Sometimes he is a "good guy," but a victim, as we all are, of a system that prioritizes men over women: financially, emotionally, and in labor. And as a result, he prioritizes his own needs, time, or money over his partner's. He may not mean to do so, but internalized patriarchy is real, and as such many men who truly feel that they love and respect their wives may still unintentionally treat them with less respect than they deserve.

In this chapter, I address some of the systemic issues that impact marriages, much of which are more obvious in cis-het-ero relationships. Because of this, I've used more gendered language here. However, because of the systemic nature of these issues, they are not unique to heterosexual relationships, and I've seen them play out in the marriages of the lesbians I've worked with as well.

Merriam-Webster defines patriarchy as: "social organiza-tion marked by the supremacy of the father in the clan or family, the legal dependence of wives and children, and the reckoning of descent and inheritance in the male line." "Con-trol by men of a disproportionately large share of power," and "a society or institution organized according to the principles or practices of patriarchy."

In other words, patriarchy is a society in which men con-trol a disproportionate amount of power, and in which wives and children are legally dependent upon such men. The United States was built on the foundation of patriarchy, slavery, and genocide. How else could cisgender, heterosexual, white men build and maintain all that power and control were it not for the unpaid labor of women and people of color?

When I talk about systemic issues of power and control, this is exactly what I mean. To my mind, we can't talk about marriage today without discussing patriarchy and white supremacy.

How Did We Get Here?

Up until the mid-twentieth century, marriages were, essen-tially, business arrangements, and in many cultures they still are. Families merged to increase power and land-holdings. If you ended up with an affinity for your spouse that was a bonus, but it certainly wasn't the premise for the union, and women had almost no choice in the matter whatsoever. Families had children, not because of a biological yearning, but because more hands were needed to support the family business, care for elders, or to carry on the patriarchal lineage. From what we understand, women's relationships with men were mostly for procreation, protection, and food. Women got their emotional and spiritual needs met by other women. They raised children in community with one another and engaged in powerful rituals like the Red Tent, in which women would come together around their menstrual cycles to celebrate and nurture one another.

In Western culture, single-family homes, while seen as early as the fifteenth and sixteenth centuries, really began to boom with the advent and proliferation of the automobile in the early twentieth century. With cars came greater freedom to commute, and housing spread into more rural areas, which led to greater and greater space between us. Women left their family homes, found partners, and moved into these new single-family dwellings, with white picket fences and all the trappings of modern society. And all that we once got from multiple sources—spiritually, psychologically, physically, emotionally—suddenly landed squarely on one person: our spouse.

However, biologically speaking, men are not wired to fill this support role. Studies have shown that women and men release different hormones under stress. Women release oxytocin (the bonding hormone that we also release during orgasm and breastfeeding), while men release testosterone. Women's instinct to bond during times of stress biologically conflicts with men's more aggressive, problem-solving approach. This is why women are so compelled to turn to other women in times of trouble and often see their husbands as little or no comfort. It's also why women feel that men don't understand them, or aren't there for them when they need them, and why men sometimes look at us like we're aliens with three heads when we tell them we don't want them to *solve* our problems, we just need them to *listen.*

For all our advances, the one thing that we've lost, and that women still instinctively crave, is coming together in ritual, sharing the burden of motherhood and womanhood itself. This is why we start book clubs and rarely read or talk about the books. It was never about the books; it was always about the gathering. It's also why, if you ask any woman, she'll jump at the idea of living in a community of other women.

This isn't simply because we want to share community and support with other women; it's because we viscerally understand that the patriarchy has its very roots in our oppression. We've come to understand that white picket fences are not the symbol of cultural achievement we were taught they were, but rather our jail bars—tools to keep us isolated, imprisoned, and compliant. If we can't overthrow the patriarchy, we can fantasize about creating a sub-, indeed, *counter*-patriarchal culture, even if it's just on a plot of land, a row of tiny houses, or a big house we all run together.

When her husband, John Adams, one of the Founding Fathers of the United States, went off to write the Constitution, his wife, Abigail, implored him to "Remember the ladies and be more generous and favorable to them than your ancestors. Do not put such unlimited power into the hands of the husbands. Remember, all men would be tyrants if they could. If particular care and attention is not paid to the ladies, we are determined to foment a rebellion, and will not hold ourselves bound by any laws in which we have no voice or representation" (National Archives).

If only he'd listened. While the 1950s are often touted as an idyllic time in our history, you only have to watch a few early episodes of *Mad Men* to know that underneath the poodle skirts, coiffed hair, and sheets of perfectly baked cookies, women were suffering from a loneliness and isolation that caused us to rise up in fierce rebellion by the late 1960s. We became tired of being forced to stay home and keep house. We became tired of being objectified. We wanted equality, autonomy, and *choice*. In 1973, after a bitter fight and millions of deaths, women were given choice over their bodily autonomy when the Supreme Court heard and upheld *Roe v. Wade*. In 1974, a woman was finally able get a credit card in her own name without her husband's signature. It wasn't until 1994 that Bill Clinton signed The Violence Against Women Act, which provided funding for programs that help victims of domestic violence, rape, sexual assault, stalking, and other gender-related violence.

Unfortunately, and as proven by Jim Crow, just because certain freedoms are signed into law or even ratified into the Constitution, it doesn't mean society won't find other ways to continue its oppression. The Equal Rights Amendment, first proposed in 1923, has yet to be ratified into the US Constitution, and in June of 2022, a woman's right to choose was upended when the Supreme Court overturned *Roe v. Wade*. No, we haven't come a long way, baby.

Not Your Fucking Job

When I interviewed Leslie Bennetts, author of *The Feminine Mistake: Are We Giving Up Too Much?* (Hyperion, 2007) for my podcast, she told me that in researching her book she learned that of the four heterosexual population groups (married women, married men, single women, single men), the happiest population group is married men. The next happy is single women. Then single men. The least happy population group? Married women. This may be a big ole "No shit, Sherlock" to those of you reading this book, and you may feel like your life is a walking case study proving this. Almost any heterosexual woman who's been married inherently knows that marriage serves men while depleting women—even those in happy marriages. In fact, Leslie also said on my podcast, "Married women do 90 percent of the giving, and men do 90 percent of the taking." While that number may not be statistically true, most married heterosexual women sure feel like it is.

But why is this? The short answer is *male entitlement.* The longer answer is, of course, about the systemic structures that are set up to keep women exhausted, overwhelmed, and broke, while supporting male advancement, achievement, and leisure. Of course, men are entitled. The entire system tells them they should be.

Let's begin with the gender pay gap.

In 2021, full-time working women earned 84 percent of what their male counterparts made, up from 73 percent in 2014 (slow clap). These numbers are far worse for Black women who only earned 63 percent, and Latina women who earn just 57 percent of what white men make. This means that, on average, women earn eighty-four cents for every dollar earned by a man, and Black women earn sixty-three cents for every dollar earned by a white man, and Latina women earn fifty-seven cents for every dollar a white man earns. Add that gap up over a lifetime and the difference ends up in the millions.

And what about the unpaid work that American women do—raising the children, keeping house, managing budgets and medical care, and everything else? As *MarketWatch* declared in their April 15, 2018 headline, "WOMEN'S UNPAID WORK IS THE BACKBONE OF THE AMERICAN ECONOMY."

The forty-hour work week was designed by and for men who had wives at home to take care of all the domestic labor. But when women entered the workforce, men didn't pick up their fair share of the domestic labor to make it possible; women just had to work two jobs, one at the office, and one at home, often called *the second shift*.

Over time, we've raised enough hell over this that more men than ever before are stepping up to the plate at home, but even those who think they do equal domestic labor have been proven wrong in scientific studies.

A Pew Research Study done in 2015 proved that, despite the fact that fathers said that they shared home and child responsibilities equally, moms actually did significantly more. In fact, after having one child, a woman's total work (including domestic and paid work outside the home) increased by 21 hours per week, while men's total work increased by only 12.5 hours.

Oh, and men tend to enjoy three more hours of leisure time per week than women do.

A study done by the *New York Times* in March of 2020 concluded that "If American women earned minimum wage for the unpaid work they do around the house and caring for relatives, they would have made $1.5 trillion last year." (In March of 2020, the federal minimum wage was $7.25—and had been since 2009.). Keep in mind that this study was concluded before the pandemic, during which women lost an estimated 5.4 million jobs, many of which they were forced to leave in order to care for their home-bound children, while their (usually male) co-parents continued to work, unabated.

We earn less while working the same jobs and do more in the house. Add a global pandemic and we lose our jobs and increase domestic labor . . . kind of like the 1950s.

Awesome.

Is it any wonder that married women are the least happy population group?

Sixty-nine percent of heterosexual divorces are initiated by women, and men are often blindsided when their wives file for divorce. They don't take their wives seriously when they beg them to step up in the house, to do more domestic labor, to go to therapy with them—because they can't understand what the problem is. After all, *the issues women have in their marriages are the very things that make married men so happy.*

Women's unpaid labor falls into four distinct categories:

1. **The Mental Load:** This is all the stuff that swirls around in women's heads taking up a ton of mental energy: the to-do lists, the shopping lists, the lists of school supplies (and when they're needed), the dog's veterinary appointments, when each kid is due at the dentist, etc. Carrying the mental load can be so taxing that it can cause anxiety and stress to the point that it causes us to become forgetful in other areas. After all, we can really only hold so much.

2. **Emotional Labor:** This is all the emotional work we do to keep our relationships intact. It's when we play therapist to our husbands because they won't call an actual therapist; when we remind our husbands to call their parents; when we're the only one who can soothe a boo-boo; when we're the only ones who read the relationship books and listen to the podcasts when things are on the fritz. Sometimes carrying the emotional labor of the family can make us feel like we do all the output with very little input, and can leave us emotionally drained and resentful.

3. **The Second Shift:** This is all the household labor you have to do before or after your actual shift at work. Prepping lunches, doing homework, bath time, grocery shopping. We all have a second shift in our lives, because that's adulting. The problem is when we have no support in our second shift, especially when there are kids involved and the person who's supposed to be sharing the load is busy playing video games or golf.

4. **Invisible Labor:** This is all the stuff no one sees but that magically happens behind the scenes. Lunch boxes are magically filled each morning, the milk and toilet paper never run out, that kind of thing.

When it comes to domestic labor, men, generally speaking, fall into three broad categories:

1. **Unicorns:** Those who actually do half of the domestic labor and whose wives feel that there is an equal balance between the two.

2. **Oblivious Enthusiasts:** Those who really think they're doing their fair share in the home, and genuinely want to, but whose wives will confirm that they are in fact, not. These men often identify as feminists, and are eager to effect change.
3. **Passive Accommodators:** Those who think that if their wives really need *help*, they'll just ask. They want us to make them to-do lists, and then they'll do whatever we want them to do.
4. **Entitled Misogynists:** Those who believe women belong in the home and in the kitchen, regardless of what other work they're also doing, and whether or not they themselves have an actual job.

My ex-husband was a Unicorn. Despite the fact that he worked outside the home and I was a stay-at-home mom, we shared domestic chores fairly evenly. Yes, I shopped and did the laundry, and handled all scheduling, but he cooked often, and whoever cooked was usually the one to do bath and bedtime with our son while the other cleaned up the kitchen. These chores rotated fairly evenly. (Clearly, being married to a Unicorn doesn't solve all marital issues.)

New York Times best-selling author Eve Rodsky's book, *Fair Play*, and its accompanying card deck, seeks to solve the issue of the Oblivious Enthusiast by outlining every single piece of domestic labor required to run a household and asking each partner to take ownership of exactly half. In the documentary of the same name, after going through the process, one dad declares, "I really didn't understand the amount that she had to endure." See? Oblivious.

Rodsky argues that when men take on their share of domestic labor, and they experience ownership in the domestic space, they have the opportunity to connect more deeply with their children and feel like active participants in their family life. These men feel empowered. Intimacy with their wives increases because their wives are not utterly exhausted, overwhelmed, and resentful. Marriage to an Oblivious Enthusiast can improve dramatically with the opening up of dialogue and with him taking the lead in doing some research.

But do we really need a card game to "teach" men how to do their fair share? And it's not like men, even Oblivious Enthusiasts, are running out to buy the books or games. *Because they don't even see the problem.* So yet again, it's one more thing that women need to do.

Feminist writer Zawn Villines said in a February 19, 2023 Facebook post, "Men are not dumb or incompetent. They can see when their partners are working. They can observe that the family needs food to survive and that someone needs to procure that food from the grocery store. Don't let society tell you this is complicated and requires even more work from you to fix." Villines argues that we support the idea that men don't know how to participate in domestic labor by asking women to take on the additional labor of teaching them what needs to be done, and how. "Endless articles suggest that if we just ask in the right way, or offer the right incentive, or use the right combination of words, or spend enough time learning about our partners to understand their motives, everything can change." All of which adds to the emotional labor of women, in our quest to reduce our domestic load.

Then there's the Passive Accommodator. He thinks that if his wife really needs his help she'll just ask. The word *help* implies that domestic labor is a woman's job, and men are merely our assistants. This mentality and language are rampant among men *and* women. I implore you to watch your use of the word *help*. Do you ask your husband to *help* with dinner or putting the kids to bed? Do you ask for *help* taking the kids to school? Notice how often you use it in your household, and try to stop. Remember, you're modeling something to your kids here. What do you want it to be?

In her viral cartoon "You Should've Asked," Emma writes, "When a man expects his partner to ask him to do things, he's viewing her as the *manager* of household chores. So it's up to her to know what needs to be done and when. The problem with that is that planning and organizing things is already a full-time job."

Realize that *it's not your fucking job* to tell a grown-ass human being that the laundry needs to be done, or that dinner needs to be made, or that the kids need a bath, or that you're out of toothpaste.

There is no genetic predisposition that makes women better at remembering all the stuff that needs to get done to run a house than men. People used to believe that women were better multitaskers than men, but it turns out that we're only better at it because we do it more. Our brains aren't naturally wired for this; we have more neural pathways developed around multitasking because we've been left to do so much of it.

Chicken, meet egg.

The Passive Accommodator will also employ a sneaky little trick called *weaponized incompetence*, or *feigned incompetence*, in which they pretend they don't know how to do basic life stuff in order to get out of doing it. Case in point: the bumbling dad of commercials, TV shows, and movies.

You should've asked is a form of weaponized incompetence in which someone pretends they don't know how something works so you have to teach them (hi, emotional labor), or better yet, they get away with not doing it because they simply "don't know how." Women have to be careful about enabling weaponized incompetence. When our partners do a chore and they don't do it to our liking, we need to *not* swoop in and chastise them for doing it wrong and then do it the way we want it done. This solidifies their feelings of incompetence and guarantees that they'll never do said chore again (which is often the goal). We must give other adults the dignity of doing things themselves, their way. It doesn't need to be done perfectly, it just needs to be done, and the only way we get things taken off our plates is by allowing them to be on someone else's.

(By the way, this goes for our kids too. When teaching children how to do chores, allow them to do them their own way, and imperfectly. This is how boys in particular learn not to become Passive Accommodators later in life.)

When Ruth Bader Ginsberg was founding the ACLU Women's Rights Project while also teaching at Columbia University while also litigating cases all over the country and in front of the Supreme Court (before becoming a Supreme Court Justice herself) while also raising two kids, she famously told her son's school, who called her often due to her son's hyperactivity, "This child has two parents. Please alternate calls for conferences."

Interestingly enough, after this conversation the calls slowed down and only came about once a semester. Justice Ginsberg concluded that the school began to think harder about calling a parent when they knew they had to interrupt a man's work rather than a woman's. (From her 1992 commencement speech at Lewis & Clark Law School)

As for the Entitled Misogynist, well... If you're married to a misogynist and you're wondering if you should stay or go, all I'd ask you to do is look back to your values and ask yourself if this is in alignment with who you are at your core, and if this is the domestic dynamic you want to model for your kids. Even if you've agreed to be a stay-at-home mom, domestic labor isn't a 9-to-5 job. A partner who goes to work 9-to-5, comes home and sits on the couch playing video games, and doesn't participate in the house or with the children after they're done with work while you run around cooking, cleaning, and taking care of the children after having done so *all day long* is, at best, oblivious, and at worst, entitled.

So, what's the solution to all of this? We must be willing to communicate in our marriages, because standing in the corner with steam coming out of our ears never solved anything. So have the conversation. But have it once, and have it in detail. Tell your partner you're dissatisfied and exhausted and that even coming up with a solution to this issue puts more on your plate. Then ask *them* to come up with ways to solve the problem. Ask your partner what *they suggest* to minimize your load. And then see what they do.

And every time they ask you for "help" say, "I'm sure you can figure it out." Rinse and repeat. "I'm sure you can figure it out." Eventually, they will. *But only if you stop doing more than your fair share.*

There's a whole host of things I've seen women do (and that I did in my marriage) that are really not our jobs. The only way we get men to step up to the plate and do their fair share is by not doing all the things that are simply *#notyour fuckingjob*.

Here's a list of other things that are not your job, and that will help alleviate some of the labor on your plate:

IT'S NOT YOUR FUCKING JOB:

- To coordinate his meals and snacks so he doesn't get hangry
- To single-handedly bring passion to your relationship
- To pack for him when he goes on trips
- To shop and cook before you go out of town for the weekend
- To create to-do lists for him
- To force him to go to therapy
- To be his therapist
- To satisfy him sexually with no reciprocation
- To be his Madonna *and* his whore
- To remind him to take his meds
- To be "attractive enough" to keep him from straying
- To dye your hair, get a boob job, cut your hair, lose weight, gain weight, exercise, etc., in order to be *enough* for him
- To be his mother
- To bend yourself into pretzels to try to fill his void
- To keep his schedule
- To heal his trauma
- To prove your worth
- To remind him to attend parent/teacher conferences
- To help him maintain relationships with his parents/siblings/children/friends

- To wake him up in the morning so he gets to work on time
- To put his happiness and comfort above your own
- To heal his addictions
- To force him to be an equal partner in your marriage
- To soothe his anxiety
- To change to avoid conflict
- To keep quiet so you don't rock the boat
- To have sex you don't want to have

And so much more. Add to your personal list here:

_____

_____

_____

_____

_____

_____

_____

_____

_____

CHAPTER 4

But I Love Him!

Defining Love in a Spiritual Context

I F YOU GOOGLE, "WHAT IS LOVE?" you'll find any number of answers, from "an overwhelming feeling of emotions," to "passion, intimacy, and commitment." But in truth, most people find that love, being a feeling, is difficult to define in words.

In his classic self-help book *The Road Less Traveled* (Simon & Schuster, 1978), M. Scott Peck defines love as "the will to extend one's self for the purpose of nurturing one's own or another's spiritual growth," and I think this is the best definition I've come across.

So often women say to me, "But I love him!" when describing their agony over trying to decide whether to stay in or leave their marriages. I then ask them to describe what it is they love about their partner. I had a dear friend who was struggling with this question, and when I asked what he loved about his wife he stopped and thought hard and then said, "She does yoga." My clients are often just as stumped. It's as if love is a reflex. *I'm married, therefore I love.* But when asked, "What, specifically, do you love about this person?" many people are hard-pressed to answer the question.

Some clients have responded to this question with, "Well, he's a good guy." Really? What exactly does that mean? Multiple times a week someone posts in my Facebook group saying, "My husband is a good guy, but he cheats on me," or "He's a great dad, but he abuses me," or "He abuses me, but he'd never hurt the kids!!"

My response to these women is always the same: a good guy doesn't betray you, lie to you, or humiliate you. A great dad doesn't destabilize the foundation of the family by cheating on or abusing his wife. A great dad is one who continually reinforces the foundation of the family by loving, honoring, and respecting the woman he married so their children can be raised in a stable home.

Is he a great dad/guy if he doesn't know who his kids' doctors are, when they had their last round of vaccines, the names of their teachers, or if he spends the weekend gaming or watching football rather than interacting with his kids? What would we call a mom who parented in this way? Is there any chance that we'd call her a "good mom?" Hell no.

Clara came to me when her marriage was in shambles. She said her husband was a really great dad, and a really great guy, but he'd been caught cheating multiple times over the years. Each time he swore he'd stop, and each time he didn't. Because he was so great in all other ways, Clara was really confused about whether to stay or go.

I asked Clara to lay out for me the reasons she thought her husband was a great guy and a great dad. She told me that he was gregarious, funny, and outgoing. He was a pillar of the community and was generous and kind. He believed in service to others and would show up for anyone when they were in need. He was completely involved in his children's lives and was an unequivocally equal co-parent in most things.

It wasn't hard to see why this could be so confusing to Clara. After all, her husband did sound like a great guy from the outside. But inside the marriage was another story altogether. Coupled with his cheating were some abusive behaviors that made Clara believe his cheating was somehow her fault. She kept trying to make herself more desirable in order to keep her husband's interest and attention. When Clara first started working with me, she confessed that she had forgotten who she once was and felt like a shell of her former self. All her efforts to recapture her husband's attentions failed, and she'd lost her identity in the process.

Rather than focus on what she could do to recapture her husband's attention, I suggested that Clara first focus solely on building back her Self. The more work Clara did on herself, prioritizing herself by digging deeply into our coaching work, the more self-knowledge Clara accumulated. The more self-knowledge she accumulated, the more self-esteem she built until she could no longer justify staying in a marriage with someone who didn't view her the way she now viewed herself. Through our work together Clara was able to recognize that her husband's outward displays were hollow and based on a false image he wanted to project to the world, but that in truth he wasn't such a great guy after all. He was, in fact, a liar and a cheat. And now that she had some really unshakable self-esteem, her life no longer held space for people to treat her badly, especially the person who was meant to love her most in the world.

The idea of a good guy, or a good dad is purely subjective; it's a label that ultimately has no meaning. What matters most is the holistic view of the marriage. Does your partner put loving and supporting you at the top of their list of priorities, so that they provide and maintain a stable and sacred container in which to raise children, and do you do the same for them? If the answer is *no,* then whether they're a good guy or not doesn't matter one bit.

Maybe I should stop asking, *Why do you love your husband?* and instead flip the script. *Does this person love you? And how do they show it?*

If we take M. Scott Peck's definition of love, "the will to extend one's self for the purpose of nurturing one's own or another's spiritual growth," as the benchmark, then is your partner extending themselves for the purpose of nurturing *your* spiritual growth? And are you doing the same for them? Does your relationship create the container for such a thing? Is it *safe* to extend yourself? Does your partner feel safe to extend themselves? Is spiritual growth possible here? Is nurturing? And most of all, do you have *the will*? Does your partner?

Clara's husband, in a bid to save his marriage, told her over and over again how much he loved her. While I believe that he believed this, I have a hard time aligning love with his actions, as did Clara. Who gets to say if love is true in a relationship? Is it the person doing the loving, or the one receiving it? Clara didn't feel loved; she felt betrayed and as if the love she thought they shared was all a sham. That matters far more than anything her husband could say.

This is the premise of Gary Chapman's commonly misunderstood *The Five Love Languages* (Northfield Publishing, 2015). The point of discovering your Love Language is to communicate it to your partner in order to teach them how to show their love for you in the way that you most want to receive it, and vice versa. It's not, as is so often thought, to find someone with the same Love Language as yourself. Love Languages are not a compatibility test. They're about empathy. Are you willing to stretch *beyond yourself* in order to make someone else *feel* the love you say you have for them? Again: do you have "the will to extend [yourself] for the purpose of nurturing [your] own or another's spiritual growth"?

My Love Language is an equal balance between *acts of service* and *gifts*. If I'm dating someone whose Love Language is *physical touch*, they may touch me a lot and think they're showing me how much they love me. Despite the fact that it might feel nice to cuddle on the couch, if he's not doing things like taking out the garbage, walking the dogs, cleaning up the kitchen, or surprising me with flowers, I may not really feel loved. Similarly, if I do all those acts of service for him but never hold his hand while we're out and about, he won't feel fully loved by me, no matter how much I say I love him. While love is an emotion that we feel inside ourselves, what matters most are the actions we take that help our partner feel it.

We must have the will to extend ourselves for the purpose of our partner's spiritual growth, because what, truly, is love, if not a spiritual experience? When I asked my friend who said he loved his wife because she did yoga to explain a bit more, I discovered that they shared the practice of Kundalini yoga and that the spiritual connection they had, fueled by this deeply resonant breath practice, was a shared expression of their love.

When I was in the *should I stay or should I go* phase of my life, I was in a personal development class in which one of the leaders asserted that for a relationship to last there needed to be something outside the relationship that both people were committed to. For my friend and his wife, it was Kundalini yoga. For some it's religion. For others it's a shared charity or social justice initiative. For some it's their children. This points to a couple having shared values, which, as I've said, is a vital component of a happy marriage.

It's often said that love is a verb. Love is action. Love is taking action even when you don't want to if it serves the relationship.

My best friend, Lamont, is an actor. He works a lot on television and has starred in a few hit shows. The first time Lamont had a red-carpet event to go to, his husband, Tobias (an introvert), didn't want to go with him. He declared that he hated such things and didn't want to get dressed up and be on display. Lamont explained to Tobias that it didn't matter how he felt about it; it was important to *him* that Tobias was by his side on the red carpet. It was a big deal, and Lamont was nervous. "You're my husband," Lamont said. "I need you."

Tobias eventually came around and now, whenever Lamont has a red-carpet event, Tobias is dressed up and ready to go without being asked. Recently, Tobias even went back and changed his outfit when he realized it clashed with Lamont's without Lamont saying anything.

On the flip side of this, Tobias is a crunchy outdoorsy type, whereas Lamont is, well, not. But when Tobias wanted to buy some land to build a sustainable garden and eco-housing (including walls made of bales of straw and clay), Lamont supported him all the way—even though Lamont would much prefer to be at the Four Seasons with 800-thread-count sheets and room-service (me too!). Their marriage works, not because they're the same, but because they honor each other and are willing to stretch *beyond themselves* in order to support one another.

So, the question is, do you do the same for your partner? Do they extend you the same courtesy? When you say you love them, is that love an action? When they say they love you, do you *feel* loved by them? More importantly, is your partner willing to have this conversation? Do they have "the will to extend [themselves] for the purpose of nurturing [their] own or [your] spiritual growth"? If so, whatever issues you're having that brought you to these pages may be solved with a good couple's therapist.

What Does a Healthy Relationship Even Look Like?

Few of us were raised with any healthy relationship models, so most of us have no idea what a healthy relationship even looks like. This isn't something that's taught in school, and many of our parents aren't of the generation that had access to the level of personal development work we do today. For many of our parents, marriage was forever, whether it was healthy and happy or not. Some of us were raised in violence and abuse that was normalized or swept under the rug, and some of us were raised in homes in which there was underlying tension that no one ever talked about. It's a sad fact that very few adults I know today were raised in loving, communicative, or empathic homes.

Psychologically speaking, we tend to choose partners who mirror the relationship we had with our initial, primary caregiver. This means that if we had a primary caregiver (most often a mother) who was emotionally distant, an addict, controlling, or any other number of issues, we will choose a partner who is the same or similar. We don't choose them consciously; that would be insane. But when the person who was supposed to love us the most abused us, neglected us, or otherwise scarred us, our developing brains naturally conflated that abuse with love. And since it's our unconscious that draws us to people, we unconsciously choose people whose love feels like the love we received as children, even if it was damaging. There's a joke in Al-Anon that says that an Al-Anon member will find the one alcoholic in the room at a crowded party and will be drawn to them like a magnet. Anyone who was raised in an alcoholic home can confirm this by sharing the number of alcoholics they've dated (or married).

So, if we're all pretty messed up because so few of us were raised with healthy relationship models, what do we do? Are we just screwed? No. But we have an increased responsibility to do the work to identify and address our trauma, wounding, and injury so we can be better models for our kids.

So, what would a healthy relationship model look like?

I think it's important, first, to ask what it *feels* like. A relationship should, first and foremost, *feel safe*. You should feel emotionally, spiritually, financially, psychologically, and physically safe with your partner. You should feel safe to be exactly who you are, at any time. You should feel safe to have and express your feelings and opinions, and you should feel safe expressing concerns within your relationship to your partner.

All relationships have conflict, but how conflict is handled and repaired is what determines the health of a relationship. You should be able to compromise and negotiate. You don't have to agree on everything, but everyone's feelings should be considered valid. In a healthy relationship, arguments are ended with compromise and authentic communication. You should allow your conflicts to bring you closer, opening up space to learn more about one another.

In a healthy relationship, if one person has transgressed or hurt their partner, they will make amends, rather than an apology. An apology is what you say when you bump into someone by accident. An amends is an acknowledgment of a wrong, with a plan for changed behavior. In her book, *The Science of Stuck* (TarcherPerigee, 2022), author Britt Frank outlines what amends should look like by outlining what she calls *The Four O's. Own, Observe, Outline, and Offer.*

The first step is to take full ownership for what you did: "I didn't show you the love and respect you deserve." "I was an hour late without calling." Taking ownership immediately puts the other person at ease by letting them know that you're not going to deflect. They can relax, knowing that you understand that what you did is entirely on you.

The second step is to observe the impact your actions had on your partner. This step is all about empathy. You might say, "I imagine you must have felt really scared/hurt/angry." This allows the other person to really feel seen and heard. You might also check in and ask, "Is that how you felt?" Allow the other person to add their feelings without comment, interruption, or judgment.

The next step is to outline how you plan to not repeat the behavior in the future. For example, "In the future, if I'm going to be late, I will call you immediately to let you know," or "Next time this comes up I'm going to really work on shutting my mouth and just listening."

The final step is to offer to listen to anything else your partner has to say about the matter. You might say, "Is there anything else you need to say to feel complete with this? I'm here to listen," and then do exactly that: listen. You may need to repeat the above steps as you move through this, until your partner truly feels emotionally heard.

Can you see how different this experience would be from a simple, *I'm sorry*?

If someone constantly apologizes for their behavior but doesn't actually *change* that behavior, they're not really sorry; they're saying what they need to say in order to end the conversation and continue to offend. That's called manipulation.

In a healthy relationship there is respect for privacy and space. You should be able to keep your journal on your bedside table and know that it won't be read. Your phone should be private—not because you're hiding anything, but because it's yours.

In a healthy relationship, you should feel comfortable going out with friends without repercussions or arguments. You should have multiple sources for emotional nourishment. You should have friends, therapists, or coaches who support you outside the marriage, and relationships with friends and family should be encouraged and facilitated.

A healthy relationship should have clear communication, clear boundaries, trust, and consent. There should be bodily autonomy, always. Your partner should be interested and curious about you, as an individual, about your hobbies and interests.

A healthy relationship should have curiosity. When we express curiosity about someone else, we're acknowledging and honoring that they are different from us, that we don't know everything about them. This should be seen as exciting and interesting, not as a threat.

A healthy relationship should have reciprocity. You should feel energy flowing back and forth between you, like the infinity symbol. You should feel energized and inspired by your partner, as they should feel by you.

A healthy relationship thrives on *interdependence*. An interdependent relationship is made up of two fully formed people who are emotionally stable by their own merit, who walk side by side along the same path, coming together intimately, while also allowing for healthy separation. Interdependent relationships rely on each person having a fully formed Self, while choosing to live life with another. Interdependence allows for vulnerability and intimacy, whereas independence may not. Interdependence shouldn't be confused with codependence, which occurs when there is an imbalance of power and one person relies heavily on the other for a sense of Self and emotional stability.

Exercise For Determining if You're in a Healthy Relationship:

CHECK THE BOX THAT SAYS YES IF YOU AGREE WITH THE STATEMENT ON THE LEFT, AND NO IF YOU DISAGREE.

	YES	NO
I feel emotionally safe in my relationship	☐	☐
I am able to freely express myself and my opinions are heard and honored	☐	☐

I feel physically safe in my relationship ☐ ☐
I feel completely free to be myself around my
    partner ☐ ☐
I feel safe to have and express my feelings ☐ ☐
I am able to safely express my concerns about the
    relationship ☐ ☐
We are able to compromise and negotiate when in
    conflict ☐ ☐
Our conflicts bring us closer ☐ ☐
I am free to go out with my friends without
    repercussions ☐ ☐
My relationships with my friends and family are
    supported and encouraged ☐ ☐
I have privacy and space ☐ ☐
My partner encourages me to try and do new things ☐ ☐
My partner takes interest in my hobbies ☐ ☐
Our values are aligned ☐ ☐
We each have sources of emotional nourishment
    outside the relationship ☐ ☐
I trust my partner and they trust me ☐ ☐
I have bodily autonomy in my relationship ☐ ☐
My partner shows curiosity about me ☐ ☐
My partner honors me as an individual ☐ ☐
My partner and I have an equal exchange of energy
    and love ☐ ☐
I feel energized and inspired by my partner ☐ ☐
We are each fully actualized beings, apart from one
    another ☐ ☐
I feel safe being vulnerable with my partner ☐ ☐

TOTAL   ____ ____

Tally your yeses and your nos. If your yeses outweigh your nos, congratulations! Your relationship may be healthier than you thought. If your nos outweigh your yeses your relationship may not be all that healthy. If your nos far outweigh your yeses, you may be in an abusive relationship. This next chapter is for you.

CHAPTER 5

Am I Being Abused?

Recognizing the Personalities and the Signs

W HEN WE HEAR THE WORDS "domestic violence," we immediately think of blackened eyes and busted lips. And this is the sad reality for many women experiencing physical violence at the hands of their spouses. But it's important to understand that domestic violence isn't just about physical violence. In fact, some advocates don't like using the word *violence* and prefer to call it *domestic abuse* in order to encompass all forms of abuse.

According to The National Domestic Violence Hotline, "Domestic violence (also referred to as intimate partner violence (IPV), dating abuse, or relationship abuse) is a pattern of behaviors used by one partner to maintain power and control over another partner in an intimate relationship." Domestic violence takes many forms:

- Physical
- Emotional/psychological/verbal
- Financial
- Sexual
- Spiritual
- Digital/cyber

Underlying all forms of domestic violence is coercive control. While there are many definitions of coercive control, here's a simple one from DomesticShelters.org that I think sums it up well: "Coercive control refers to any pattern of behavior an abuser uses to dominate their partner and limit their freedom." The most important word in this definition is *dominate*, as this is how abusers maintain power and control. Any form of domination in an intimate relationship that is used to limit the freedom of another person is coercive control—and *that* is domestic violence.

Despite the fact that coercive control underpins all forms of domestic violence, it has only been specifically criminalized in Ireland, England, Scotland, Wales, and France. As of 2022, only five states in the US (Washington, Colorado, Connecticut, Hawaii, and California) have codified coercive control as being a form of domestic violence, but it has yet to be criminalized in the US at all.

Of all forms of domestic violence, physical abuse is the most dangerous, not only because of the physical violence involved, but because it is more likely to lead to serious injury or death. Physical abuse doesn't only or always include someone physically assaulting their partner. It can be throwing something at or toward you, punching a wall either next to you or across the room. Physical abuse can even be the clenching of a fist if the victim feels threatened by it.

Abusers tend to escalate only to whatever means are necessary to maintain control. If they can maintain control by clenching their fist, that's where they'll stop. But as soon as you become inured to the clenched fist, they'll need to escalate beyond that. Next time they'll punch the wall. After that they'll punch your face. Escalating beyond that could mean your life is in danger. It's important to recognize that abuse doesn't *de*-escalate. Each time it escalates, that's the new level.

Let me make one thing clear: *If you are in a physically violent relationship, you need to escape.* There is no question about it—but it needs to be done safely and strategically.

Failure to escape a physically violent abuser can have dire consequences beyond your physical safety. Most states in the US have *failure to protect* laws, which give the state the legal right (and often the mandate) to arrest victims of domestic violence for failing to protect their children from their abusive partners. Oklahoma has the strictest of these laws, which can, and often will, incarcerate victims for life—while their abusers are sentenced to just a few years. (Laws like these—and so many others—drive home the systemic misogyny victims and advocates are fighting against.)

However, as imperative as it is to escape a physically abusive relationship, it can be so incredibly dangerous to leave. Seventy-five percent of all domestic homicides occur when a victim escapes because that's when the abuser feels they've finally lost all control. Murder is the final act of power and control. According to the National Coalition Against Domestic

Violence, "The presence of a gun in a domestic violence situation increases the risk of homicide by 500%."

For this reason, it is incredibly important to work with a domestic violence shelter or advocate to create a safety plan *before* escaping a violent relationship. Safety plans are created over time, before a victim escapes, so that when they do get out, they do so in the safest way possible and are prepared with everything they need. I talk more about creating a safety plan in Chapter Eight.

Most of us believe that domestic violence happens to "other people." We have a vision of the type of woman who is abused by their partner. We think abused women belong to a certain socio-economic class, a specific race, or education level. We don't think it could possibly happen to *us*. We think the same of abusers: they're menacing, poorly educated, and come from lower economic statuses. We somehow think that they wear signs, so we'll clearly recognize them. Nothing could be further from the truth. Statistically speaking, domestic violence can happen to and by anyone, in any socio-economic class, of any race, and of any education level—at any time. It happened to me. Perhaps it has happened to you. These next chapters will help you identify whether or not you're a victim of domestic violence and tell you what to do if you are.

Owning your victimhood doesn't mean that you are labeling yourself as a *victim* in any negative sense of the word. In fact, I believe understanding that we've been victims of any form of domestic violence can be incredibly empowering. Once I was able to name my abuse and fully accept that I was a victim, I was able to heal from it. After all, we can't heal from trauma we haven't identified. Many people advocate for the use of the word *survivor* over *victim*. If you're a victim/survivor,

I support you calling yourself whatever you want. I choose the word *victim* because it makes it clear (to myself and others) what happened to me, and doesn't let me sidestep the important work of owning the fact that I was, in fact, the victim of domestic violence.

Over the last decade I've been shocked to discover that almost all the women who come to me seeking help and guidance have been victims of some form of domestic violence, whether emotional abuse, physical, digital, sexual, financial, or all of these combined. This isn't because I talk about it so much that victims of domestic violence are drawn to me. I talk about it *because* it's the most common topic among the tens of thousands of women who follow me, join my programs, are in my Facebook group, and those who've worked with me privately. It's become my focus out of sheer necessity. The more time I spend in the divorce space, the more evidence I have that this is a global crisis that we're not paying nearly enough attention to, and that we still have so much work to do to educate the masses on how these power and control tactics work to undermine women's autonomy and freedom.

Women I work with often feel a desperate need to know if their partners are abusers or just assholes. In an attempt to reconcile themselves with the idea that they may be in an abusive relationship, women try to make sense of their husband's behavior. They wonder why he does what he does. They question if his behavior is due to substance abuse, mental illness, or his own unhealed trauma. I always ask if it matters. "Do you really want to remain married to someone who treats you terribly? Does it really matter what their (unofficial) diagnosis is?" For many women it really does. For them the diagnosis isn't to help them understand their partners, but rather to understand *their experiences.* They feel less crazy, and less alone. To these women, this knowledge is clarifying and empowering, and I help them find it.

But for many others, it's a distraction from the harder work of shoring up their sense of Self, which is necessary work when you're the victim of any form of abuse. These women tend to believe that if they can understand their partner better, then they can get to work convincing them to change (*You're an abuser! Don't you get it?*) or getting their partner the help they need. What they don't realize is that men who abuse women don't change, nor do they want to (because their tactics work for them). Additionally, it tends to be a person's core beliefs that drive their behavior. Sure, alcohol and drugs may some- what alter someone's personality, but their conduct while intoxicated is still determined by their underlying beliefs and values. Sometimes, it's the alcohol or drugs that allow what's already inside them to come out. And while I feel compassion for anyone who has experienced trauma in their lives, a per- son's pain does not justify hurting someone else. I urge you to have more compassion for yourself than for someone who con- tinues to hurt you, no matter the reason. If your partner struggles with post-traumatic stress disorder (PTSD), he should definitely seek professional help. The same holds true if he suffers from mental illness or addiction. But to be clear, noth- ing excuses his bad behavior. We are all responsible for our own actions, and it is not your job to fix anyone, convince them to seek treatment, or be a martyr to their suffering. It *is* your job to protect yourself and your children.

This chapter is for the women who need to understand their partners so they can clarify their own experiences, and make their decisions based on that information. This chapter is *not* intended for you to bring to your partner to explain to them who or what they are in an attempt to get them to finally see what they're doing, and change.

Narcissist, Abuser, or Sociopath?

Narcissism has become a buzzword these days. Ask any divorce attorney and they'll tell you: *everyone* is divorcing a narcissist. But are they? Is it possible that there are suddenly so many narcissists in the world? Or are we simply recognizing the signs and therefore more able to name it when we see it, suggesting that there have always been this many?

It's possible that the number of narcissists is growing because our culture cultivates, and applauds, narcissism. From reality TV to social media, celebrities to politicians, we foster and reward narcissistic behavior. Narcissists tend to be charismatic and likeable and are often successful in their careers. The more rewarded the narcissist is in life and work, the more their egos tend to grow. Because narcissists are created, rather than born, our cultural acceptance and wide-spread adoration of narcissistic behaviors most certainly exacerbate the problem. It's also possible that there have always been this many narcissists in the world, but our increasing recognition and decreasing tolerance for their behaviors is allowing us to call them out more regularly and openly. The *#metoo* movement was a turning point in our cultural willingness to continue to turn a blind eye to the deeply entitled behavior of male aggressors.

It's important to note that narcissism exists on a spectrum. On one end of the spectrum is perfectly healthy self-image. As you move along the spectrum, you'll find benign narcissists, such as those who are self-centered and always turn a conversation back to themselves. Further along you'll find more malignant narcissists, such as those who hurt other people in the pursuit of getting their own needs met. And at the far end of the spectrum is narcissistic personality disorder (NPD). One in sixteen people claim to have been impacted by someone with narcissistic personality disorder, and yet only 1 to 5 percent of the population has been *diagnosed* with NPD. This discrepancy is due to the fact that most people with narcissistic personality disorder don't seek treatment, so never get diagnosed. Those who are diagnosed have often sought treatment for any number of co-occurring disorders, such as alcohol use disorder, bipolar disorder, or depression, and once those issues are identified, medicated, or otherwise treated, the NPD is left exposed.

If they aren't diagnosed, how do the people impacted know their friend/spouse/coworker/parent/sibling has NPD? According to the American Psychiatric Association's *Diagnostic and Statistical Manual of Mental Disorders*, Fifth Edition (DSM-5), narcissistic personality disorder is defined as having "a pervasive pattern of grandiosity (in fantasy or behavior), need for admiration, and lack of empathy, beginning by early adulthood and present in a variety of contexts." To be diagnosed with NPD, a person must display at least five of these nine symptoms:

1. Has delusions of grandeur, exaggerating their accomplishments and abilities
2. Has fantasies of ultimate success, power, genius, or love; believes they're entitled to the best
3. Believes themself to be so unique that only a select few could ever understand or be on par with them

4. Requires special attention and ego-stroking
5. Believes they're entitled to special treatment in all circumstances
6. Takes advantage of others in order to increase their own gain
7. Lacks empathy
8. Is often jealous of what others have, or expects others to be jealous of them
9. Is self-important, vain, and arrogant

Whether officially diagnosed or not, most people can assess whether their partner has five or more of these traits. And if someone doesn't meet the criteria for narcissistic personality disorder, they may still have *narcissistic traits*, which can make them a narcissist, narcissistic, or an asshole. For simplicity, I'll use the word *narcissist* going forward, which encompasses those with NPD and those with narcissistic traits. I'll also use the word *sociopath* but this can also include psychopaths as there's very little difference between the two that's relevant for our purposes here. In fact, there's very little consistency across the board on the difference between the sociopaths and psychopaths, and neither is an official diagnosis; diagnostically, both fall under the umbrella of *anti-social personality disorder*.

Symptoms of narcissism "present in a variety of contexts" (per the DSM-5 definition), meaning that they occur at work, at home, on the golf course—anywhere. Someone with narcissistic personality disorder has a disorder that cannot be contextualized, as it's an overarching disorder of the entire personality. In other words, they'll be equally impacted at work and at home, which causes the narcissist to be unhappy. Unfortunately, because of their entitlement and need for external validation, narcissists will usually pin their unhappiness on others rather than think there's something wrong with them. In other words, they're unhappy, but it's all your fault.

Underneath their arrogance, narcissists actually have incredibly low self-esteem. In fact, their arrogance and entitlement are rooted in the fact that they have such a limited sense of self that they require validation from others to build up their identity. Narcissists rely on others to tell them who they are, and when we don't (because we can't), they can turn on us with intense rage. This is why it can feel like the narcissist in your life has a bottomless pit of need that you can never fill, or that the solution to their misery is a moving target that you can never seem to hit, try as you might.

Once victims of narcissistic abuse understand that their partners suffer from low self-esteem, they tend to feel bad for them and naturally want to help. Victims (falsely) believe that they can help their partner raise their self-esteem by loving them enough, and the *right way*. But there is no right way to love a narcissist, other than from afar. No matter how much you empty your soul into a narcissist, they will never feel fulfilled—and you will always feel empty. This is because most narcissists are victims of intense childhood trauma that fractured their psyches in ways that only very long and very intense trauma therapy *might* be able to help, but the general consensus among experts is that narcissists cannot change, even if they want to. (And before you go feeling bad about their childhood trauma, again, this is *#notyourfuckingjob* to fix, it's theirs.)

Narcissists will begin a relationship with you by exalting you and putting you on a pedestal. They've projected onto you that you are their savior and the one who will finally make them whole. You're *The One*. And for a while it feels like it's true because new love tends to feel that way. But as the shine wears off and you settle into day-to-day life, they become angry that you've failed to fulfill your *duty* (as they see it). When they meet someone else, they feel fully justified in embarking on an affair because they've convinced themselves that this new person is actually *The One* who will heal them and fulfill all of their needs. And since you didn't, it's your fault they had to stray. Then the lies begin. And if there's a long-term relationship with children involved, this can become a complex web of lies that will often cause the narcissist stress-related disorders, chronic health conditions, and crippling anxiety. It doesn't stop them from lying or cheating though, because they still feel completely justified in their behavior, and entitled to their lies, and any discomfort they feel is your fault anyway.

While narcissists have low self-esteem, sociopaths, on the other hand, have extremely high self-esteem. They have no fear of consequences and they have no remorse. They can (and often do) pass lie detector tests because they have no stress or anxiety around telling lies. They view the world and other people solely as pawns to be used for their own gain. On brain scans of sociopaths, not only do the empathy centers of their brain not light up when faced with someone else's pain, but very often the pleasure centers of their brains *do*. This means that not only do they have no empathy, but they actually derive pleasure from the pain of others.

Sociopaths will behave one way in public and another way in private because they are absolutely aware that their abuse is wrong. They use it as a tool to control you, but put it away when in view of others. This makes them harder to identify and harder to break free of. To the outside world, they may be charismatic, loving, wonderful people—but only because they know how to play the part. While narcissists will hurt you and even try to destroy you, they do it from a place of trying to get their impossibly deep abyss of needs met. Sociopaths will destroy you simply because they can.

There are a few schools of thought on how abusers may be different from narcissists or sociopaths. Many experts will lump everyone into either the narcissist or sociopath bucket. Others believe that all narcissists are *abusive,* but not all abusers meet the diagnostic criteria for narcissism. However, these people also may not be sociopathic. Lundy Bancroft, author of *Why Does He Do That: Inside the Minds of Angry and Controlling Men* (Berkley Reprint edition, September 2003), asserts that abusers have a separate identity. He believes that while narcissists are shaped primarily by childhood wounding, "abusers are overwhelmingly influenced by attitudes, values, and behaviors that they've learned from key role models (male relatives, their own peers, men in pornography, cultural icons) and from the misogyny of the society at large." Bancroft believes that if we identify all abusers as narcissists, then we place blame at the feet of mothers who raise boys (perpetuating misogyny) and let the society that shapes abusers off the hook.

I believe there are three distinct buckets:

1. **Narcissists,** who are *created,* usually by childhood trauma and wounding, who abuse because they have an insatiable need, and an entitled desire, to get their needs met and their identity supplied by others.

2. **Sociopaths,** who are most often *born* (although sometimes created), who abuse because they have no

remorse, no empathy, and while they may have a sense of right and wrong, they don't particularly care. They see you as a tool to be used to get whatever it is they want. Life is a game, and you're just a pawn on their chessboard.

3. **Abusers**, who are *created* by social conditioning that teaches boys and men that they are superior and entitled to women's labor, servitude, adoration, bodies, and unconditional love.

Because humans are complex and rarely fall squarely into one box or another, your partner may not fit perfectly into one of these categories. Please don't let that trip you up in your quest for answers. If your *experience* of your marriage is such that one of these labels helps put things in perspective, that's all you need to know. Narcissists, sociopaths, and abusers have one important thing in common: they are all abusive and dangerous to be in a relationship with.

CHAPTER 6

I Think I'm Going Crazy

Unraveling the Tangle of Emotional Abuse

EMOTIONAL ABUSE IS THE MOST common form of intimate partner violence, and nearly 50 percent of all relationships experience lifelong emotional abuse by an intimate partner, according to a report from the National Library of Medicine (Karakurt & Silver, "Emotion Abuse in Intimate Relationships: The Role of Gender and Age" 2013). Emotional abuse is also one of the most baffling forms of abuse, and hardest to identify, because emotional abusers use confusion as one of their main tactics of power and control. They rely on your inability to recognize what's happening as abuse in order to continue to abuse you.

Gaslighting is one of the more common tactics of emotional abusers, and one of the most dangerous. It's also become a buzzword that's over- and improperly used, so it's important to understand exactly what it is—and what it's not.

Gaslighting is defined in the dictionary as "manipulating someone by psychological means into questioning their own sanity." Gaslighting is intentional. It's designed to erode your sense of Self by forcing you to question your own perception of reality. (This is why the work laid out in Chapter One of this book is so important. Strengthening your Self is the only way to be able to objectively view your relationship.) Gaslighting is not the same as lying. It's lying for the purpose of making you begin to second-guess your own perception of reality, with the end result being that you actually think you might be going crazy. In extreme cases, people lose their grip on reality, and indeed go mad. Gaslighting is a tactic of all types of narcissists, sociopaths, and abusers, and has become so common that it was Merriam-Webster's Word of the Year for 2022.

Benita and her husband had an argument in which her husband called her violent and ugly names. In couples therapy the next week, when Benita brought it up, her husband denied it ever happened. Not only did he deny it happened, he expressed concern to the therapist that Benita could be making up such lies. He said he was worried that perhaps there was something wrong with her that she would remember something that never happened.

Benita knew it had happened, but she was confused and scared by her husband's seemingly genuine concern. Either she was misremembering the events, or he was pathologically lying to her and their therapist. Since she couldn't possibly wrap her mind around her husband being a complete sociopath, the only option was for Benita to doubt her own perception of what had occurred. Maybe it wasn't as bad as she remembered it after all. She'd had some wine and she tends to get emotional when she drinks, so maybe she was just overly sensitive.

Over time, these episodes repeated in varying contexts and to varying degrees, but with the constant being that Benita was left feeling confused and second-guessing herself to the point that she started to genuinely question her own sanity. During the course of our work together Benita came dangerously close to a severe mental breakdown because of her husband's extreme gaslighting. Fortunately, she still had enough of a grip on reality that I was able to help her see what was happening. Although she'd been avoiding it for almost a year, that was the moment she finally realized she needed to leave her home. Once she had some distance, she was able to objectively see just how badly she'd been abused for years.

Emotional abuse takes many other forms. An emotional abuser may say something mean, claim they were *just joking* when you express hurt feelings, and then accuse you of having no sense of humor. They'll refuse to accept responsibly for their actions, or worse, accept partial responsibility only as a tactic to get out of having to change their behavior or face real consequences. They'll withhold love, communication, or celebration for achievements. They'll shift blame back onto you for things they've done. They'll accuse you of things that they have no evidence of (often this is projecting what they've done onto you—for example, a cheater will often accuse their partner of cheating). They'll play the victim, or say things such as, "You're right. I'm the problem. It's all me," in order to avoid genuine accountability, because where can you take the conversation from there?

If you google "what are the signs of emotional or verbal abuse" you'll often get answers that seem quite apparent, such as these from The National Domestic Violence Hotline:

- Telling you that you never do anything right
- Insulting, demeaning, or shaming you, especially in front of other people
- Preventing or discouraging you from spending time with friends, family members, or peers

However, most abusers are far more covert than this, and these definitions often lead women to believe they're not really being abused when in fact they are. This can be extremely dangerous and can keep women in abusive relationships far longer than is necessary or safe. In order to ascertain whether or not you're being abused, it can be more useful to look at how you *feel* in your relationship, rather than focusing on what your partner is *doing*.

IN A HEALTHY RELATIONSHIP YOU FEEL:

Safe, protected, vulnerable, trusting, relaxed, completely free to be yourself, free to express your opinions, free to communicate things about the relationship that are bothering you, safe to be independent, respected, interesting.

IN AN ABUSIVE RELATIONSHIP YOU FEEL:

- **An imbalance of power.** Your partner will use control tactics to make you feel emotionally powerless and as if they have dominance over you. You feel scared of the person you're supposed to be in a loving relationship with. You feel you're always walking on eggshells, afraid to upset or anger your partner.

- **That you can never do anything right.** Your partner will tell you what you need to do to make things okay, but when you do the thing, it's not the *right* thing, or it's not done the *right way*—and then it's your fault for missing the mark. In an abusive relationship the mark is a moving target that you'll never hit because you're not meant to. It's never about your behavior; it's always about the abuser's need for control.

- **Extreme highs and lows.** You feel like you're soulmates one day, and the next day you feel completely destroyed. There's always the promise of deep connection, but with that comes the threat of decimation. You do everything in your power to maintain the connection because that's the part of your relationship you love, but soon enough, you hit a snag and you spiral into the depths of despair.

- **That you never know who's going to walk in the door.** Are they going to be the nice version today, or the nasty one? You feel like if you do everything "right" before they come home then they'll be pleased and be nice, but it's never guaranteed and you're constantly on edge.

- **That you're always to blame.** Abusers will make you feel as if you're to blame for everything that goes wrong in the relationship. Even if they take responsibility for some of the issues in the relationship, somehow it always flips back onto you. They'll often say that if you'd only do x, then they wouldn't have to do y. They'll cop to the front 5 percent, which makes it look like they're working on their issues, but you quickly realize that they're not making any changes—all while you're bending yourself into pretzels to try to please them.

- **Confused, foggy, or unclear.** Emotional abuse can take a mental toll on the victim. You can get brain-fog from the trauma, which makes you unable to remember things, and since your reality is always shifting, you can become easily confused. This is one of the main symptoms of gaslighting.
- **Like the relationship is one-sided.** You give and you give, but you don't seem to get a lot in return. *You* read the relationship and parenting books. *You* call the therapists. You'll do anything to make this work, but it feels like you're the only one putting in the effort.
- **Like you are always sick.** It's very common for victims of abuse to report having chronic health problems, even autoimmune diseases, that defy diagnosis or treatment. It's also common for victims to report symptoms vanishing when they're out of their toxic homes.

If you relate to some, many, or all of these descriptions, you are likely experiencing some form of emotional abuse.

The National Domestic Violence Hotline defines domestic violence as "a pattern of behaviors used by one partner to maintain power and control over another partner in an intimate relationship." It's incredibly important to remember that all abuse is rooted in *power and control.*

In an interview on my podcast, my friend Rhian Lockard said, "If you can't make sense of the way someone is treating you (because if they loved you, surely, they wouldn't treat you this way), then ask yourself if it would make more sense if you replaced the word *love* with *control*. If they were trying to *control* you would their behavior make sense? If the answer is yes, you may have your answer."

In order to recognize abusive patterns in your relationship it can also be helpful to identify *the cycle of abuse*. The cycle of abuse is present in many cases of domestic violence but will look different in every relationship. The cycle has four distinct phases:

1. **Tension building.** Communication begins to break down, and the environment becomes stressful. You begin to walk on eggshells, fearing your partner's explosion.
2. **The explosion.** The trigger is pulled and the abuse is set off. This could mean the silent treatment or a verbal or physical assault.
3. **Reconciliation.** This doesn't always occur, but when it does there are often apologies, gifts, or flowers, and the promise that it will never happen again. Sometimes this step is skipped altogether and the abuser will act as if nothing has happened.
4. **Calm.** In some cases, usually those in which there are gifts and proclamations, this is the return to the honeymoon stage. In other cases, it's simply a period of calm in which there is no abuse or tension.

My client, Heather, was in an emotionally abusive marriage with Don. Don had serious rage issues and Heather never knew what would set him off. I asked Heather to map her own cycle, to write out in detail what it looked like in her marriage. Heather recounted a typical episode that happened the year before.

It began when Don came home from work one night. Heather could tell he was tense. She could see his jaw working, and he was slightly snippy and impatient, but nothing too serious. At that point, Heather started walking on eggshells. She tried really hard to soothe Don by making his favorite meal and being sure the kids were behaving. Anything to try to avoid setting him off. Then one night, when he'd had a little too much to drink, Don blew his top. He screamed at the kids and called Heather a dumb bitch. He got verbally violent, calling her names and attacking her character. Heather didn't know what she'd done wrong, but as far as Don was concerned, she'd done *everything* wrong.

At that point, Heather crumbled. She sobbed uncontrollably, begging him to stop, but Don took her vulnerability as weakness and escalated his abuse, calling her pathetic. Sometimes when he acted like this Heather would take the kids and go to her parents' house. Other times she'd sleep in her kids' room with the door locked. She stayed home this time, but she resolved that this would be the last time he would treat her like this. She knew that she couldn't go through this anymore and that she had to leave.

But the next day Don came home with flowers. He was ashamed. He was utterly heartbroken that he could ever treat his wife, the mother of his children, whom he loved more than anything in the world, so terribly. He vowed to do better. He admitted he had an anger problem and promised to get help. He swore he'd stop drinking. He begged, cried, and promised. Because Heather loved Don, and wanted to believe in him, she agreed to give him another chance. If he was willing to go to therapy, if he promised to stop drinking, how could she just turn her back on him? Heather resolved to work on her issues too. After all, marriage is a two-way street, so whatever she'd done to contribute, she would work on.

For the next few weeks, life was glorious. Don came home from work and dove in with the kids and the dishes. He bought Heather gifts like he used to—a bracelet, flowers, her favorite chocolate. He left notes on the bathroom mirror. Heather felt like she had the old Don back. She was on cloud nine. She went back to therapy herself so she could work on her code-pendence. Then things settled down. No more giant, overt shows of love and affection, but no outbursts of rage. Don started drinking again, but only a little. Life was simply *normal.* Heather was relieved, but she did wonder if Don had ever called that therapist.

Within a couple of months, Heather noticed that Don was starting to get tense again. He was becoming more irritable, and he was drinking more than he had been. She was afraid to mention it to him, lest she set him off. She was so happy with the way things had been, she really didn't want to rock the boat. She started amping up her caretaking, working hard to ease Don's stress. Whatever it was, she could soothe him. She knew she could.

But over the course of a week or more, Don's irritability grew, until one night, in a drunken rage, he exploded again. Heather begged and cried. She reminded him of his promises. She asked if he'd called the therapist and Don scoffed and said that therapy was for wimps with mommy issues and there was nothing wrong with him. He said she was the one who needed a head shrinker. Heather moved into her kids' room for a few nights, trying to figure out her next move, until the day Don came home with flowers...

You see how this goes. And you can substitute just about anything for Don's rage. Amelia's husband was a serial cheater. He'd cheat, he'd get caught, he'd promise and beg and even go to Sex Addicts Anonymous (SAA). But within a few months he'd cheat again. This cycle repeated for four years before Amelia came to me for help.

The reconciliation stage isn't always so grandiose. Sometimes there are no presents, no grand gestures; it's just a period of getting along really well, of being intimate in the ways you used to be. It could be laughing together, sharing inside jokes, flirting, or having more sex. It could be going on dates. And sometimes there is no reconciliation. There's simply calm, like nothing ever happened. To a victim of abuse, the calm is all we want, and we lap it up desperately, like finally having found water in the desert.

Not all experts like to use this model because it can be turned around and used to blame victims. *If it's a cycle, how come you didn't see it?* implying that abuse is predictable, when it can be anything but. I put it forth here because my clients find it useful to identify certain patterns in their marriages, which helps them recognize, and name, abuse.

The Power and Control Wheel, created by The Domestic Abuse Intervention Project in Duluth, MN, is a model that many advocates prefer to use. At the center of the wheel are the words POWER AND CONTROL, which all abuse is centered around. On the outer ring of the wheel are the words *physical and sexual violence,* with eight spokes connecting the center to the outer ring. These eight spokes represent the often-subtle behaviors abusers use to exert power and control. They are:

- Using coercion and threats
- Using intimidation
- Using emotional abuse
- Using isolation
- Minimizing, denying, and blaming
- Using children
- Using male privilege
- Using economic abuse

Emotional abuse can be one of the most confusing forms of abuse to endure, precisely because of these behaviors. This is why it can be helpful to use these models.

Making this even more confusing, an emotional abuser may not seem like an abuser at all; they may simply seem damaged and have childhood wounding that you have great compassion for. You may be in couples therapy with your partner and the couples therapist may even ask you to go further out of your way to indulge your partner's feelings in an effort to help them heal. If you're in an abusive relationship this will only fan the flames of abuse as the abuser has just been told that they're even more entitled to your excessive caretaking. (This is why you never go to therapy with an abuser, which I discuss more in a later chapter.)

One of the most complicated issues regarding any form of abuse is wrapping your mind around the fact that abusers have a different worldview than the rest of us. While you and I may be in a relationship in order to connect and love and create a life with another person, abusers are in a relationship in order to control you and get their own needs met. They may mimic love and connection just so they can get what they want. And we so desperately want the love and connection that abusers dangle like a carrot at the end of a stick that we suffer through years of misery and confusion trying to capture it—all because we don't understand this very important difference in the mindset of the abuser. Additionally, there's a distinct, clinical difference in the way narcissists process shame. When a non-narcissist experiences shame, they internalize it (*what's wrong with me?*), but when a narcissist experiences shame, they externalize it (*what's wrong with everyone?*). This keeps them from taking responsibility and secures their spot as a victim in a world hell-bent on vilifying them.

Many people who don't understand the dynamics in abusive relationships ask, *Why don't they just leave?* The answer is deep and complex, but the simplest answer is, *we don't leave because we don't want the relationship to end; we just want the abuse to stop.* Throughout the cycle of abuse, the promise that it will stop is intoxicating. This is why it can take an average of seven tries before a victim finally escapes their abuser—and stays gone.

Exercises for Identifying Emotional Abuse in Your Marriage:

If you've seen some of your marriage in this chapter, it might be useful to map the cycle as it plays out in your relationship. Here are some questions you might answer in your journal that can help you map your own cycle:

- How does it feel when the tension begins to build?
- What do you notice in yourself or your spouse?
- How do you know when the tension is building? What are some signs you might look out for?
- What does the explosion look like in your marriage? Does your spouse yell, throw things, or give you the silent treatment?
- Is there reconciliation? Are there grand gestures that might be considered *love bombing* or does everything just get swept under the rug?
- How do you feel in the calm period?

Here are some additional journal prompts to help you make sense of what you have learned in this chapter:

- What do you see in your own cycle?
- Is there an imbalance of power and control in your relationship?
- Do you feel that you can never do anything right?
- Do you feel extreme highs and lows?
- Do you feel that you never know who's going to walk in the door?
- Are you walking on eggshells?
- Do you feel that you're always to blame?
- Do you often feel confused, foggy, or unclear?
- Do you feel like the relationship is one-sided?

Emotional abuse is one of the most complex forms of abuse, and often one of the worst. Many survivors of physical abuse have said that they can heal from the broken bones, but the emotional abuse leaves lasting scars, while many victims of emotional abuse declare that they wish their spouse would hit them so their decision would be clearer. Having the person who is supposed to love you the most cause you to second-guess your own reality can completely erode your sense of Self. The confusion and brain fog you may be feeling is not your fault. You're not dumb or ditzy or flaky. You're being abused. But there is help available, I promise.

CHAPTER 7

I Feel Trapped

Understanding Financial, Spiritual, Sexual, and Cyber Abuse

THERE ARE OTHER FORMS OF abuse that are not often discussed but are quite damaging and can leave women feeling trapped. It's important to recognize the signs so you can protect and empower yourself.

Financial Abuse

Financial abuse is an extremely common tactic of abusers because controlling finances is one of the most effective ways to maintain power and control over a partner.

Here are some sobering statistics:

- Financial abuse occurs in 99% of domestic violence

cases (Adams, "Measuring the Effects of Domestic Violence on Women's Financial Well-Being" 2011).

- Victims of financial abuse collectively lose a total of eight million days of paid work each year.
- 59% of people's credit is negatively impacted by their abuser.
- 70% of domestic violence victims are forbidden to work by their abusers (Pennsylvania Coalition Against Domestic Violence, World Health Organization).

FINANCIAL ABUSE CAN TAKE MANY DIFFERENT FORMS:

- Not allowing you access to accounts, statements, or other financial information
- Blocking you from working or having financial independence
- Depositing your paycheck into an account you can't access
- Giving you an *allowance*, and monitoring all spending
- Stealing financial aid checks
- Taking out loans or credit cards in your name
- Ruining your credit
- Spending lavishly on themselves while restricting your spending
- Getting you fired from a job by harassing you or other employees

As with emotional abuse, the signs of financial abuse may be covert or overt, and they may escalate over time. At first a partner may appear kind or chivalrous when they suggest you don't need to worry about money and that they'll handle it and take care of you. After all, isn't this one of the fairy tales we grew up with? A knight in shining armor rescuing the damsel in distress, sweeping her off her feet and taking care of her every need? Over time, however, you may notice that you have less and less access to money, or none at all. Your *allowance* begins to shrink, and when you ask for more money, your partner demands to know what it's for. They comb over the grocery receipts, asking you to account for each purchase. They become more and more controlling over time until, when you finally realize what's happened, you have no access to money whatsoever, and no resources to escape their control. Even if you are able to leave, financial insecurity is cited as one of the main reasons victims return to their abusers.

When women stop working and give their financial power over to men who abuse them, it can create large gaps in employment, which makes it harder for a victim to secure work down the line. When an abuser uses his wife's credit to rack up debt, it can leave the victim with a ruined credit score, making it increasingly difficult to secure food or housing should she leave. Then, when she can't afford to adequately care for their children, she could lose custody of them to the abusive partner.

Currently three states, Maine, Texas, and California, have laws on the books that protect victims from *coerced debt*, meaning that their credit can be protected if they've suffered domestic violence. New York and Connecticut are poised to pass coerced debt laws soon, and we can only hope the rest of the nation will follow suit. Until then, victims are left unprotected.

If you're suffering from financial abuse the first thing you should do is to become financially literate. Most abusers control the purse-strings because their victims don't know a lot about money (or the abuser makes the victim feel that they don't). Understanding the basics about money can go a long way to helping you feel more empowered so you can regain some control over your finances. Read books on personal finance, such as Amanda Steinberg's *Worth It: Your Life, Your Money, Your Terms* (Gallery Books, 2017) and anything by Suze Orman. Suze Orman's website (www.suzeorman.com) is also a wealth of information (pun intended). Bari Tessler's book, *The Art of Money: A Lifechanging Guide to Financial Happiness*, (Parallax Press, 2016), is wonderful, as is her podcast of the same name.

Here are some other financial resources available specifically for survivors:

- The *Allstate Foundation Moving Ahead Curriculum* "has been designed to help domestic violence survivors achieve financial independence and rebuild their lives." The curriculum offers a variety of information, from basic money-management principles to advanced financial planning, and it's free on their website, www.allstatefoundation.org.
- *FreeFrom* is a national organization whose mission is "to dismantle the nexus between intimate partner violence and financial insecurity." They have a peer network of survivors, do community advocacy work, and work with banks, employers, and other institutions to help support survivors' financial safety and security. You can find them at www.freefrom.org.

The next thing you should do is work to become financially independent. This means having your own bank account and access to your own money. It also means having some form of work so that you have your own money coming in. Ideally this should be done before leaving so you have a cushion before you leave. There is no set amount you should have saved before you leave—if you're in any form of danger, a domestic violence shelter will take you in free of charge—but having a few hundred dollars or more stashed away can help immensely. Here are some ways you can begin to build your financial independence:

- Start a secret cash-stash somewhere safe. This might be in the glove-compartment of your car or at a friend's house; just be sure it's completely private.
- Find work so you can begin to build your secret cash-stash. Fiverr or Upwork are great places to find small jobs that you can do online from home or in secret.
- Open an Etsy store and sell your amazing crafts.
- Open a secret bank account in your name only and deposit your checks into it. Stash other money into it as well, even if it's only five dollars a month.
- Connect a private PayPal, Zelle, or Venmo account to your secret bank account.
- Clear your browser history every time you log into your bank account.
- When you go to the grocery store, get cash-back or purchase Visa Gift Cards and store them with your secret cash-stash.

Domestic violence shelters across the country have free resources available for women who are experiencing abuse, such as financial literacy programs, personal empowerment programs (PEP), and legal aid. Even if you don't go to live in their shelter, their resources will be available to you. Websites such as The National Domestic Violence Hotline (thehotline.org) and The National Coalition Against Domestic Violence (ncadv.org) have information and resources available to victims and survivors.

Financial abuse is a serious form of domestic violence. Financial abuse is the cage in which your abuser keeps you captive. It should not be taken lightly. Breaking free can be very challenging, but not impossible.

Spiritual Abuse

Spiritual, or religious, abuse occurs when someone uses spiritual faith or religious practice as a way to assert dominance over another. This could show up as a religious leader inflicting abuse on a congregation by using their position of power to shame, ridicule, or control. The leader might also use their power to manipulate members of their faith into giving them money, or into sexual submission. At its extreme, this is how cults are formed.

In "Fighting Abuse in the Faith Community" (Spectrum, 2013) Sarah McDugal, an expert in spiritual abuse, says that "spiritual abuse is the misuse of theology, scripture, church position, or spiritual influence to control, cause harm to, exploit, or reduce the personhood of another. At its core, spiritual abuse is any action that breaks the third commandment—where someone takes the name of God and then misrepresents his character using His name."

In many conservative religious communities women are indoctrinated to be submissive, gentle, and meek, and are considered responsible for setting the tone of their home. This means that if a man is angry, it's because his wife hasn't done her duty to make him happy. She's brainwashed into thinking that if she just prays more, studies more scripture, and works harder at being more submissive and enlightened, then her abusive husband will be nicer and treat her with more respect. In other words, any abuse a wife is experiencing is her own fault for not being a good enough Christian/Muslim/Jew/fill-in-the-blank.

A client of mine who was a member of a conservative Christian faith group told me that her husband had punched her in the face numerous times, and had felt entitled to do so because, in his eyes, and in the eyes of God, she was his property. When my client finally left her abuser, and subsequently her faith, she was shunned by her community. She lost all her friends because she was deemed unfaithful, led astray by the Devil himself.

Because in many faith communities it's believed that women are responsible for their husbands' emotional happiness, when victims of domestic violence go to their faith leaders for help, they're often told to try harder to please their spouse and to *forgive their sins*. The victim is re-victimized by being told that the abuse is her fault for not being a good enough wife, or that she can make it stop by working harder to please her man.

Many conservative faith communities also espouse the belief that it is a wife's duty to have sex with her husband whenever the mood strikes him, whether she wants to or not, and if she doesn't, it's perfectly appropriate for him to force himself on her (otherwise known as rape). But a wife who tries to initiate sex with her husband is a sinner, as a woman of faith is not meant to have such ungodly urges.

Spiritual abuse is difficult to escape because it's firmly upheld by an entire community. Reporting often leads to being shunned, which can isolate you from the community as a whole—including friends and family. I worked with a woman who was part of a very insular and deeply connected Islamic community, of which her husband was the de facto leader. After years of emotional and verbal abuse she discovered that he'd been living a double life with another woman. At that point, she knew she had to leave. Despite his infidelity and abuse, she was the one who was shunned by her community, leaving her with no friends, no family, and no support system. Even those who believed her couldn't support her because of the threat of being ostracized themselves. Sadly, even her own children turned against her.

If you're the victim of spiritual abuse the first step, of course, is to recognize it for what it is. The second step is to get help from outside the institution that is perpetrating or upholding the abuse. If your faith is important to you, find a community that better aligns with your values, that honors you, and that actually aligns with the true teachings of your faith (hint: I'm fairly sure Jesus, who was the original social justice warrior and fought for inclusion and love of all, wouldn't condone abuse in His name). There are many more progressive religious institutions that will love and support you while also giving you a place to practice your faith. I also recommend joining a support group for people who are healing from spiritual abuse. Check out Sarah McDugal's Instagram, @sarahmcdugal. It is rich with teachings that help unravel this knot. I also recommend her book, *Myths We Believe, Predators We Trust: 37 Things You Don't Want to Know About Abuse in Church (But You Really Should)* (Wilder Journey Press, 2019).

Sexual Abuse and Marital Rape

Sex in marriage should always be a consensual act that is an expression of love, trust, and unity. That doesn't mean that sex always needs to be *lovemaking*. A quickie in the shower or an afternoon delight can be just as special and important in a relationship, as long as it rests on the foundation of trust, love, and unity—and most importantly, *consent.*

Unfortunately, this isn't the experience for many, and, as with most forms of abuse, women suffer sexual abuse in marriages at a disproportionate rate to men.

Here are some signs of sexual abuse in a marriage:

- You agree to have sex because you're afraid of what will happen if you say no.
- Your partner wants to engage in sex acts you find uncomfortable, but they do it anyway.
- Your partner refuses to practice safe sex.
- Your partner forces their decisions about pregnancy, birth control, or abortion onto you.
- Your partner withholds sex as a punishment.
- Your partner touches you in ways that are demeaning or unwanted.
- Your partner persists even after you've said "No."
- Your partner insults or criticizes your body.
- Your partner coerces you to watch porn with them.

- Your partner uses insults about your body to justify cheating or watching porn.
- Your partner withholds resources, such as money or food, until they get the sex they want.
- Your partner only satisfies themself sexually and doesn't attend to your sexual needs.
- Your partner demands sex regardless of your physical or mental state (illness, surgery, pregnancy, recent birth, mental illness, exhaustion).
- Your partner has sex with you when you are unable to consent, either because you're drunk, asleep, mentally or physically impaired, or otherwise unable to consent.
- You partner physically forces you to have sex that you don't want to have.

Between 14 and 25 percent of women in the US are raped by an intimate partner during their relationship, and between 10 and 14 percent of married women are raped by their husbands. One-third of married women report having sex they don't want to have, and between 40 and 46 percent of women in abusive marriages will be raped by their partners (Bergen & Barnhill, "Marital Rape: New Research and Directions," VAWnet 2006). According to the findings of a 2006 research brief by the National Resource Center on Domestic Violence (NRCDV), women who are raped by their spouse are likely to be raped many times, with some reporting being raped twenty or more times.

Up until 1993, rape statutes defined rape as "forced sexual intercourse with a woman not your wife," which made it completely legal for a man to rape his wife, in any context. In 1993, marital rape became a crime in all fifty states. However, in thirty states there are still exemptions given to a husband who doesn't have to use force because his wife is mentally or physically impaired, unconscious, or asleep, and therefore unable to consent. (Lambert, "Marital Rape is Criminalized, but not Upheld," *Psychology Today,* March 2022). You read that right. In thirty states, if he doesn't have to use force, it is perfectly legal for a man to rape his wife.

Let me be absolutely clear: Just because it's legal doesn't make it right. When my college boyfriend had sex with me while I was passed out drunk after a party, that was rape. If your husband does the same to you, that is also rape, whether he can be prosecuted for it or not. This is a gross violation, not just of your body, but of your spirit, trust, and marital vows. No one is entitled to your body, at any time, ever, or for any reason. All sex and sexual touch must be consensual at all times. Someone who uses scripture or any other form of manufactured entitlement to pressure you into sex doesn't see you as an individual worthy of love, honor, or respect. They see you as their property.

The way out of this isn't to try to convince your partner that you're not their property, because this worldview of theirs is skewed—and static. The way out is for you to do the work on your Self so *you believe you're no one's property* and believe that you are worthy of dignity and respect. In that light, marriage to someone who rapes you no longer aligns with your self-esteem. Almost all domestic violence shelters provide Personal Empowerment Programs (PEP), which are designed to help the victim build their sense of Self in order to gain the strength to not return to their abusers. These programs are very similar to the exercises put forth earlier in this book and that I do with my clients, and they are free.

Digital or Cyber Abuse

Cyber abuse, also known as digital abuse, or digital domestic abuse, involves the use of digital technologies to control, intimidate, or harm a partner. Here are some examples of cyber abuse that can occur in an abusive marriage:

- **Monitoring and Surveillance:** If your spouse is constantly monitoring your online activities, including checking your emails, text messages, social media accounts, or location, this is an invasion of privacy that can be used to control or manipulate you.
- **Harassment and Threats:** Sending you threatening or abusive messages, emails, or social media posts is cyber harassment. This can include derogatory comments, explicit language, or threats of physical or emotional harm.
- **Revenge Porn:** Sharing intimate or explicit photos or videos of you without your consent, often as a means of revenge or control, is illegal in almost all states. In the states that don't have specific statutes against this, Massachusetts and South Carolina, offenders can be prosecuted under privacy or obscenity laws. This is a form of digital exploitation that can cause significant emotional distress and harm.
- **Identity Theft:** Illegally accessing and using your personal information, such as your social media accounts, email accounts, or financial details, without your permission is considered cyber abuse. This can lead to financial loss, reputational damage, or other consequences. I see this often when men hack

into their wives' social media accounts and access their posts in my Facebook group. Often these women think someone in the group outed them to their husbands, when in fact, their husbands are to blame.

- **Online Isolation:** Restricting your access to the internet or social media platforms, isolating you from friends and family, and controlling your online interactions is abuse, and is not okay. Isolation is one of the top tactics abusers use in general; online isolation is just another way to limit your social connections and maintain power and control over you.

- **Cyberstalking:** This is when abusers engage in persistent online monitoring, harassment, or threats, which can involve constantly sending messages, tracking your online activities, or making you feel unsafe or intimidated.

- **Digital Gaslighting:** Manipulating or distorting your perception of reality through digital means can cause you extreme distress. This can include deleting or altering messages, photos, or other evidence to make you doubt your own experiences or sanity.

It's important to remember that cyber abuse in a marriage can have severe emotional, psychological, and sometimes even physical consequences. If you are experiencing cyber abuse, it's important to seek support from trusted individuals, organizations, or authorities to ensure your safety and well-being. Fortunately, you don't have to be a tech expert to fight cyber abuse. In fact, most cyber abusers aren't tech wizards, so protecting yourself doesn't have to be all that complicated.

Here are some steps you can take to protect yourself from cyber abuse:

- Change all your passwords frequently.
- Log out of all social media accounts after each use.
- Set up two-factor authentication on all accounts.
- Run a full-factory reset on your phone, which will often (although not always) delete spyware.
- Go through all your apps and delete anything you don't recognize.
- Check to see if there are any parental controls set on your phone that might allow tracking. If so, call your carrier to have them removed.
- Set up your own Apple ID, Prime account, or other shared accounts that allow a spouse to see your online activity.
- Turn off the metadata function for your camera and location services (like Find My Friends) on your phone. Metadata can be used to help pinpoint your exact location.
- On both Apple and Android phones, turn on the Air Tag Alert, which will alert you if an Air Tag is moving with you. If you get an alert, empty all purses, and thoroughly search your car.
- Open a new email account on an encrypted platform such as Proton Mail, and link that account to all of your social media and financial accounts.
- Take your car to the dealer and ask them to disable your car's connection to any functions that allow your vehicle to be tracked remotely.

- Use a VPN (virtual private network) whenever using wi-fi.
- Use incognito mode whenever possible and delete your browser history each time you go online.
- Disconnect or reset all smart devices.

While this list is quite exhaustive, it is by no means complete. Cyber abuse is extremely prevalent in our society, and just another tool abusers use to exert power and control over their victims.

CHAPTER 8

Do They Know It's Abuse and Can They Change?

Inside the Mind of the Abuser

O NCE SOMEONE HAS THE dawning realization that they're in an abusive relationship, one of the first questions they invariably ask is, *Does my partner know that what they're doing is abuse?*

They believe that if their abuser *knew* it was abuse, they'd surely stop. After all, their partner says that they love them, and if someone loves someone, they wouldn't want to abuse them, right? As I said in Chapter Six, abusers have a different worldview, so expecting them to abide by the conventions of love when what they're really after is control, is futile. (And no, they're not going to admit they want to control you; you have only to look at their actions to determine this. Someone who has put a tracking device on your car absolutely knows what

they're doing.) I beg you: stop trying to get the abuser to understand what they're doing. The only person who needs to
understand this is you.

A great litmus test as to whether or not someone knows
they're abusing you is to look at how they behave in other areas
of their life. Do they treat the people they work with the way
they treat you? Do they yell, explode, and berate their co-
workers? Or are they able to keep up the appearance of being a
normal, decent person to the outside world? Do they attempt
to exert power and control over other people in their life, or just
you? If they are able to maintain the image of being a kind, generous person out in the world, and only abuse you in private,
then they know exactly what they're doing. The proof is in the
fact that they know not to do it in public and are perfectly capable of holding themselves back in other aspects of their life.
They know what they're doing isn't acceptable. They just think
they can get away with it *with you.* This person is either an
abuser or a sociopath. In either case, they're unlikely to stop.

If they're not able to maintain this kind of image to the outside world, if they have trouble holding down a job and
maintaining relationships because of their abusive behavior,
they're likely a narcissist. Narcissists may not realize their behavior is abusive (partly because they lack the empathy
necessary to understand this), but they'll never *not* be a narcissist, and they too are unlikely to stop.

So, do they know they're abusive? Usually, the answer is yes,
although they don't see it as abuse. They simply feel entitled to
control you. But if the answer is no, should you explain it to
them so they understand and stop? Don't waste your time. Even
if a narcissist were to hear your diagnosis/complaint/request
and agree that they need to go to therapy (which they may

agree to do because it feeds their love of navel-gazing), the amount of work that's needed for someone to actually change on a systemic level could take years, if not decades. The kind of work necessary is a complete reprogramming of the belief systems that support the level of entitlement narcissists hold, and it would require a very compelling reason for them to get completely honest about their feelings and experiences in the world—usually profound loss or hitting some form of *bottom*—not just you explaining it or threatening to leave. Everyone's bottom looks different, but for most, it's having lost everything that means anything to them: job, marriage, kids, family, usually all of these. Almost no one truly does the work to change unless they've experienced profound loss.

In Alcoholics Anonymous literature there's a passage that talks about holding on to the principles of AA "with all the fervor with which the drowning seize life preservers." (*Twelve & Twelve*, Alcoholics Anonymous World Services, Inc.; 1st edition, 1952) Your partner should have that same fervor about changing his behavior so he stops hurting you. I know someone who recently lost everything: his wife, a good portion of his work, the respect of his children and wider community, friendships, and more. Even though he's been told numerous times by multiple people (including me) that his behavior was dishonest, abusive, and damaging, it wasn't until he lost absolutely everything that he finally checked into a rehab facility and began to do the work on his issues in earnest. He truly had the fervor of a drowning man because he was, in fact, drowning. This phenomenon is called a *narcissistic collapse*, which occurs when all the structures put in place to uphold the narcissist's inflated ego no longer work. This can result in extreme anxiety, depression, and shame. Up until his collapse, my friend was able to justify his behavior by projecting his shame outwardly and blaming other people for his actions. When it all crashed down on him, he had no choice but to face his shame and seek help. But let me be very clear: *it wasn't until he had lost everything that he was willing to change.* And even now, it will take years for him to reach any kind of true healing—and only if he continues to do the really deep, daily work.

If I've heard it once, I've heard it a thousand times: "I told him I was going to leave and now he's doing everything right. He's being perfect, saying all the right things, helping with the kids [there's that *helping* word again], and doing more in the house. He's being so loving and kind!" Nine times out of ten the woman believes that her partner has magically changed, and she doesn't leave. Then, within weeks, her partner reverts back to the old behaviors because they got *exactly* what they wanted: *She didn't leave.*

If you tell someone you're going to leave, and they start saying and doing all the right things, then it's a good bet they knew all along that what they were doing was wrong, and could have stopped earlier, but chose not to. When a client of mine finally left her husband, he came to her two weeks later and said, "I'm so sorry. I just never thought you'd leave," meaning, *I knew what I was doing was wrong, I just thought I could continue to get away with it.*

If your partner starts doing all the right things, follow through on your end. Separate, and give it *at least six months.* Watch what they *do,* not what they *say.* Do they go to therapy? Do they buy *and read* the relationship and parenting books? Do they give you the space you asked for and focus on their own recovery while you focus on yours? Or do they beg and plead for you to come back, rage when you don't, get on a dating site the night you leave (men do this more often than you'd ever want to know), and ramp up the abuse when they realize they're not getting their way? Unfortunately, this is all too common and a perfect indicator that they never had any intention of doing the work; they just wanted to maintain control.

If you want someone to change, you've got to give them the chance and a reason to do so. Give them time and space and don't do anything for them. Listen to their words but watch their actions more closely. Hold firm to your boundaries. I promise, someone who truly loves you—and doesn't want to control you—will hear your requests and *show you their love* by giving you the space you're asking for and doing the hard work themselves. Someone who wants to control you will freak out when they realize that they no longer can and will likely escalate their abuse. If there's a history of physical abuse, this time can be dangerous and should include no contact and a restraining order—and it should in no way be temporary.

Am I the Abuser?

When women I've worked with begin to understand the dynamics of abuse, they'll often stop in their tracks and say, "Wait …am *I* the problem? I've hit my partner. I've said terrible things to him or given him the silent treatment. Am *I* the abuser?" The short answer is, if you're asking the question, then no, probably not. The longer answer is this: In order to establish who the abuser is in any dysfunctional relationship, look to who has the power and control. Statistically speaking, men are far more likely to be aggressors than women because in our society men tend to have a lot more power and control (and money) overall. They also tend to be far more entitled than women, and entitlement is one of the key elements of abuse. They can also be larger and stronger, putting women in far more physical danger than men usually are from women.

So, are you exerting power and control in your relationship? Or are you reacting to it? Victims will often behave terribly, sometimes violently, when they're being manipulated and abused by their partner. It's at that point that the abuser will accuse the victim of being the abuser, and, because we're often so surprised by our own violent behavior, we believe them. The technical term for this is DARVO. DARVO stands for *Deny, Attack, Reverse Victim and Offender.* First the abuser denies their abuse, then they attack the victim for accusing them of abuse, and then they reverse victim and offender by claiming that they are the real victims of the abuse that they're perpetrating.

We saw this dynamic at play in the much-publicized and tragic case of Gabby Petito and Brian Laundrie. The couple was stopped by the police in Moab, Utah, and body cam footage shows Petito an emotional wreck. She blames herself for the argument they were having, saying she was the one grabbing his phone and that she was hitting him. She says she has anxiety and OCD and was having a hard time that morning. She's hyperventilating, and clearly in great distress. In contrast, Laundrie is calm and collected. He never once takes responsibility for any part of their argument. He subtly plays Petito off as the unstable one that he's just trying to keep calm and help, and when the officer erroneously names Laundrie the victim of domestic violence, *he laughs.*

This footage was released when Petito was still missing, and Laundrie had gone home to his parents' house in Florida.

Domestic violence experts watched that footage in horror. We could see all the signs that Laundrie was the primary aggressor, yet the police missed those signs and believed Laundrie to be the victim. At that point, experts were fairly certain that Petito was dead and that Laundrie had killed her, and we were, sadly, correct. What Petito was displaying were signs of gaslighting, and what's sometimes known as *reactive abuse*, or *mutual abuse* (which isn't a thing, because abuse is about power and control, which by definition negates mutuality). I don't believe it's abuse at all. I believe it's a perfectly appropriate response to *being* abused, otherwise known as *self-defense*.

I've seen this demonstrated in my own practice. One night, toward the end of Jessica's marriage, she and her husband got into an enormous fight. Jessica was really triggered, and so, using skills from their couples therapy, she told her husband she needed to leave the house to calm down. At that point, her husband blocked the door and went into lawyer mode, saying that if she left it would be abandonment, and she would not have no legal right to their home in the divorce (this is not true). Jessica tried to tell him that she needed to leave so that the fight wouldn't escalate, but her husband took her car keys and continued to block the door (which in the domestic violence field is called *false imprisonment*, and is illegal), all the while speaking to her in calm, "reasonable" tones, ostensibly to sooth her, but actually gaslighting her. Jessica became more and more hysterical until she tried to wrestle her way out the door, clawing at her husband's arms in the process. When she couldn't get out, she ran into the kitchen and slammed a glass cabinet door and, as shards of glass rained down onto the counter, her husband looked at her and said, "Wow, Jess, you're insane. Do you realize how crazy you are? You have a real problem."

Jessica's husband was calm; she was hysterical. But was Jessica the abuser? No. She was defending against *his* abuse. When someone is trapped and asking to get out, and the other person is pushing them, goading them, patronizing them, becoming more and more calm as they become more and more unhinged, it's a perfectly appropriate human response to completely lose your ever-loving mind. If you are in a dynamic in which one person has clear power over you, and you are (legitimately) reacting to their dominance, you are *not* the abuser.

Will Couples Therapy Help?

You should *never* go to couples therapy with an abuser. *Abuse isn't a relationship issue, nor is it a communication problem;* it's an abuser problem, and no amount of couples therapy will help. In fact, it's considered contraindicated by most experts. In effective couples therapy, the therapist will take a neutral position and treat the issues of the relationship as fifty-fifty. Dr. Judith Herman, author of *Trauma and Recovery: The Aftermath of Violence—from Domestic Abuse to Political Terror* (Basic Books, 2022) says that victims of any kind of abuse need to experience a therapeutic alignment that is one hundred percent on their side, which by definition makes couples therapy contraindicated.

Most therapists aren't trained to recognize the signs of domestic violence. Therapists' basic training consists of zero hours of mandatory domestic violence training. *Zero.* The same is true of family law attorneys, family court judges, and doctors. The only therapists who have had training in recognizing abuse are those who have sought out additional training and continuing education in this area, and if they see that abuse is present in a relationship, they won't work with you as a couple (they will usually pull you aside and tell you why, and might even offer private counseling).

Because abusers are doing everything in their power to continue to exert power and control over you, they're not able to engage in therapy in the way that's necessary for progress and growth. Because abusers aren't capable of, nor interested in, communication or compromise, they approach therapy the way they approach every conversation you've already tried to have with them: as a game they need to win.

If you're being abused, please don't go to therapy with your abuser. Find a good therapist for yourself (one trained in domestic violence), and learn to empower yourself with knowledge, information, and most of all, healing. If an abuser really wants to stop abusing, they should seek out a therapy program *for themselves* that understands the work necessary to unravel the faulty belief systems and entitlement that underpins abuse. The Marriage Recovery Center (www.marriagerecoverycenter.com) is one such option.

When It's Time to Escape

Once you recognize that you are in an abusive relationship, you really do need to get out. It's not your job to save or heal your partner. Your only responsibility is to yourself and your children.

As I said earlier, in order to escape safely, you should work with a Certified Domestic Violence Victim's Advocate or your local domestic violence shelter for help in creating your safety plan. Here is everything you need to think about when creating that plan.

Exercise for Creating a Safety Plan:

This is also available to download at www.kateanthony.com/ book-resources

1. Decide on the safest time to escape. Make sure that your abuser has no idea where you're going. Consider leaving at a time when your abuser is least likely to be aware of your movements.
2. If possible, pack clothes, money, important documents, and evidence. While some things like clothes and toys are replaceable, having personal belongings can help ease the transition and make life in a shelter feel more comfortable.
3. Keep it all in a safe place, such as behind boxes in the garage, in the fake bottom of the trunk of your car, or with a trusted friend. Some essentials to pack include:
   - Identification, including children's
     - Birth certificates
     - Social Security cards or numbers written on a piece of paper
     - Driver's license
     - Photo identification or passports
     - Welfare identification
     - Green card
   - Important personal papers
     - Marriage certificate
     - Divorce papers
     - Custody papers
     - Legal protection or restraining orders

- Medical records for all family members
- Health insurance papers and medical cards
- Children's school records
- Investment records / Account numbers
- Work permit
- Immigration papers
- Rental agreement or house deed
- Car title, registration, and insurance papers
- Funds
  - Cash
  - Credit cards
  - ATM cards
  - Checkbook and bank account info
  - Login and passwords for all accounts
- Keys
  - House
  - Cars (if the car is in your name, or both of your names, you can take it. If it's only in your partner's name, you can't because they can report it stolen)
  - Safety deposit box
  - Mailbox or post office box
  - Gate
- A way to communicate
  - Notify a trusted friend or family member
  - Cell phone
  - Burner or disposable phone, fully charged and loaded with important numbers such as DV shelter, the DV Hotline 1-800-799-SAFE (7233), and safe friends and family

- Address book with important contact numbers
- Medical Supplies
  - At least one month supply of all medicines
  - Copy of prescriptions, including children's
  - Doctor's contact information
  - Pharmacy contact information
- Self-Care Items
  - Pictures
  - Keepsakes
  - Small family heirlooms, i.e., jewelry
  - Children's small toys or books (comfort items)
- Restraining Orders
  - Gather evidence to substantiate need for legal protection
    - Police reports
    - Photos of injuries
    - Print harassing/threatening texts and emails (some states won't accept screenshots as evidence)
    - Save harassing/threatening phone messages
    - Written statement, including dates and times, when partner caused harmful/dangerous behavior
4. Plan your exact escape route. Have plenty of gas in the car and your cell phone fully charged. If you do not have your own vehicle, look into bus routes or get in contact with a safe friend or family member who can provide transportation.

5. Inform *safe* family members or friends not to worry. It's important to keep this list as small as possible and limited to those who you completely trust.
6. Keep electronic use to a minimum. If an abuser is especially technologically savvy, take extra precaution by turning off your cell phone as you travel to a safe location, and follow all the recommendations in Chapter Seven about keeping yourself safe from cyber abuse.

Remember: no matter what type of abuse you're experiencing, the most dangerous time is when you leave. This doesn't mean you shouldn't leave your abuser; you simply must do it in the safest, most planned way possible.

Break Trauma Bonds and Stop Going Back

One of the most frustrating and heartbreaking things for domestic violence experts is to see victims go back to an abusive partner. Unfortunately, it is an all-too-common phenomenon. As difficult as it is to escape an abusive relationship, it's even harder to stay away. As I've said, it takes victims an average of seven times before they are finally able to stay gone. While some of this is because of financial abuse, trauma bonds also keep victims tied to their abusers. A trauma bond is an addictive pattern that's created through the cycle of abuse. When the *incident* portion of the cycle of abuse happens, the victim hungers for nothing more than to return to the intimate, loving, often intense connection she shares with her abuser. When the abuser comes back for reconciliation, the victim gets her wish, and with it a hit of dopamine in her brain. Dopamine is a neurotransmitter that plays a role in the reward center of the brain. Dopamine is released when we get notifications on our phones, when we level up in a video game, or when we do certain drugs, like cocaine. The reason these things can be so addictive is because the brain wants to chase the high of a dopamine hit. With cocaine, for example, the dopamine hit is very high and very sudden. We naturally want to experience that again, but over time it takes more and more cocaine to achieve the feeling of the first time, which leads to addiction.

Similarly, we become addicted to the high of reconciliation in the cycle of abuse. The bond is created in that reconciliation phase, when the abuser convinces you that you're everything and that it's you and them against the world. You've just come through the lowest of lows, and you're now in the highest of highs. You're bonded through the trauma of the cycle you've just gone through, and addicted to the high of the dopamine hit you get each time you reconcile.

As with any addiction, the best way to break a trauma bond is to go cold turkey, and that's the advice that's given all over the internet and social media: *Go no-contact!* However, if you share a child with the person to whom you're trauma bonded, you don't have the luxury of going no-contact, because you have to co-parent your children. In this case, it's important to *limit* contact as much as possible. Remember: you can't break a trauma bond while you're still engaging in the relationship. That's like trying to heal a cocaine addiction while still doing cocaine.

Use a co-parenting app like Our Family Wizard or FAYR in order to communicate with your co-parent and keep all communication about the children only. *Do not* respond to messages that aren't about the kids. If you can have a judge mandate the use of a co-parenting app, you'll be legally supported in setting this important boundary. When communicating, use Bill Eddy's BIFF (Unhooked Books, 2020) method for communication. BIFF stands for *brief, informative, friendly, and firm*. Your communication with your co-parent should follow that guideline (more on BIFF in a later chapter). Treat all your communication with your co-parent as you would a business transaction. Keep all emotion out of it and keep it polite, as you would with a business associate—regardless of how they're treating you. Remember: Keep your side of the street squeaky clean.

Block your co-parent on all social media. There is absolutely no reason you need to see their goings-on, or for them to be able to see yours. Do pick-ups and drop-offs of the children at school as often as possible (you drop them off at school in the morning, and your co-parent picks them up in the afternoon), and drop off any kids' stuff (soccer gear, stuffed animals, etc.) when you know your co-parent won't be home by leaving it on their porch or in a hidden spot on their property. (Don't send children to school with a huge bag full of their belongings. That will stigmatize and embarrass them, and this isn't their burden to bear.)

Remember, your abuser will want to maintain a connection with you because up until now they've managed to lure you back in every single time. They'll use multiple tactics to try to destroy any boundary you set. If you want this time to be different, *you'll* have to do things differently (the definition of insanity: doing the same thing over and over and expecting a different result). It will be hard because you have a very real emotional addiction to this person, and you want nothing more than to believe that things will be different *this time*. But remember what I said in Chapter Seven about the likelihood of an abuser changing: little to no chance. This is where your boundary work from Chapter Two will come in very handy.

One of my clients, Stella, experienced what was clearly a trauma bond with her ex-boyfriend, Arnold. She said it was the most intense and beautiful love she had ever felt. For decades, women had said that they wanted to crack the code to unlock Arnold's heart, but Stella had cracked it without even trying, and it was intoxicating and romantic to be his. She had met Arnold at her daughter's school, so they'd always see each other at drop-off and pick-up. They broke up and got back together so often over the course of two years that it became a running joke between the other parents. The pick-up gate was often where they would begin to rekindle after a breakup. A look. A comment. And then later a text. And the cycle would begin again. The highest of highs. The promises. The makeup sex. The Crazy Love, as they called it (hello, red flag).

What made this bond so hard to break was that Arnold wasn't what most people would classify as an *abuser*. However, he had so much childhood trauma that he was emotionally unable to function in a relationship. He'd been completely locked up for over forty years, and suddenly he was cracked wide open. Except Arnold didn't know how to be that vulnerable. The world wasn't a safe place for his tender heart, and he was a classic avoidant. Arnold would open his heart to Stella and his fear would overwhelm him and shut it down. He was so (unconsciously) terrified of being abandoned the way he was in infancy that his unconscious response was to try to decimate Stella first. And he did. Over and over again.

The irony was that Arnold wanted nothing more than to love Stella; he was just fully incapable of doing so. He later told her, "If I couldn't do it with you, Stel, I'll never be able to do it.

I know that. You were and always will be my One True Love." I usually don't believe such things about people; I tend to think they're more capable than they think (and Stella did too, which is why she tried so hard with him; she was sure she could love him enough to heal his fractured psyche), but after all was said and done, I believe Arnold was right. He was just too broken.

Arnold may have been broken, but he was also abusive to Stella. No matter the underlying reasons, the way he treated her was abusive. He was a narcissistic abuser. His fractured psyche was from a classic narcissistic wound, and no amount of love Stella poured into him would heal his broken heart.

At some point during our work together, Stella accepted that she needed to sever her bond with Arnold completely. We devised a strategy to support her decision. She asked a friend to pick up her daughter from school each day. This way, Stella couldn't see Arnold and be sucked back in. Not necessarily by him, but by her need to be connected to him. By her addiction to the highs of that relationship, which were the most intense she'd ever experienced. Luckily, school ended a few weeks later, and she had the summer to begin to heal. Stella's daughter only had one more year at that school, but as it turns out, Arnold didn't come back in September. Stella heard through the grapevine that Arnold and his daughter had moved out of state. However, the relationship had taken a toll on her. Stella and I have kept in touch, and she says it took her a full five years to feel like she wasn't completely broken from that relationship, and she's not sure she'll ever be the same.

If you have children with the person to whom you are trauma bonded, expect your healing journey to be long. You'll have to be extremely diligent in setting and holding your boundaries with them. Each time you break a boundary and get back together, even for a night, you set your healing back to zero. This is your work to do. Your abuser will want to suck you back in (also known as *hoovering*, after the old vacuums). It's your job to hold your boundaries firmly, putting your healing first, above all else. This is your self-care priority.

Trauma bonds are no joke. They're real, and they're devastating. Healing is possible but will take enormous work on your part. If you've ever given up an addiction, you know how hard it can be. This is no different. Except, while you can quit a drug, cigarettes, alcohol, or other substance completely, you can't fully quit your co-parent. This is why limiting contact is so incredibly important.

Leaving any relationship is difficult. Leaving an abusive one has a unique set of challenges. But it is imperative that you protect yourself and your children by walking away from your abuser... for good.

CHAPTER 9

What If They're an Addict or Mentally Ill?

Navigating Complex Challenges

THE 2011 "MULTINATIONAL Study of Mental Disorders, Marriage, and Divorce" (J. Breslau et al., National Center for Biotechnology Information) showed that marriages in which there is addiction or mental illness have a much higher rate of divorce. Depending on some variables, the study put the increase between 20 and 80 percent. Alcohol abuse, major depression (including bipolar disorder), and PTSD had the largest impact

When deciding to stay in or leave a marriage in which there is addiction or mental illness, the most important questions you should ask are: *Does your partner recognize that they have an addiction or mental illness? Do they want help for their addiction or mental illness?* and *Are they actively seeking that help on their own?* If the answer to these questions is yes, then there's hope for the marriage, but that doesn't mean it will be easy. The largest factor for the increase in the divorce rate in affected marriages is someone not seeking treatment. Someone who seeks treatment is aware of their problem and is taking responsibility for it. That's the first (crucial) step.

If the answer to the questions above is no (or yes, yes, no), then all may not be lost; you just have to realistically consider what kind of marriage you can have with this person, which may mean adjusting your expectations for emotional intimacy. In this chapter, I help you break down all you need to know about being married to (or divorced from) someone with mental-health or addiction issues.

Addiction

Addiction is one of the most widely misunderstood diseases in the world. Many people believe that addicts lack the will-power to quit their bad habits, and that if they really wanted to, they could stop at any time. Nothing could be further from the truth. For most addicts, the addictive cycles in the brain cancel out all choice whatsoever.

Addiction is, in essence, like any other disease, such as diabetes, heart disease, or cancer. As with other diseases, one of the most common signs for diagnosing or predetermining a propensity toward addiction is family history. This fact negates the idea that addiction could be a choice at all. No one would wake up one day and choose to become an addict, any more than they would choose to become diabetic. Addicts may make a choice to use initially, often because of some other mental or physical health issues. But over time, and often not very much time, the genetic predisposition for the disease takes over, and choice is eliminated. Supporting the idea that addiction is a mental disease rather than a choice are the ideas that addiction affects the addict's brain, impacting their ability to function normally, and that even when the substance is removed from the addict, they usually require ongoing recovery work so as not to relapse. If it were just a choice, their brains would go back to normal, and once they stopped using, it would be as if they'd never used at all. Add the genetic factor, and it's clear this is no choice.

So, it's right and necessary to have compassion for an addict. That being said, it's also right and necessary to recognize that you have no power to make another person get the help that's needed to recover from their disease. If you loved a diabetic and they refused to see a doctor and continued to eat too many carbs, even though they knew it would kill them, there would be little you could do to stop them. You could cook only healthy, low-carb foods at home, but if they walk out the door and go to the donut shop on their way to work, you're powerless to stop them. Just as you can't do medical work for a diabetic, you can't do recovery work for an addict.

But if it's not about *choice*, how do addicts make the *decision* to get help? It's a bit of a catch-22, isn't it?

Sometimes addicts don't decide to get help, and that's one of the hardest things to wrap your brain around. It's agonizing when you love someone so much and you can see their potential, but they continue to spiral deeper into their addiction. It's painfully difficult to come to understand that you can't control them or their actions.

For those who do seek help, sometimes it's because the pain of using ends up outweighing the pain of not using. For example, if they lose their job, their home, their marriage, or their kids, that pain will sometimes kick-start someone into rehab or a recovery program. For others, the shame of their addiction might outweigh the pain that's being covered up by using their drug of choice. For example, if they suffer from a crippling anxiety disorder and they use prescription drugs or alcohol to manage their anxiety, the shame or consequences of their addiction needs to outweigh the fear of facing their anxiety head-on.

Almost no one gets clean or sober because their spouse nags them, begs them, shames them, or otherwise tries to convince them to do it. In fact, that can often make things worse. It has to be the addict's choice, plain and simple. When they hear this, many people then try to figure out what they can do to force their spouse to make that choice. When you're married to an addict, they can seem like Dr. Jekyll and Mr. Hyde, and you know how wonderful they'd be, and how happy your marriage could be, if they could just be their good side all the time! Let me reiterate: *there is nothing you can do to control whether or when they get help.*

The best thing you can do—for yourself, your children, and yes, your spouse—is to focus on your own recovery. Addiction is a family disease, not just because it's genetic. Addiction affects all aspects of a family, and we learn to adjust our behavior around the addict just as we do an abuser because we're scared of rocking the boat. We worry that one thing we do may set them off on a bender, so we walk on eggshells trying not to trip the wire. When they're on a bender, or using, we cover for them, making excuses with friends and family, telling lies to cover our own secret shame. Just like the addict is changed through their addiction, so too are we. This is what makes it a family disease.

These are codependent behaviors which should be dealt with in your own recovery program. If you're in a relationship with an addict of any kind, please seek out an Al-Anon meeting in your area. Al-Anon is a 12-Step program for friends and families of alcoholics, although loved ones of all addicts are welcome. In Al-Anon, you'll learn to keep the focus on yourself. In Al-Anon, you'll learn that it's okay to love an addict. In Al-Anon, you'll be given the tools to enable you to live your life to its fullest, no matter what the addict in your life is doing. For many of us, this seems completely unimaginable. (Al-Anon meetings can be found at *www.al-anon.org.*)

I went to my first Al-Anon meeting in April of 1999. I had an incredibly deep fear that my boyfriend at the time (now my ex-husband) was going to break up with me. A man at a meeting said to me, "So what if he does?" And I was like, "*What?* So what if he does? I'll be shattered! I'll lose everything! I'll *die!*" He smiled and said, "Will you, though? Will you die? What if you're okay?"

I was angry about this conversation at the time, like, actually *enraged,* because it seemed this guy didn't understand how much being broken up with would hurt me. I loved my boyfriend! If he broke up with me, *I wouldn't be okay!* But this stranger did understand; it was I who didn't understand. I came into that relationship so codependent that I derived my entire sense of Self from my boyfriend. If he broke up with me, removing my total identity in the process, it actually felt like I would die. But this man was telling me that I wouldn't die. If I got dumped that night, or any other, I would be okay because there was more to me than I knew. The concept was literally unfathomable to me at the time. It was another six months before I finally understood and accepted what this guy was trying to tell me, and many more years before I metabolized it. Al-Anon taught me that no matter what someone else is doing—drinking, using drugs, breaking up with me, cheating on me—*I* have choices, and *I* will be okay. Al-Anon gave me the tools to begin building my Self. This doesn't mean I won't have feelings about things that happen to me; it just means that my entire soul won't be crushed to smithereens.

There are members of Al-Anon who happily live with active addicts for many years. These people are able to have full and flourishing lives and have complete acceptance for their loved one's addiction. There are also members of Al-Anon who leave their addicted spouses because they choose something different for themselves. But we can't recognize this ability to make choices when we're codependent and engaging in codependent behaviors.

If you can *choose to accept* your partner exactly as they are today, without trying to change them, you may be able to continue to have a happy life with them but this will only come through your own recovery work. If you are constantly trying to change them, trying to get them to get clean or sober (with threats, tears, begging, etc.), then neither of you are going to have a happy life, and in fact, you may push your partner deeper into their addiction due to stress and shame. (Almost all addicts suffer from an immense amount of shame, which they mostly project outwardly. The more you push them to feel that shame, the more likely they will be to keep using in order to suppress that feeling, or blaming you for it.)

If you keep covering for an addict, fixing their mistakes, cleaning up their messes, hiding their addiction from others, you're getting in the way of them hitting the bottom they need to hit in order to make the decision to quit. It may seem like you're helping them, but in the long run, you're cushioning their bottom so they don't have to feel the direct impact of their actions. Sometimes the most loving thing to do is get out of the way and let them hit bottom as hard as they can. This is often the only path to a clean and sober life.

It should be stated that if you have children with an addict, it's imperative that you protect them from any volatility this may create. An active addict should never have unmonitored parenting time with a child, nor should they ever be allowed to drive your children anywhere unless they've used a breathalyzer such as Soberlink in advance.

If They Quit, Will Everything Get Better?

In a word: maybe. Because addiction is a disease, it's not the substance that's at the core of the addict's issues; it's the addict's brain. If an addict goes into active recovery, life can indeed change for the better for all involved—as long as you, too, engage in your own recovery work, either through therapy or a codependency recovery program such as Al-Anon or Codependents Anonymous (CoDA). (More on codependence in Chapter Ten.)

Often, when someone first gets clean or sober, their friends and family members believe that all the family problems are finally over, when in fact they're just beginning. The addict now has to deal with whatever mental-health issues they were drinking or using to cover, along with withdrawal and an intense discomfort at being in the world without their crutch. They can feel extremely exposed and vulnerable, and be even more volatile than before. This is why it's so important for them to have a recovery group and program to lean on. And why it's important that you do as well.

When Bill Wilson and Dr. Bob first founded Alcoholics Anonymous in 1939, the wives of all the alcoholic men gathered in the kitchen, making coffee and preparing snacks for the meetings. As they talked in the kitchen, many of these women realized that now that their husbands were sober, they'd lost much of their purpose in life. They'd spent so much time, energy, and effort trying to get their husbands sober, now that they were they felt a gaping hole in their own existences. In addition to this, their husbands now had this community of other men to support them, and the wives were left feeling a bit resentful. After all the time they'd poured into supporting their husbands, surely their husbands should be spending their time with *them*, not these men? Didn't they owe them that?

Year after year, there became no denying the AA program worked, so eventually Bill Wilson's wife, Lois, and Dr. Bob's wife, Anne S., suggested that perhaps the same twelve steps that were helping the men get sober and live these new, vibrant lives might also work to help the women with their loss of identity. And thus, in 1951, Al-Anon was born.

I tell you this story, not for historical relevance, but to highlight how alone so many people feel when their spouses get sober. It can be a crushing blow to realize that all of the coping strategies you employed while the addict was active in their addiction are no longer needed, and just how taken over your life had become by the addict and their addiction. When all you could think about all day every day was whether or not the addict was using and what consequence that would have at home or work, and now you don't have to think about that, it can leave a pretty big void in your life. What's more, your partner may be spending more time in recovery rooms than at home, and while this is necessary for their recovery, it can make the partner of the addict feel like an AA widow/widower and like nothing has really changed. This is why doing your own recovery work is so important. Addiction is a family disease in that it alters the way everyone in a family functions as a result of the addiction. Take away the addiction, and those functions no longer work. We all need retraining.

If an addict quits their drug of choice but doesn't seek the emotional treatment or support of therapy, rehab, or a 12-Step program, it's almost guaranteed that life will become much worse over time. There may be a period of elation and relief, but, because addiction is a mental disease, it will soon devolve into something far darker. Alcoholics who don't drink but also don't seek any treatment or support are often called *dry drunks*. They exhibit all the behaviors they did when they were drinking, just without the alcohol. They may rage or engage in risky behaviors. These people don't drink, but they're far from *sober*. Webster's New World College Dictionary defines sober as "characterized by reason, sanity, or self-control; showing mental and emotional balance." This has little to do with not drinking, and everything to do with the recovery needed to rejoin society in a safe and meaningful way. Addicts need help to recover from their mental disease, not just their drug of choice.

If an addict chooses their own path to sobriety, incorporating some sort of therapeutic program or process, and you do this as well, the marriage has a very strong chance of surviving. Two people who are committed to creating and living a sober life together have a strong sense of purpose outside of their relationship, and this can strengthen almost any bond.

Mental Illness

According to the American Psychiatric Association, "Mental illnesses are health conditions involving changes in emotion, thinking, or behavior (or a combination of these). Mental illnesses are associated with distress and/or problems functioning in social, work, or family activities."

The APA also says that every year

- About one in five (19%) US adults experience some form of mental illness.
- One in twenty-four (4.1%) has a serious mental illness.
- One in twelve (8.5%) has a diagnosable substance use disorder.

These numbers skyrocketed during and after the pandemic, which make it frighteningly clear how many people suffer from mental illness in the United States today. It also highlights how little shame or stigma there should be around seeking treatment, and yet, so few actually do.

According to the CDC:

- Nearly one in four women received any mental-health treatment (24.7%) in the past twelve months, compared with 13.4 percent of men.
- Women were more likely than men to have taken medication for their mental health (20.6% and 10.7%, respectively) and to have received counseling or therapy from a mental-health professional (11.7% and 7.2%) in the past twelve months.

Why don't men seek treatment as often as women? Because we've conditioned men and boys that their emotional lives are shameful and should be hidden at all costs. We teach boys from a very early age that showing (or feeling) any of the softer emotions, such as fear, sadness, regret, or pain makes them "feminine" or "gay," and that these are the worst things for a boy to be. When boys are babies and toddlers they have full access to a wide range of emotional expression, but as early as four years old, boys are shamed into hiding their feelings, often being told to "man up," or "don't be a sissy." This forces their outlet for emotional expression to narrow to the point that almost nothing can get through. But the feelings don't stop; simply their expression does. The stress and pressure build up inside, "resulting in epidemic levels of social isolation, illness, and early mortality as men reach 45+," says Mark Greene in his 2016 book *Remaking Manhood, Stories from the Front Lines of Change* (CreateSpace Independent Publishing Platform). The ensuing result is an explosion of rage, abuse, depression, suicide, mortality, addiction, and alcoholism. All because we don't think men should have feelings.

This is the definition of toxic masculinity. That doesn't mean that men are toxic. It means that we've conditioned boys and men to suppress their emotions to the point that they fester and become toxic inside of them, and when the pressure builds, the toxins explode all over society. Women aren't the only ones hurt by toxic masculinity; men are far more damaged by it, even resulting in a shorter lifespan.

The best way for us to combat this is to remove as much, if not all, of the stigma as possible from men or boys seeking treatment for their depression, anxiety, or any other mood disorder or mental illness. Fortunately, we've seen an enormous shift in this in recent years with our current youth. For all the horrors of the pandemic, one thing that came out of it was epic numbers of teenagers, boys included, seeking treatment for their pandemic-related mental-health issues. I have a lot of faith that toxic masculinity is going to be greatly reduced in Gen Z and beyond, but we also see a rising tide of toxicity with school shootings, white supremacist gangs, and alt-right militias.

If your partner suffers from mental illness, knows and accepts this, but is resistant to treatment, see if you can find out why. If it's rooted in this toxicity, remind them that vulnerability is stronger than any form of holding it all in, and that you will support them in any way possible through the process. If they refuse to get a diagnosis, or follow through on a prescribed treatment plan, there's not much you can do to help or change the situation. As with an addict, the best thing you may be able to do for them is to let them hit their bottom, as long as your children are spared any direct repercussions. If they have a breakdown, lose their job, are arrested, or end up hospitalized, they'll have to face their illness head-on. Again, as with an addict, it must be their choice.

If there is a danger of suicide, it's imperative that you call the Suicide and Crisis Lifeline at 988 to get help. Your partner may need to be admitted for a seventy-two-hour hold for observation, assessment, and treatment. As with addiction, it's also imperative that you have your own support system in place for dealing with a loved one with mental illness.

Melinda's husband was diagnosed with bipolar disorder. His moods were extreme, and he had a hard time regulating his emotions and actions. He was abusive to Melinda, but she thought it stemmed from his bipolar disorder. Melinda went to therapy with her husband, and on her own, to try to make sense of what was happening, and also to truly assess whether or not change was possible. When she met with her husband's therapist alone, he told her that if her husband was consistent with his medication *and* therapy, he could make some shifts, but not to expect anything too dramatic, too soon. This would take time.

Melinda's husband was on and off his meds numerous times in the time we worked together, and his behaviors, on and off meds, were abusive. But because he had a medical diagnosis for which he was pursuing treatment, Melinda felt terrible about leaving him. Through our work together, Melinda began to realize that the work her husband had to do was his and his alone, and that hers was her own. Part of her work was realizing that she couldn't control his responses to her within their marriage, nor was she responsible for them. She began to realize that he was abusive completely separate from his bipolar diagnosis (there are plenty of bipolar people in the world who don't emotionally abuse their spouses).

Eventually Melinda filed for divorce. It's been almost four years, and her ex-husband is still attempting to control and abuse her and has delayed their divorce for years with his manipulation tactics. He still sees his therapist and is confirmed to be on his medication. Clearly his bipolar disorder wasn't the issue. If Melinda hadn't done the work to shore up her beaten down Self, she would have continued to have more compassion for her husband than she had for herself by putting his mental illness above her and her small child's emotional safety, even though his mental illness was only part of the problem.

When dealing with a partner with mental illness, it's really important to ascertain what's the mental illness versus what's just bad (or abusive) behavior. There are millions of people in the world who have various forms of mental illness and who are living happy, successful lives, and are in happy, successful relationships. These people are addressing their issues, seeking treatment, and are open to sharing their emotional struggles with their partners in appropriate ways. Mental illness is not an excuse for abuse or neglect, nor should it be the reason you put up with it from your partner.

CHAPTER 10

Is He a Cheater or a Sex Addict?

Clarifying The Impact of Infidelity

G ENERALLY SPEAKING, MEN and women appear to cheat for different reasons. Women often cheat because they're seeking something missing in their marriages, usually emotional intimacy. Men often cheat because they're looking for more sexual gratification than their (presumably exhausted) wives can give them—and because they *can.*

In the book *Cheatingland: The Secret Confessions of Men Who Stray* (Atria Books, 2022), the anonymous author did in-depth interviews with over sixty men who cheat on women with whom they claim to have "very happy marriages." (You read that right.) The author concludes from these interviews that men cheat because they want two women in their lives with whom they can have two distinct relationships. He says,

"A man wants a wife who helps build a happy, close-knit family, who helps him to be seen as someone who has a loving unit that is a valued part of their community, thus making him look good. She helps him forge his legacy. When men cheat, they want to have another woman in their lives who pumps up their ego, helping them feel attractive, sexy, and powerful. They want to be both the proud patriarch with an unforgettable lady at their side and the sexual animal they felt like when they were younger." In other words, men who cheat want a madonna and a whore, and what's more, they feel entitled to both.

The idea that it is somehow a woman's job to fulfill either of these needs for a man is, in a word, disgraceful. It's not a woman's job to make a man feel like a patriarch, nor is it her job to make him feel like a stud. If a man can't feel like a man without the help of (at least) *two women to pump up various* parts of his ego and anatomy, perhaps he's not much of a man to begin with.

And what's more, these men claim to love their wives. I know it sounds crazy, but most cheaters believe that infidelity doesn't mean they don't love their wives. In the cheater's mind, having sex with another woman has nothing to do with his wife. Absent from this exploration is what the unsuspecting wives of these men think about their husbands fooling around, because, of course, *they don't know*. The lack of empathy is staggering. According to *Cheatingland*, the number one reason men *stopped* cheating is to spend more time working. Not because they realized it was *wrong*, or because they want to spend more time with their wives and children. Nope. Because it was taking up too much time and energy that they wanted to devote to work.

Sex Addiction versus Cheating

When some men are caught cheating they'll often claim that they're a sex addict—as if that somehow absolves them of the responsibility of being faithful to their spouse. *I'm a sex addict! I can't help it. I have a problem. Help me!* And now they're the victim and all focus must turn to them and their pain, rather than the pain they just inflicted on their spouse. Sex addiction is real, and probably more prevalent than we know (or even want to know), and if someone realizes that they have such an addiction, admitting it is the first step to getting help. Hiding behind a sex addiction for the purposes of continuing to cheat, with no intention of getting help, however, is bordering on sociopathic.

The prevalence of sex addiction is difficult to assess, mostly because it's self-diagnosed and highly stigmatized. Early research suggests that between 3 and 5 percent of the population suffers from some form of sex addiction, but with the introduction of the internet and other societal factors, it's believed that number has increased greatly. It's now estimated that there are anywhere between twelve and thirty million people in the US affected today, a majority of them being men (*Sex Addiction Facts and Statistics*, Recovery Village, 2022).

Sex and porn addictions usually go hand-in-hand, as porn is often more accessible than sex partners or sex workers (not to mention, less expensive), and most addicts don't consider watching porn to be cheating. Their partners, on the other hand, usually disagree. (Note: in a healthy relationship these things are discussed and the boundaries of what's considered cheating or not is co-created between the partners. I know many women who love porn and consider it a healthy part of their sex lives with their spouses.)

For many, the compulsion to seek outside partners has less to do with sex, and more to do with a love or relationship addiction. In many people, this manifests as desperately seeking validation and confirmation of Self through the attention of others. Many of these people are also narcissists. Sex addiction is powerfully correlated with childhood trauma, with 97 percent of sex addicts reporting to have been emotionally abused as children, 81 percent sexually abused, and 72 percent physically abused. Recovery from sex and love addiction can be long and difficult, given the underlying conditions associated with them, and addicts often have many co-occurring conditions, such as anxiety, depression, OCD, substance abuse disorder, bipolar disorder, borderline personality disorder, and more (*Sex Addiction Facts and Statistics*, Recovery Village, 2022).

These statistics support my earlier assessment that humanity is in deep trouble. Because we don't tend to support men in processing trauma, we have a broad swath of the population turning to dangerous and terribly unhealthy behaviors as an outlet for their pain. And these behaviors destroy marriages. They also do real damage to the women these men claim to love. According to Recovery Village, an addiction rehab center, "Romantic partners, especially women, often suffer emotionally when they discover their partner has a sex addiction or has committed infidelity. As many as 80 percent develop depression, while 60 percent develop an eating disorder. Partners of people with sex addictions are also much more likely to contract an STI, such as HIV or HPV."

If someone truly does have a sex/love/relationship addiction that they want to stop, they'll seek treatment and do the work required. The trauma work that underlies all addiction is deep and challenging, and few people really want to face it, but it's the only way this cycle will ever stop. That being said, the recovery work needed can take *years* to really process, and it is a challenging undertaking. There's a saying in 12-Step programs that says, "First it gets better, then it gets worse, then it gets good, then it gets real." Often people stop the real work when things start to get better, but that's only the beginning. As with an alcoholic or any other addict, just quitting the substance or behavior doesn't lead to a sober life and quitting without doing some form of recovery work (12-Step, trauma therapy, or something else) is likely to lead to relapse. Staying in a relationship with someone going through this process will be hard, and you should be in your own recovery as well, as I said in the previous chapter.

Claire's husband was a sex addict. He was hiring sex workers at an alarming rate (sometimes multiple times a day) and had racked up over $250,000 in credit card debt that Claire knew nothing about. As soon as it was discovered, her husband went to Sex Addicts Anonymous (SAA) and began seeing a therapist who specialized in this level of addiction. Soon, Claire was asked to join the therapy so they could begin the arduous journey of recovering their marriage. It was clear that her husband had an addiction; his behaviors were clearly compulsive. And, as is so common, Claire's husband also had a history of being horribly abused as a child. All of this made Claire a compassionate and willing participant in their therapy sessions, despite the trauma the discovery had caused her.

Early in their couple's work, their therapist asked Claire to make a list of her non-negotiables, the things she needed her husband to do in order to make her feel safe. On her list were things like, *share your location on your phone, don't take your phone into the bathroom,* and *if I ask, show me your phone right away*. Given her husband's indiscretions, these were all very reasonable requests that were designed to help rebuild trust in the relationship.

Her husband had two jobs: continue his recovery work in earnest and comply with her requests. In their couples therapy sessions, they were only allowed to talk about their relationship and how his addiction had betrayed their bond. In his personal therapy and 12-Step work, he could talk all he wanted about his wounding and his childhood trauma, and all the things that went into bringing him to this moment. But in couples therapy, that stayed at the door, unless used as a way to help Claire understand how they got there. *The couple's work centered on Claire, not her husband's trauma.* Only in this way could Claire begin to feel safe again.

When Claire and I began working together this process had been in motion for some time, but their therapist had retired, and they weren't seeing anyone new. As time went on, Claire began to notice little things shifting. Her husband, who had been going to meetings daily, was now only going occasionally, and was becoming more and more tense. He began bringing his phone into the bathroom again, and when Claire would ask him not to, he would get defensive. At that point she'd ask to see his phone, and he'd become enraged. When she asked about his meetings, he was dismissive. I told Claire that these were red flags to notice and keep an eye on, but she also told me that at that point she didn't think she could ever trust him again; that even if he never reverted back to old behaviors, these micro-betrayals made her feel as if her marriage was over.

Claire and I set upon crafting a plan to enable her to safely leave the marriage on her own terms. Claire and her husband have stayed together, but they live like roommates now. Claire has a long-term plan to raise her kids, start working again, and get to a place where she can support herself on her own. She keeps a close eye on the family finances and has created a full life for herself outside of her marriage. Claire's decision to stay in her marriage was strategic, conscious, and temporary.

So, are they a sex addict or just a cheater? It's very difficult to know. What you can take to the bank, though, is that if someone claims that they're a sex addict and doesn't do the work to heal their addiction, they will cheat again. And again. And again.

Healing from Betrayal

If a partner has cheated and it wasn't a sex addiction, and they want to save the relationship, there is a very specific therapeutic process that needs to take place, and it should happen with a therapist who specializes in affair recovery. The first question a therapist should ask is, *Do you both want to recover this relationship*? As the betrayed party, you may not see the path forward; you may not know *how* you'll be able to recover this relationship, but that's not important at this juncture. The only question should be, do you *want* to save this marriage? If the answer from both parties is *yes*, then there is a path forward. If the answer from the betrayed party is, *I'm not sure*, there might also a path forward, which affair recovery therapy can reveal.

I would also ask the question, *Why do you want to save your marriage*? because men and women often want to save their marriages for different reasons, and now might be a good time to reveal this. The obvious answer is, *because I love him*, but I'd dig more deeply:

Why do you love your partner?

What are some qualities about your partner you respect?

How does your partner nurture your spiritual growth? How do you nurture theirs?

What do you bring to the marriage that you believe is worth your partner fighting for or forgiving?

This begins to open up space to determine someone's true commitment to the relationship, rather than a commitment to get past the cheating episode. It can also reveal a partner who doesn't want to lose a meal ticket or a housekeeper.

An affair can be a wake-up call for a couple, and an opportunity for them to look at how both parties have neglected the marriage. If both parties are committed to the marriage and willing to learn new relationship skills, this could be a time for them to deepen their intimacy and fidelity.

Another important question to ask is whether the affair was discovered or disclosed. If an affair was disclosed, you likely have a partner who very much wants the relationship to work. They probably feel guilty and are taking the biggest risk possible by laying it on the table. If an affair was discovered (which is more common), your partner's reaction to the discovery may be the bellwether of healing. If they turn it back on you, blaming you for neglect, not enough sex, or *anything* else, then you may have a partner who isn't willing to do the work to come back from the betrayal. That being said, affairs don't usually occur in a vacuum, so a skilled therapist will be able to help you identify the fractures in the relationship that led to the infidelity, and if they're healable. If your partner's reaction to being discovered is guilt and shame and they take responsibility for their actions, this is good news for your ability to heal, but affair recovery therapy is still necessary.

One of the most common things I hear from members of my groups is that when an affair, or chronic cheating, is discovered, after a few weeks the betraying party will get angry that their partner hasn't *gotten over it already*, while having put in almost no effort to try to heal the betrayal. They think just because they apologized and bought flowers, it should be over.

Betrayal like this can only be gotten over with hard work in affair recovery therapy. Anything that's swept under the rug simply creates instability in the foundation (a lumpy rug), and a marriage with instability in its foundation can't last. The betrayed party is the *only one* who gets to say when they're over it, or when they trust again. The betrayed party is the one who gets to say what they need in order to heal, and the betrayer's job is to do everything in their power to make their partner feel loved and safe again.

As with almost everything else, healing from betrayal is an action-based process. Watch what your partner does, rather than listening to what they say. They may say all the right things, but do they take actions that back up those words? Or do they make it all about themselves, their process, their feelings, or their wounding, and get angry with you for not getting over it sooner? Sadly, this is much more common, and a pretty good indicator that your partner is just trying to move forward without taking responsibility and will likely cheat again.

The C Word

Pia Mellody, Senior Clinical Advisor for The Meadows, a residential treatment center in Wickenburg, AZ, and author of *Facing Codependence* (Harper & Row, 2003), defines codependency as, "A complex subject that many describe as a disease, similar to alcoholism, with its roots in childhood trauma." Codependency is, at its core, the state of defining yourself through the eyes of another. It's the lack of a true sense of Self, the result of which is seeking to know, love, and understand yourself through the love, attention, or affection of someone else. Frankly, almost everyone has some codependent traits due to the fact that codependence is rooted in childhood trauma, and I personally don't know anyone who hasn't been affected by some form of childhood trauma. Women are especially prone to be codependent because codependence is a function of the patriarchy, in which we socialize men to be entitled and women to be compliant.

I don't believe codependence is the shameful thing it's been made out to be. In fact, I think there's great power in owning and understanding your codependency so that you can work to heal from it.

According to Pia Mellody, all codependents.

1. **Have difficulty experiencing appropriate levels of self-esteem**, which can mean we have too much or too little self-esteem, depending on the trauma we experienced. For example, if we were neglected as children, we may have too little; if we were enmeshed, and our parents set no boundaries with or for us, we may be grandiose or narcissistic. Fun fact: all narcissists and addicts are codependent; not all codependents are narcissists or addicts.

2. **Have difficulty setting functional boundaries**, which means that we don't know where our boundaries lie. This can lead us to have unhealthy sexual relation-

ships, to be taken advantage of, or to inappropriately trample other people's boundaries by trying to
control their feelings, thoughts, or behaviors.

3. **Have difficulty owning and expressing their own reality.**
According to Mellody, our reality is made up of our
thoughts and feelings. When we have difficulty owning and expressing our reality, it means that we
either understand our own thoughts and feelings
but don't want to tell anyone for fear of rejection, or
we're so disconnected from our own thoughts and
feelings that we don't even know what they are (as I
discussed in Chapter One).

4. **Have difficulty taking care of their adult needs and
wants,** which means that we wait for others to take
care of our needs or wants, usually without expressing what they are, because we don't know what they
are, or we're too independent and take care of them
ourselves, cutting off intimacy, or we confuse our
needs and wants, for example drinking a bottle of
whiskey when what we really needed was love.

5. **Have difficulty experiencing and expressing their reality moderately,** which means that we can be overly
expressive, really loud, really big over-sharers, or become invisible so others don't know we exist.

These core symptoms give rise to all sorts of extended
symptoms, such as process addictions (sex and love addiction,
relationship addiction, gambling, eating disorders, and more),
mood disorders (depression, Bipolar), anxiety disorders (OCD,
panic attacks, PTSD), and chemical addictions (drugs, alcohol).
Codependence is the underlying cause of almost all addictions and

mental-health disorders. Without addressing the root issue of codependence and the childhood trauma that created it, overcoming such addictions or disorders will be almost impossible. This is why people who try to quit drinking or drugging without the support of some kind of trauma therapy program usually relapse. Similarly, without addressing the trauma at the root of our codependency, we will have difficulty moving beyond these core issues.

The Traits of Codependency

Here are some more examples of what codependence might look like in your life. As codependents we:

- Put other's needs before our own because we believe that if we pour ourselves into others, they'll love us enough for us to feel good about ourselves.
- Compulsively caretake other people because we believe that if we take care of the other person, they'll love us, and then we'll feel complete.
- Have trouble identifying our own feelings because we are so often focused on how others feel that we don't even *know* how we feel.
- Don't honor the feelings we do have, often minimizing or altering them to suit another, because we're scared of being abandoned if we speak our own truth.
- Have trouble making decisions because we don't know what we want, we put others' wants before our own, or we're scared of making a choice someone else won't like.

- Believe we don't need anyone to take care of us; we're fine!
- Often carry around a lot of resentment so we lash out passive-aggressively, or in ways that aren't appropriate to the situation.
- Need to be "right" about almost everything so we look good to others, even if we lie or make up stories about things that we actually don't know anything about.
- Pride ourselves on being chameleons, when what's really happening is that we don't have a solid sense of our own Self, so we adapt to fit the people we're with.
- Compromise our own values in order to avoid being rejected.
- Are in charge or in control of everyone else's life, and rarely of our own.
- Quickly abandon our own interests or plans in favor of someone else's so we're loved and accepted.
- Confuse sex and love, and have a lot of sex we don't want to have in a vain attempt to be loved.
- Are spiritually bereft, having a difficult time connecting with a higher power because the *not knowing* (the essence of faith) is such a terrifying place for us to be.
- Offer advice and counsel to others because we truly think we know what's best, even if the other person hasn't asked, and then become resentful when they don't heed our advice.
- Are at once overly compliant, and overly controlling. It's a confusing dichotomy but makes complete

sense in the context of the childhood traumas most of us have suffered.

Healing Codependency

The best way to heal codependency is to seek out the trauma it's rooted in. Most of us developed certain coping mechanisms when we were trying to survive terrifying or chaotic childhoods. When we're out of that situation, however, those mechanisms become problematic, and can be seen as disordered. The trauma responses we developed in order to save our life when we were in danger served us well then, but now they get in the way of healthy function. In order to release them, we first need to identify them, and their root causes.

For many, codependency comes up later in life, when we're married to an addict, although I'd assert that most of us marry addicts because we unconsciously recognize the behaviors and personality of the addict from our childhood and are drawn to them as a way to try to heal the wounds of our past. It can be easy to blame all the relationship problems on the addict, but the fact of the matter is that codependency can be just as disruptive to relationships as the addict or their addiction. No one likes to be controlled, and every healthy person wants a partner who has a solid sense of Self.

The very best way to heal codependency is through trauma therapy and the various support groups available for codependents, including Al-Anon, and Codependents Anonymous (CoDA). There are meetings all over the world, and since the pandemic, many of them are on Zoom so you can attend meetings virtually from anywhere! It's recommended in almost all

12-Step programs that you try six different meetings before deciding if the program is right for you. Each meeting will have different people and a different feel. If one meeting doesn't feel right to you, another might. (Pro tip: this applies to therapists as well!) Melodie Beatty's book, *Codependent No More* (Spiegel & Grau, 2022) and Pia Mellody's book, *Facing Codependence* (Harper & Row, 2003) are also great resources.

CHAPTER ELEVEN

How Does Divorce Even Work?

Understanding the Legal and Financial Aspects of Divorce

IT'S REALLY IMPORTANT TO understand the mechanics of divorce before entering into it, and often people want to know how it works before making their final decision to leave a marriage. Divorce is a complex and tricky business, with laws that vary country to country, state to state, and sometimes even county-to-county. In this chapter, I talk about how divorce works—generally speaking—in the United States, but you should absolutely consult an attorney in your area to get the full understanding of how divorce works where you live.

The most important thing to know about divorce is that you're making the biggest legal and financial decisions of your life in the midst of the biggest emotional upheaval of your life, and that is a *terrible combination.* If you choose this path, in order to avoid complete disaster, it's really important to give yourself—and your spouse—time to process the emotional aspect of what's happening before diving into the legal and financial aspects of the divorce process. This can be really hard for those who've been thinking about this for years. Once you finally make the decision to leave, you naturally want to get the ball rolling as fast as possible. Unfortunately, this will make you more likely to get sucked into the kind of contentious divorce that harms children and can cost tens of thousands of dollars. No matter how long you've been thinking about this, no matter how many times you've told your spouse you're thinking about divorce, when you finally tell them this is the end, *this will be news to them.* So please be sure to let the dust settle before moving forward with any plans.

In the meantime, you should be doing some due diligence about the various options available to you as you move forward, and that's what this part of the book provides.

Different Types of Divorce

When deciding whether or not to get divorced, it can be helpful to understand what the process looks like, not just the sensational stories you read about in the tabloids, but what it looks like in reality, for you.

There are, essentially, four different ways divorce can be done, depending on your relationship with your soon-to-be-ex and how complicated your assets are.

1. The least expensive, and most simple, is the **kitchen-table** divorce, in which you and your partner sit

down together and hammer out all the details between you. You can then either file at your local courthouse or use one of the many online divorce filing platforms available today, such as Hello Divorce, which I highly recommend (www.hellodivorce.com). This option works best if there aren't very many complicated financials involved, if your relationship is mostly collaborative, and your parenting plan straightforward. This is not an option if you're leaving an abusive marriage, as it gives your abuser further opportunity to try to control you.

2. The option I most recommend is **mediation**. In mediation, you and your partner will sit with a mediator who will help you come to agreements about all the various decisions that need to be made: how will you split assets, liabilities, property, parenting time, and more. It's important to note that a mediator is a *neutral third party*. It's their job to help you and your spouse come to a consensus on things that need to go in your divorce decree. It's *not* a mediator's job to advocate for either party, or to give legal advice. For this reason, you should each have a *consulting attorney* whose job it is to advise you on what you should be asking for in mediation. This is the person who tells you what the law is, and what you should be mediating *toward*. You might end up bringing your consulting attorneys into mediation if things get sticky. Your consulting attorney is also the person who will read your final decree before it's filed, just to be sure you've covered all your bases and aren't making any glaring mistakes.

Mediation is about coming to a middle-ground on various points that might be contentious; it's not about getting everything you want. As in all negotiations, you should expect that both of you will be unhappy about a few things, and comfortable with others. For the most part, mediation will occur with both parties present, unless the proceedings get contentious, in which case a mediator may choose to *caucus* you both, which means that you'll each go into a different room (or a breakout room on Zoom), and the mediator will go back and forth between you.

Choosing a good mediator is critically important. Mediators are often attorneys, Certified Divorce Financial Analysts, or therapists, all of whom have undergone training to become mediators as well. If you have a tricky legal case, an attorney-mediator may be your best choice. If your case is highly emotional, a therapist-mediator might be best for you.

Not all mediator training is created equally, so I highly recommend finding someone who has been trained by a reputable mediation training organization, such as The Mosten Guthrie Academy. Forest "Woody" Mosten is one of the pioneers of the mediation field and has written a number of books on the subject. Susan Guthrie, Esq. is one of the top family law attorneys and mediators in the country. Together, Woody and Susan have created the most comprehensive 40-hour mediation training in the world. Anyone who comes out of their academy is sure to be top-notch.

3. **Collaborative Divorce** is a specific process that takes the team approach to divorce. People often confuse the term *collaborative divorce* (as in, we want to get along amicably through this) with the official process, *Collaborative Divorce.* In the Collaborative Divorce process, you'll each have a Collaborative Attorney. Collaborative Attorneys have special training in the Collaborative process. There will also be a Certified Divorce Financial Analyst, one or two Collaborative Coaches, and a co-parenting Specialist if needed. (It should be noted that Collaborative Coaches are always licensed mental-health professionals, not certified coaches, such as myself.) The International Association of Collaborative Professionals (IACP) is a great resource for finding Collaborative Professionals in your area.

   Collaborative Divorce is similar to mediation in that you'll be working with your partner to come to agreements, but different in that the entire team will usually be present at each meeting. When things get tough, your Collaborative Team may also caucus you both, but in that case, you'll be caucused with your Collaborative Coach who will help you work through your feelings in order to come to a reasoned agreement.

   One thing to note is that if your Collaborative Divorce negotiations fall apart, none of your Collaborative team can work with you in litigation—meaning you'll have to start from scratch with a new team of professionals should you need to litigate, and you'll have lost all the money you've already spent if you end up throwing out everything you've already agreed to. This *disqualification clause* is critical to the Collaborative process, however, because it seeks to ensure that everyone is invested in working together, even when things are difficult, and because it releases the attorneys from their obligation to always be preparing for litigation, which they would need to do if the disqualification clause wasn't in place.

4. The most expensive, most contentious, least desirable, and yet most common option for divorce is **litigation**. In litigation, each party retains their own attorney, and the attorneys duke it out on your behalf. Where this gets tricky is that sometimes attorneys will fight for things their clients don't even know about. I've heard of cases in which the parties spent thousands of dollars on their attorneys only to find out that what the attorneys were arguing about the clients were actually in agreement about.

   If you, your partner, and your attorneys can't come to agreements on certain things, you'll then end up before a judge in family court who will simply rule on any disagreements. For example, if you can't agree on who gets to keep the house, a judge may simply rule that you have to sell it and split whatever profit or loss that may incur.

   Litigation is the worst for kids because it can put them squarely in the middle of a vicious court battle. Unfortunately, many abusers will do almost anything to keep a case in litigation because it provides them with another tool to continue their abuse, post-separation. Cases against abusers are hard to settle because while you're there to come to an agreement, they have an entirely different mind-set: they're there to create conflict. Some people call these cases *high-conflict*, but it's important to recognize that usually only one person in this scenario is high-conflict, and they should in fact be called what they are: *domestic abuse cases*. Court battles with abusers can go on for decades, and until the family law system learns to recognize abuse and abusers, victims will continue to be victimized by these vexatious litigants.

No matter what kind of divorce you choose, do your due diligence by checking your state laws and consulting with a good, qualified, recommended attorney.

How to Choose an Attorney That's Right for You

No matter what kind of divorce you choose, you'll likely need an attorney at some point in the process, whether as a consulting attorney for your mediation, your Collaborative Attorney, or your litigator. Choosing your legal support during this delicate and emotional time can be difficult and should be done carefully. Something I see often with my clients is that they use the same mechanism to choose their attorney that they used to pick their spouse. They end up with an attorney who neglects them, or worse, abuses them, and that they ultimately have to fire.

Your attorney is not your coach or therapist, but they should still make you feel supported and taken care of. They won't always tell you what you want to hear, but when they're laying down some difficult truths they should do so with kindness and compassion. Your attorney should never yell at you, belittle you, or make you feel that you're a burden on their time. Remember: *your attorney works for you.* If at any time you don't feel that they're working for your best interests, you can (and should) fire them.

You should interview at least three different attorneys in your area, and come prepared with a list of questions, which I've outlined at the end of this section. If at all possible, get recommendations from people in your area who've had the kind of divorce you want. For example, if you want an amicable divorce, don't consult with the shark litigator who handled your friend's super-high-conflict case. At the end of each consultation, ask yourself if you're more educated about the law in your area than you were going in, and if you feel supported. This is a good time to check in with your Inner Guide. What does she tell you about this person? If the attorney seems overworked and frazzled during your meeting, or if they don't give you their full, focused attention during a consultation, don't hire them. If they don't have the capacity to focus on you during a consult, they don't have the capacity to take on your case. If they become aggressive and immediately want to make bold, contentious *shark* moves, move on. Shark attorneys thrive on (and often create) conflict, and you want to avoid that at all costs. You're looking for someone who will clarify the law and give you reasonable expectations for your particular divorce. You may need someone assertive, but try to stay away from someone too aggressive.

You also want an attorney who has experience with your particular kind of divorce. If you're divorcing any kind of domestic abuser, you want to be sure your attorney has experience with this. They should answer the question, *Have you worked with cases of domestic violence?* with *Yes, I have a lot of experience and training in this,* not, *Yeah, I've dealt with it a few times,* or, *No, but it doesn't really matter.* It matters. If you're divorcing someone with addiction issues, make sure your attorney is experienced in this and knows the ins and outs of how this might be handled in your state.

Exercise for Hiring the Best Attorney for You:

Here's a list of questions you should ask an attorney in a consultation. You may add your own questions, based on your specific circumstances.

COMMUNICATION:

- How will we communicate about my case?
- Will I communicate with you directly?
- How often will we communicate, and through what means?
- Will I be communicating with a paralegal?
- What is your usual response time?

FINANCES:

- What is your hourly rate?

- How much of a retainer do you require?
- If I speak with a paralegal, is that billed at a different rate?
- Other than being cooperative, how can I keep my divorce costs down?
- How might you handle it if my spouse seems to be working to drive my costs up?
- How often will you bill me?
- What are the chances of getting my legal fees paid by my spouse, especially if they're the one escalating matters?

EXPECTATIONS:

- How long might my divorce take?
- What does the typical divorce process look like?
- How does the court usually rule in cases like mine?
- Do you have time to take on my case?
- What does the law say about [certain things pertaining to your case]?
- Can I get temporary orders?
- What temporary orders should I try to get?
- How does the process of getting temporary orders work?
- What child custody and parenting plan makes sense in my case?
- What does state law say about how much child or spousal support I should expect?
- Do you have references I can contact?
- Who will be working on my case? If we need to go to court, who will be making court appearances?

Remember to add any questions that pertain to your case specifically, such as use of Soberlink, drug-testing, monitored parenting time, and anything else legally relevant.

Understanding Support

Divorce can cause a lot of financial fear. People who don't have or make a lot of money are scared about whether or not they'll have enough money to live on and support their children. Those who have more money are often worried about a dramatic change in lifestyle. Whatever your financial circumstances, when all is said and done, you'll have to turn the finances available to support one household into supporting two households. This is an enormous shift for most people to make, and enough to cause anxiety in even the most frugal of parents.

Since fear is best eradicated by knowledge, and usually exacerbated by not being clear on the facts, laws, and your rights, let's break this down a bit. There are two different kinds of support you may receive or have to pay: *child support* and *spousal support* (also known as alimony, or spousal maintenance). Usually these are calculated separately, as child support is meant to be for the support of the children, and spousal support is meant as a way to even out a financial inequity that may have been built during the marriage.

Let's start with child support, as that's often the most straightforward. Because all states differ in their approaches and calculations (for example, Texas doesn't have spousal support, proving once again that Texas is one of the least friendly states to women), it's important that you consult with an attorney in your state to find out what your rights or responsibilities may be.

What Is Child Support and What Does It Cover?

According to the Judicial Council of California, "Child support is the amount of money that a court orders a parent or both parents to pay every month to help pay for the support of the child (or children) and the child's living expenses." (This definition is fairly consistent across all states.)

If one parent makes significantly more money than the other parent, or if one parent has been the stay-at-home parent and needs to get back on their feet financially, child support is there to ensure that the children are provided with basic necessities in each household. In most states, you don't need to account for how you spend your child support, as it's generally accepted that the funds are being spent for the reasonable needs of the child. In some states, however, the parent receiving child support may have to show an accounting if there's a reasonable doubt as to how the funds are being spent.

Just because someone receives child support, it doesn't mean they're then responsible for all extra activities or incidental expenditures related to the children. Anything additional, like extracurricular activities, sports equipment, and back-to-school shopping, should be shared between parents, often equitably, rather than equally. (For example, if one parent makes 25 percent more than the other, that parent will pay 25 percent more for additional child-related expenses.) *This should be negotiated and clearly stated in your divorce decree as most states do not have laws that cover the sharing of these expenses.*

Many people mischaracterize child support as *paying my ex*. With this mindset, people often resist paying and fall behind. *Child support is for children.* Failure to pay child support is considered a crime, and each state has its own child support enforcement agency which operates separately from the individual parties involved. In other words, if you go to court for failure to pay child support, the child support enforcement agency (not your ex) comes after you, the idea being that someone who is owed child support shouldn't have to bear an even larger financial burden in order to recoup what's owed to them. In 1992, the Child Support Recovery Act was passed, making it a federal crime to fail to pay child support. According to the Department of Justice, "Federal law makes it illegal for an individual to willfully fail to pay child support as ordered by a court in certain circumstances. Convicted offenders may face fines and imprisonment." Sadly, despite these laws, it can still be very difficult to collect unpaid support.

How Is Child Support Calculated?

All states have a child support calculator you can look up online. These calculators will often ask for the income of each parent, allowable deductions, the number of children, and in many states, the percentage of custody you're seeking. Tying child support to custody can create a lot of conflict around parenting time. As noted in the introduction to this book, many litigators will urge a parent to fight for more custody so they can get more support or have to pay less. This is how children become pawns, and, in extreme cases, has led to cases of *parental alienation* in which a parent accuses the other parent of horrific and often unfounded abuses in order to take a child away from that parent altogether to avoid having to pay child support. (More on parental alienation later.) For example, if Parent A makes $100,000 a year, and Parent B makes $30,000 a year, and they plan on having fifty-fifty custody of their three children, the state calculator will spit out a number that Parent A will need to pay Parent B in order for Parent B to effectively care for their three children. As I've said, where this gets tricky is when Parent A realizes that if they fight for seventy-thirty custody, then they'll have to pay less child support to Parent B. If Parent A cares more about money than what's best for their children, or simply wants to *win* at the game of divorce, then the kids get put in the middle of that fight.

Not all states tie child support to percentage of custody, so check the laws and Child Support Guidelines in your state. (There is a grassroots movement afoot to sever parenting time from the calculation of support nationwide, which will hopefully take hold soon.)

All states have criteria for determining when child support will end, usually based upon the age of the child; however, parents can agree to pay child support for a longer period of time and in many states, if the child has special needs, child support can be ordered to be extended beyond the usual cutoff age of eighteen.

What Is Spousal Support and What Does It Cover?

Spousal support can be much trickier than child support, and the laws vary widely from state to state. Spousal support was originally created in the 1950s when women overwhelmingly didn't work and stayed home to care for their children. If a woman got divorced, she had few options to support herself, so she was paid alimony, usually for life, or until she got remarried. Nowadays, spousal support is designed more as rehabilitative support for a spouse who chose to become a stay-at-home parent (or who didn't pursue their career in the same way as they may have if they had not had children to care for) and needs time to rebuild a career, when there is a discrepancy in the incomes of the two parties, or for other reasons that the court deems necessary (most states have twelve or more factors that a judge can take into consideration in determining alimony at their discretion).

The two main questions people want answers to are how much will I get, and for how long? The answers to both of these questions depend on a lot of factors, state law being one of them. In California, for example, spousal support is given for 50 percent of the duration of a marriage, if you've been married for ten years or less. If you've been married for more than ten years, no term is set, which many people take to mean they'll get support for life, but that's very rare (more on that in a minute). So, in California, if you've been married for nine years, you're eligible to receive spousal support for four and a half years. (That's not to say that you can't negotiate your own amounts in mediation if you both agree and a judge is willing to sign off on your agreement.)

In Connecticut, however, the duration and amount of spousal support is based on the rehabilitative need of the recipient and is discretionary (by the parties or a judge), based on things such as the income of each party, their level of education, the health of each party, the age of the children, and who the more available parent is. A couple with young children, or children with special needs that will require at least one parent to be more available on a daily basis, may decide that the parent who's been the stay-at-home parent should continue to not work in order to care for the children, in which case they may be awarded more spousal support to make this a possibility. This may continue until the children are at an age at which they can come home from school on their own and are old enough to take care of themselves. In these cases, a *step-down* approach may be used, in which the total amount paid is stretched out further by being lowered incrementally every few years as the children grow and the recipient eases into the workforce.

As you can see from just these two examples, state law varies widely, so again, be sure to consult an attorney in your area on your local laws.

He Cheated on Me. Can I Get More Money?

Currently all states in the US are no-fault states, which means that no one has to prove fault to get a divorce. There are, however, a handful of states in the union that have fault clauses in them, and in those states proving fault may result in a more favorable distribution of assets or increased spousal support for the wronged party.

Now, if your spouse cheated on you and spent $130,000 paying his affair partner's rent, taking her to dinner at country clubs, and traveling the world, then yes, your spouse will have to reimburse you for the marital assets he spent on another woman, even in no-fault states.

Usually, however, just because one person cheated, is an addict, or any number of things that make the divorce their *fault*, it doesn't mean that filing for a fault divorce will make any difference in the outcome. While it may seem only fair that the party at fault should shoulder more of the financial burden for a divorce you never wanted, it's simply not how the law works at present.

All that being said, however, there is a recent conservative movement afoot to eliminate no-fault divorce because they believe it makes it too easy for spouses (read: women) to end their marriages, often citing *traditional family values* as their main concern. This movement follows quickly on the heels of other conservative movements such as the overturning of Roe v. Wade, attacks on same-sex marriage, and limiting access to contraception. In a family court system that already overwhelmingly favors men (despite what fathers' rights activists want you to believe), this will be disastrous and dangerous for women, especially those trying to leave abusers. If we go back to fault-based divorce only, women would have to prove their spouse was at fault in the breakdown of the marriage just to be able to get a divorce. If they cannot prove it, which is harder than it sounds, then they would have to stay married. Clearly, we need to do all we can to stop this from happening. Keep an eye on this and lobby your state representatives to vote to keep no-fault divorce on the books.

The states that allow you to ask for divorce based on fault grounds are: Alabama, Alaska, Arizona, Arkansas, Connecticut, Delaware, Georgia, Maryland, New Jersey, New York, North Carolina, South Carolina, Vermont, Virginia, and the District of Columbia. You don't *have* to prove fault in these states, or in D.C., but you can, if it will benefit the financial or custodial outcome of your divorce.

Can Support Be Modified?

In most cases, support can be modified based on a substantial change in either party's income or circumstances. If the payor of support loses their job, for example, then they may petition the court for a downward modification of both child and spousal support. If they change jobs and their income significantly decreases, they may also request a modification, although the judge may ask them to prove the job change was necessary as there are many people who will get a lower paying job out of spite. If the recipient begins to make more money, the payor may petition to lower the amount of support. It's advisable that you have a *safe harbor* clause in your decree that states that there can be no modification up to a certain amount. In other words, as your salary increases, you'd be protected from modification until you reach a certain agreed-upon threshold.

Can I Get Spousal Support for Life?

These days it's very unusual for someone to be awarded spousal support for life. These cases generally occur only if someone hasn't worked for many years *and* is over an age at which entering the workforce would be feasible, or has a disability or some other factor that would prevent them from becoming self-supporting. For example, if you've been married for thirty years, have never really worked outside the home, and are now in your sixties, you may be awarded spousal support for life—but only if the money is available. When your ex-spouse retires, however, your support may be dramatically reduced. Another case in which support may be awarded for life would be in the case of a catastrophic accident that occurred during the marriage that would make it impossible for the person to work.

Many people believe that if they live in California and have been married for more than ten years, spousal support for life is automatic. Friends and relatives will even tell you to stay married until you hit that magical ten-year mark so you can get spousal support for life. Unfortunately, this is false information, and not good advice.

What About the Lifestyle to Which I'm Accustomed?

Many people believe they're entitled to enough support to keep them in the standard of living to which they became accustomed during the marriage. The issue with this is that few people can stretch the budget that supported one household to support two households in the same manner. Generally speaking, there's only so much money to go around. Most people's lifestyles take a hit during divorce, but statistically speaking, women's lifestyles take far more of a hit than men's.

One of the ways this manifests is in giving up our homes. When I got divorced, I opted to give my husband the house. I did the math and recognized that since we'd been married for only five years, I was only going to get spousal support for two and half years. I'd *just* be able to cover the mortgage for that time, but after that I'd be screwed. I also knew that if there was any damage to the house, or if it needed any repairs, I'd have a hard time paying for them. It didn't make financial sense for me to fight for the house., But since it was underwater from the housing crash, I also didn't get any sort of payout for giving it up. And so, in May of 2009, I moved from a beautiful, albeit small, house with freshly manicured lawns, rose bushes, a gazebo, new granite countertops, stainless steel appliances, and glass cupboards in one of the most desirable parts of town to a run-down rental in the sketchy part of town. There simply wasn't enough money for me to buy another house commensurate with the one I left. If I'd demanded to keep the lifestyle to which I'd become accustomed, I would have been hit with some harsh math realities down the line.

But what I did gain was a fresh start and clean energy, which was absolutely priceless. The financial struggles I faced in the decade I was building my business proved that I made the right choice. Had I fought to keep my house, it would have been a financial disaster. In fact, fighting to keep the marital home is one of the biggest financial mistakes women make in divorce.

Mortgage Consultant and Certified Divorce Lending Professional, Tami Wollensak, told me in an interview on my podcast that even if you legally get the house in the divorce, if you've been a stay-at-home-mom and are relying on spousal and child support, you may not even qualify to refinance the mortgage into your name. And even if you do, a refi may increase your monthly payment, depending on mortgage rate fluctuations.

When pleading his case to keep our house, my husband said to me, "Kate, wherever you go is home to our son. I'm already disenfranchised because I see him so much less than you do. If I stay in the house, at least the house is familiar. If I get a rental somewhere, nothing will feel familiar to him and I'll be further disenfranchised." I couldn't argue his point, and it's something I repeat often to clients and followers who've been stay-at-home parents. *Don't fight to keep a home you can't afford to maintain long-term. Live somewhere you know you can afford and infuse it with all the love you have in your heart, and your kids will be more than fine. Wherever you go is home to your children.*

I'm still in the rental I moved into in 2009. My landlord eventually did some renovations on the house, and the neighborhood has improved dramatically. I've painted and decorated every room to my liking and built a deck out back. I now live in one of the most desirable neighborhoods in Los Angeles, and I've been in this house for so long that my rent is about half of market value. Because I moved into a house that cost less than my mortgage would have, I was also able to squirrel away a good portion of my spousal support each month in order to make it last longer than the two and half years I'd been allotted. I can't tell you how quickly that time goes, and how little money I was making by the end of my third-year post-divorce. Having that savings to tide me over a bit longer was invaluable.

A Certified Divorce Financial Analyst can help you begin to think long-term about your financial security, and a Certified Divorce Lending Professional can walk you through whether you would qualify to take over your mortgage in a refinance. I highly recommend hiring these kinds of professionals as part of your divorce process.

What if I'm Sure My Spouse Is Under-Earning Just to Spite Me and Get Me to Pay Support?

If your spouse is a chronic under-earner, you may want to have an employment evaluation done as part of your divorce proceedings. Often a judge will look at employment records, education levels, mental and physical health, and give someone a certain amount of time to begin earning to their potential.

Betsy was a high-achieving high-income earner who was divorcing John, a chronic under-earner. John had a master's degree but was working at a building supply store making minimum wage. There were no chronic illnesses or mental-health issues holding John back. He simply had earning potential he was choosing not to reach and was asking Betsy to pay spousal support based on the difference in their incomes. I recommended that Betsy ask that John have an employment evaluation as part of their support negotiations. The judge agreed and the evaluation found that John was willfully under-earning. Betsy generously offered to give John a year of additional support in order to get himself back into the workforce earning a salary commensurate with his education, after which he'd have to be earning to his potential or suffer his own consequences. With Betsy no longer enabling his entitled under-earning, John chose to get a job in his field of study, and now makes a decent living on his own. Betsy still has to pay some support, which she does willingly, but it is nowhere near what John was asking for in the beginning.

Will My Support End if I Get Remarried?

In most states, if you remarry, your spousal support will end. In some states, the payor will need to petition for a modification, but in many states, termination of spousal support is automatic. In many states, cohabitation is also grounds for termination of spousal support unless expressly written otherwise in your divorce decree. Child support should remain unaffected.

On a crossover series Susan Guthrie and I did on our podcasts, Susan told the story of a divorced woman she knew who had a baby with her new partner. The couple lived next door to each other for a good amount of time in order for her to keep her spousal support coming from her ex. They had a newborn and didn't live in the same house! I know a woman who's been living with her fiancé for over a decade in a state which doesn't penalize for cohabitation; she has no intention of marrying him because it will cut off the significant amount of spousal support she receives from her very wealthy ex. The problem here is that these laws keep women from moving forward with their lives in ways that would be meaningful to them while keeping them financially tethered to their exes. While a cost-benefit analysis is always prudent, keep in mind what you're really giving up if you choose not to move forward in your life because of money, and what it might be worth to you, emotionally and psychologically—not just monetarily.

Should I Turn Down Spousal Support Because It Keeps Me Complacent?

Some people argue that women who receive spousal support are less ambitious and assertive when it comes to job-seeking. I find this theory offensive, reductionist, and, frankly, privileged AF. Almost all women I know, have coached, or are among the over tens of thousands of women currently in my Facebook groups or following me on Instagram want to work. They want nothing more than to be free of their exes, and to not feel tethered to them financially. Almost all of them would love to be able to say, *Hey, you know what? I'm good. I got this. I don't need your money.* To them, being fully self-supporting would be empowering and vindicating. In fact, a great number of them are willing to walk away from any support just to be free of their spouses. I always caution against this.

Unfortunately, far too many women are in the position of needing spousal support because they chose to opt out of the workforce in order to care for their children and are now left with very little return on the significant investment they made in their families. If they have worked outside the home throughout their marriage, the gender pay gap and other patriarchal systems have kept them economically disadvantaged. For these women spousal support is absolutely necessary to help them ease the transition into singlehood, and most of them don't get nearly enough, or for nearly as long as they actually need.

I had support for two-and-a-half years. At first, I thought this would definitely be enough for me to start a new career, or maybe even get remarried (if I'm honest, that was the real plan). What I didn't take into consideration was how much healing I had to do before I'd even be able to wrap my brain around a new career, and how many frogs I'd have to kiss before meeting my Prince Charming (still waiting). Sure, I could have gotten a job, but what I wanted was a career, a passion, a *purpose*. And after dedicating myself to other people for years, I deserved it. And so do you. The spousal support I received wasn't a handout. It didn't make me lazy or apathetic. It wasn't a *luxury*. It was *rehabilitative*. It allowed me to rehabilitate my life and afforded me the ability to create something meaningful. In fact, had I not had the support that I was, yes, privileged enough to receive, I would not be writing this book. I would not have touched the lives of the thousands of women who listen to my podcast and follow my work. I would have had to get a job, and wouldn't have had the chance to go back to school, to study, and to create. I'd assert that *not* taking the spousal support that's due to us can keep women from becoming our best, most potent selves.

The Reality of Having Been a Stay-at-Home Mom

Let's take a moment to talk about the bill of goods we've been sold about the charmed life of the stay-at-home mom. Before I start, I want to make it very clear that I have the utmost respect for the women who dedicate their lives to raising children and running a household. It's the hardest job I ever had. But believe me when I say this myth is the greatest cause of the subjugation of women.

When I became pregnant, I had just lost my job managing a successful fitness studio that was being financially mismanaged (they're now a huge chain, which makes me a certain kind of rage-y, but that's a story for another time). I was also an actor, and while I still had to have a day job (as most of us do), I'd been doing pretty well in theater and television most of my life.

Bottom line, I had a career, and not an insubstantial one. But pregnant, I wasn't exactly taking Hollywood by storm.

At the same time, my husband's work began to pick up. After years of struggle, our finances were starting to be in a really good place. So good, in fact, that we decided that it wouldn't be necessary for me to try to find stable work while pregnant, and that we could actually have that idyllic life where I stayed home to raise our child (and maybe a few more) while my husband supported us financially.

I felt like I'd hit the jackpot. This was everything I could have dreamed of. I imagined baking cookies, creating fancy dinners, snuggling with my baby as he cooed up at me, frolicking in his pack-n-play while I did all things domestic and feminine. I fancied myself a real up-and-coming Martha Stewart.

Here's what happened instead:

- **My baby had severe colic,** one of the worst cases our doctors had ever seen. He screamed for sixteen hours a day for six months straight; that's not an exaggeration. A very sympathetic doctor at Children's Hospital of Los Angeles looked us deep in the eyes and said, "I've seen very good people go very bad in cases like yours. What is your support system like?" *It was that bad.*
- **I suffered postpartum depression** and had to go on medication when my son was two weeks old. (Thank

God, because otherwise, I may not have been able to handle the aforementioned colic.)

- **There were no cookies or fancy meals** because I couldn't take my son to the store to buy groceries without him screaming bloody murder. Oh, and I was fucking exhausted. There was a lot of takeout, and even more tears.

- **I actually hated being a stay-at-home mom.** I hate domestic chores. I have no idea why I thought I'd suddenly turn into the kind of woman who liked them, other than the fact that I'd been conditioned to believe that I would and moreover, that I *should*.

- **I suffered a loneliness and isolation only a new mom knows.** There is a special kind of insanity that comes over you when you try desperately (and usually unsuccessfully) to meet up with friends and their babies only to have naps completely misalign, or your baby is screaming too much for you to even think about getting into a car, and you instead spend another day solo, exhausted, covered in puke, not having slept, showered, or spoken to an adult in days.

As I fought each day just to survive and keep my head above water, the rest of me was slowly fading away.

At first my husband would come home and we'd talk about how lucky we were. His work schedule was erratic, but there was no pressure for us to coordinate childcare and work schedules. He once said when he came home from work, "It's such a relief to know that you have all of this handled. I feel like we're really sharing the load here. I go to work and fill our coffers, and I know our son is 100 percent cared for by you, and you don't have to worry about work or where the money is coming from and can just focus solely on raising and nurturing our son."

It seemed like the perfect partnership and balance.

Except that three-and-a-half years later, when we divorced, I had nothing.

No job.

No career.

No money.

No Self.

After our divorce, my husband kept going to work every day. He was as financially stable as he'd been when we were married. He had a group of friends from work who supported him and helped him through. He had daily distractions and *a purpose*. His biggest concern was that I wasn't there to cook and do laundry for him anymore (he actually asked me when I moved out if, since he was paying me spousal support, I would still come over to do his cooking and laundry... Uh, no). Besides the loss of family, besides not having a wife to come home to each day, dinner cooked, and laundry done, ultimately my husband's life didn't change a whole hell of a lot.

But mine?

Every day I woke up in a panic about what the hell I was supposed to do with my life now. How does a 38-year-old mom with a three-and-a-half-year-old even begin to rebuild her life from scratch? I knew I didn't want to continue with my acting career, even though I'd spent the previous three years on the top-rated prime-time show, *Grey's Anatomy*. I couldn't drag my three-and-a half-year-old around on auditions, driving what can amount to three hours round-trip in rush-hour traffic to callbacks that are always on the other side of town at the worst time of day. Plus, it wasn't exactly reliable income; actors book about one out of every hundred auditions. The risk/benefit/traffic analysis didn't add up.

What no one tells you when you sign on for that *partnership agreement,* or *joint venture,* is that you end up deeply subjugating yourself to your husband and marriage. As a stay-at-home-mom you relinquish almost everything in service of raising your children while your husband's path remains fairly unaltered. In fact, men's careers are bolstered by having wives at home doing all the domestic labor. Fun fact: 70 percent of top male earners in the US have a spouse who stays home. These men literally couldn't have the careers they have were it not for the unpaid labor of their spouses.

In her 2016 *Atlantic* article "The Divorce Gap," Darlena Cunha writes, "Despite the common perception that women make out better than men in divorce proceedings, women who worked before, during, or after their marriages see a 20 percent decline in income when their marriages end, according to Stephen Jenkins, a professor at the London School of Economics. His research found that men, meanwhile, tend to see their incomes rise more than 30 percent post-divorce. Meanwhile, the poverty rate for separated women is 27 percent, nearly triple the figure for separated men."

So, with these numbers, why would any woman choose to become a stay-at-home-mom? Well, for one, when you make this choice, you're not thinking about divorce. These aren't statistics women are investigating while planning a wedding or baby shower. They're thinking about the *American Dream* that they've been sold for decades. Perhaps they're thinking about the ideal put forth in Lisa Belkin's 2003 *New York Times Magazine* article, "The Opt-Out Revolution," in which she interviewed Ivy League-educated women who gleefully opted out of their high-power careers to stay home and raise their children *because they could.* They're certainly not thinking about the follow-up story in 2013 that revealed that many of these women were unhappy, unfulfilled, divorced—and most hadn't been able to reenter the workforce anywhere near the level at which they left. No one wants to think about divorce when they're happily married any more than they want to think about a prenup before getting hitched. And yet, such things are wise and prudent.

Now, if this is a choice you made, no one here is judging you. After all, I made the exact same choice! I'm simply here to pull back the curtain on the lie we've all been sold and present the reality of what being a stay-at-home-mom usually (and statistically) means in the long-term for most women—whether we get divorced or not.

Choosing to be a stay-at-home mom is often a choice of luxury, where there's enough money for the woman to not have to work and stay home and raise children. This was my situation. For others, though, it can be a power and control move, with money used as an enticing carrot (or karat, as the case may be), and a form of financial abuse. When Ashton married Elizabeth, a second marriage for them both, a friend asked Ashton why Elizabeth had abruptly quit working. They didn't have children together, so their friend didn't understand the choice. His response was, "Why *should* she work?" The friend was confused as she thought Elizabeth had really enjoyed her career. *Why wouldn't she?* she thought. While Ashton showered Elizabeth with expensive cars, jewelry, and designer shoes and handbags, making her feel special and taken care of, it soon became clear that these were actually Ashton's control tactics that made it harder for Elizabeth to leave when his abuse escalated.

But for many more women, this isn't a choice of luxury. It's a choice of economic need. With the rising costs of daycare and a stalled minimum wage, many women simply cannot afford to work and raise children. And, because of the gender pay gap, the logical parent to stay home is usually the mother.

The average cost of daycare in the US is $11,896 per year, or $991 per month for an infant. A full-time employee earning minimum wage brings home about $1,000 a month. How could a lower-income-earning mother possibly afford to put a child in daycare on that salary? So, it makes sense that she'd choose to stay home with her baby, relying on the financial support of her husband, her family, or federal or state assistance programs—many which require that she prove she's actually looking for work in order to qualify, which she can't do because of the math laid out above. Even worse, when she applies for benefits, she's called *lazy* or a *freeloader.* It's a national atrocity that women are forced to make this kind of choice.

According to a 2018 Pew Research Center analysis of US Census Bureau data, around twenty-eight million American children are living in single-parent homes, and 81 percent of those are single mothers. With so few social safety-nets in our country, how are these single mothers supposed to work and raise children?

In her book, *The Feminine Mistake* (Hyperion, 2007), Leslie Bennetts asserts, "It has become inescapably clear that choosing economic dependency as a lifestyle is the classic feminine mistake. No matter what the reasons, justifications, or circumstances, it's simply too risky to count on anyone else to support you for the long haul. In an era of disappearing pensions, threats to Social Security, high divorce rates, a volatile labor market, and attenuating lifespans, the social safety net continues to erode even as the need grows—particularly for women, who are twice as likely as men to slide below the poverty line in their later years." Many women look to their bleak financial futures and feel unable to even address the question of whether they should stay in or leave their marriages. This isn't a sign that their marriages are healthy, happy, or even safe. It's a sign that the economic structures that are meant to support all of our citizens are deeply flawed and tether women to marriages that they no longer want to be in because to leave would cause financial catastrophe. That's not freedom. That's jail.

We need to address the structures that put women in this position, starting with raising the minimum wage, eliminating the gender pay gap, increasing and destigmatizing federal welfare programs, and increasing financial literacy for all women. We also need to educate our children (daughters *and* sons) about these inequities and help them make *informed* choices down the line.

Disability, Health Insurance, and Other Really Good Reasons to Stay

Given the state of healthcare in the United States, there are many women who are trapped in unhealthy or unhappy marriages because if they leave, they'll lose their health or disability insurance. "Health Insurance and the Risk of Divorce: Does Having Your Own Insurance Matter," by Heeju Sohn in the Journal of Marriage and Family shared a 2007 study (before the Affordable Care Act) that found that being dependent on a spouse for health insurance lowered the likelihood of divorce by nearly 70 percent. This isn't because these marriages are happier. If the marriage isn't dangerous, and if it is safe to do so, it might make a lot of sense to stay in a marriage just for the insurance. Ideally, this would be discussed and a general agreement would be made to continue to cohabitate, or even separate, but remain married. I know people who have remained married for years while living fully separated lives, just for the health benefits one spouse provides.

Many women today simply can't afford to leave their marriages. Inflation, mortgage rates, and an over-inflated housing market make it almost impossible for most people to afford two separate homes. This keeps many women in dangerous partnerships, but it leaves far more in unhappy ones. In these cases, I recommend what Zawn Villines refers to as *quiet quitting your marriage*. This means emotionally detaching as much as possible, or completely, and functioning in a transactional, businesslike manner within your home.

You'll have to do some deep inner work to become content with your choice, and again, the work in the early chapters of this book will help.

This might be a complex process of weighing pros and cons. You might even create a pros and cons list, but you'll want it to be one in which you weigh each item. For example, if health insurance is the only pro of staying, how much weight does that hold versus the cons of having to sleep in the same bed with a partner you hate, or continuing to walk on eggshells? You may have to do a revised budget to see if getting your own place and your own insurance is at all financially feasible. If you're disabled and unable to work, you really may not have an option. But if insurance premiums are going to hold you back, you might be able to negotiate this as part of your divorce settlement. My ex-husband paid my insurance premium for six months at one point when I was really struggling financially. In his words, "The mother of my son can't be uninsured." This wasn't part of our settlement, but when I hit a rough patch, he was there to support me.

If, however, there is any active abuse happening, and if you're in any physical or psychological danger, getting to safety is paramount. Seek out the help of your local domestic violence shelter to create a safety plan, and utilize their support systems, such as legal aid and advocacy programs.

Fear of cultural isolation or shunning is another very valid reason people may choose to stay in a marriage that's unhappy or even unhealthy. As I've discussed in previous chapters, the threat of being shunned, while manipulative, patriarchal, and toxic, isn't an idle threat. In some cultures, a man can immediately claim custody of children and even take them back to their country of origin. (While this is against US law, unless there's an extradition agreement, it might be very difficult to win this battle.) In these cases, waiting until children are older, and using the interim to plan and save, might be your best, and safest, option.

While I always advocate for freedom, happiness, and fulfillment for all women, there are cases in which divorce may make things exponentially worse. In these cases, I recommend continuing to do the Self work needed to strengthen your foundation, and finding a support system around you to help when things get difficult, or when you begin to feel defeated. And remember: if this is where you're at today, this may not be where you stay forever. Sometimes simply taking the next right action toward a goal can help you feel as if you're moving in the right direction. Baby steps are still steps.

CHAPTER TWELVE

I Think I'm Ready, Now What?

Difficult Conversations and Awkward Living Arrangements

I F YOU'VE READ TO THIS POINT and you've decided that you want to stay in your marriage (or at least try to make it work), find yourself a good couples therapist that specializes in whatever issues are most pressing in your marriage. If it's communication, an Imago therapist might be the best choice. If it's healing from infidelity, a therapist who specializes in healing from betrayal is your best bet. Remember: not all therapists are good, and not all are specialists in all things. Get recommendations from reliable sources, and interview a few to see who you both like best. Look outside your immediate area as many therapists are still working virtually since the pandemic ended. State licensure requires therapists to work with clients in their state, but they don't need to be in your city or even in your county.

If you've decided to stay for logistical reasons, follow all my advice on how to *quietly quit* your marriage by setting up as many boundaries and silos as possible, creating a strong support network, and shoring up your sense of Self.

If you've read to this point and it's clear that ending your marriage is your best course of action, there are a few steps you should take in order to not have things get contentious right away. The first thing you should do is *not* take divorce advice from anyone who hasn't been divorced in your state, nor from anyone who isn't a divorce professional. The minute you tell people you're getting divorced, you'll start to get all sorts of unsolicited, and usually very bad, advice, such as *Lawyer up! Start hiding money!* or *Take the kids and run!* all of which will set you up for nasty litigation, if not jail.

When my ex and I first separated, my father-in-law, who until that point loved me like a daughter, told my ex that he needed to change banks and make sure I didn't have access to the new accounts, lest I wipe him out. I got divorced before Gwyneth Paltrow and Chris Martin made *conscious uncoupling* a household term. At that time, the media showed nothing but bitter, nasty celebrity splits; custody battles dragging on for years; children's lives being upended by spiteful, fighting parents; and perfectly good parents losing custody of their children because of a wild accusation by a resentful ex-spouse. Everywhere we turned were divorce horror stories, so it was no wonder that my father-in-law was so scared.

But my father-in-law was not a divorce attorney, nor had he ever known anyone who'd gotten divorced. His *advice* came from a well-meaning place (wanting to protect his son), but it was extremely misinformed and dangerous. Had my ex followed his advice, he would have been in pretty deep legal hot water, and it would have forced me to retain an attorney to fight for what was legally mine. As it was, my ex simply said to his dad, "That's not how we're doing this, Dad, and that's not how divorce works. You love Kate, and you know she's not going to clean out our bank accounts." Ever a doomsayer, my father-in-law likely didn't respond well to this, but over time he became grateful for the co-parenting relationship and eventual friendship my ex and I forged, and the very close relationship he and I shared until his death. In fact, a few years into my divorce I introduced him to someone as my *ex-father-in-law*, and he took me aside and said, "Cake [his pet-name for me], I am your father-in-law, not your ex-father-in-law. Until the day you remarry, I will be your father-in-law." And so he shall always be, whether I remarry or not.

Taking divorce advice from people who don't know your situation, the laws in your state, or your desires, can be dangerous. I even see it in my Facebook group: women will project their experience and fears onto someone else and give advice based on their narrative, not that of the person they're advising. For example, a woman once posted a question about shared parenting time. It was innocuous, and she shared no information about abuse or that her divorce was high-conflict. But the answers she got in the comments were all from women telling her how she needs to fight for more custody, to document his actions, and to record him during exchanges. I quickly put a stop to it, but if I hadn't, this woman's divorce might have been seriously impacted.

The next thing you should do is take significant time to process your emotions—and give your spouse the same respect. This can take years, of course, but before you begin any divorce proceedings it's important for you to get your emotions in check. As I've said, though it bears repeating, when you get divorced, you're making the biggest legal and financial decisions of your life in the midst of the biggest emotional upheaval of your life, and this is a *terrible* combination. If you go into divorce in the heat of emotions, it could cost you tens of thousands of dollars more than if you and your spouse cool off for a bit before moving forward.

No matter what kind of divorce you anticipate (amicable or contentious), having all your financial ducks in a row before dropping the bomb is probably a good idea. If you're in a financially abusive marriage, this step is paramount. If you're not, it's still a prudent move. You'll need copies of all financial documents available to you. If you're married, all financial documents *should* be available to you. If they're not, you are likely being financially abused, but you still have the legal right to access all accounts on which your name appears. In this case, you'll need to go into the bank with your ID and ask for the latest statements for all accounts that have your name on them. If statements arrive in the mail for your spouse that are from accounts you don't know about or have access to, photograph the envelope. It's a federal crime to open someone else's mail, but documenting the existence of these accounts will be important. This might be a good time to move some money into an account only you have access to. You're not *hiding* this money; you're simply putting some marital funds where you know you'll have access to them when needed, particularly if you're at risk of your spouse cutting you off. You'll still have to disclose this account when you do your financial disclosures as part of your divorce.

Make copies of all current bank statements, mortgage statements, investment account statements, credit card statements, tax returns, and retirement account statements. This might be a good time for you to hire a Certified Divorce Financial Analyst, who can help you sort through your financials and make a solid plan for you moving forward.

The last step you should take, possibly before telling your spouse (depending on your relationship), is to consult with at least three attorneys in your area. Notice I didn't say *hire* an attorney. I said *consult* some. Getting information from an attorney in your area about the divorce laws in your state, child and spousal support laws, how assets are divided, etc. will help you stay out of a spiral of *what-ifs*. Putting down a retainer and hiring an attorney may set your divorce off on the wrong foot if they start pushing you in a direction you don't want to go.

Remember, knowledge is power, and right now, you likely need a lot of that.

Once you've done all of the above, it's time to have some difficult conversations.

How to Tell Your Spouse You Want a Divorce

Telling your spouse you want a divorce will undoubtedly be one of the hardest conversations you'll ever have. Getting it right can set the tone for your entire divorce process. Getting it wrong can add layers of toxicity that could take years to clean up.

While you want to be kind and compassionate, this is not a conversation. *This is a declaration.* You're not asking for permission to end your marriage. You won't get agreement or understanding; in fact, you'll likely get a lot of pushback, because your spouse probably doesn't want this—at all. You may have had this conversation multiple times, and it's likely failed because you've been waiting for some sort of agreement. That's why you need to do this differently this time. Even if this isn't an abusive relationship, even if your partner is *fine*, but you just don't feel you can continue to be married to them, *you still get to make this choice*—and they don't have to understand it or agree to it.

This conversation should have *one objective*: to get the information across that you've made this decision. This is not the time to make any decisions about the myriad things you'll need to figure out down the line. You won't decide who will keep the house, who will have more parenting time, or when you can start dating again. In this conversation, you simply need to relay one very simple, yet life-altering fact: you no longer want to be married to your spouse.

In order to relay this piece of information without the conversation going off the rails, you'll need to maintain tight control of the narrative—which can be extremely difficult in the face of another person's pain, fear, and possible rage. Making a clear declaration while keeping control of the narrative allows you to relay this information as a statement of fact, rather than as a point to be argued with. That being said, you should also lead with empathy and kindness. I liken this to telling your tantruming child that it's time to leave a party they don't want to leave. Your objective is to leave the party. Your narrative never wavers from, *it's time to leave*, while also empathizing with your child's sadness about leaving: "I know you don't want to leave. It's so hard to leave a party that's been so much fun. Unfortunately, the party is over, and we need to go now." The grace you show the person with whom you've shared a life and children will go a long way toward creating a collaborative co-parenting relationship with the person you'll be connected to for the rest of your life.

Many people ask me if they can send an email or a text to their partner because they're worried that they won't be able to keep control of the narrative. Sometimes they've tried to have this conversation so many times to no avail that they feel there's no way they'll be able to do this in person. To these people I always say, "If it's safe to have the conversation face-to-face, you must do so." This will be hard. It may be the hardest thing you've ever done. But on the other side of it you'll have grown, and you'll have shown your partner respect and kindness in the process. A client who was about to embark on having this conversation for the fourth time, recently remarked, "I have to remind myself that I'm not the same person who's had this conversation three times already. Each time I've had the conversation I've grown." And so have you.

If you fear an outburst, you may opt to have this conversation in therapy, or in a public setting like a coffee shop or restaurant—but it will still have the same design. If you fear for your physical or emotional safety, then a safety plan is in order, and you shouldn't have the conversation directly at all. In this case, working with your local domestic violence shelter is your safest option.

The other question I get asked a lot is, "Should I file before I tell them and then just have them served?" to which I respond, "If you are safe, *absolutely not.*" This is the most disrespectful (and cowardly) way to start off the divorce process and will immediately trigger your spouse to hire an attorney which will send you off to the litigation races faster than you can say *divorce*. If you are unsafe, however, this may be the best way for you to proceed, but this will also need to be accompanied by a safety plan and the assistance of your local domestic violence shelter.

If it is safe to do so, you *must* have this conversation face-to-face. Here's how it should go: First, you'll need to choose the right time—but remember that there will never be a *perfect* time. There will always be a vacation planned, or a birthday coming up. If you wait until the calendar is completely clear, you'll be waiting forever. That being said, you don't want to have this conversation five minutes before the kids come home from school, or before dinner at your parents' house. You also don't want to wait so long that you end up blurting it out on Christmas Eve, like I did. Believe me, that makes for a really shitty Christmas for years to come. Find a time when you're both calm and free of distractions. You may want to plan to have someone watch your kids for a few hours to give you some space, or to have the conversation in couples therapy.

Start the conversation by showing appreciation for your partner as your co-parent and the parent of your children. Find a few things you can list that you're grateful for. Some examples might be, *I'm so grateful that I get to co-parent with you* or *You are an amazing father to our children.* This not only softens the blow, but it will create a container of kindness for the conversation as a whole, and make it clear that you intend to have this go smoothly and peacefully.

Once you've greased the wheels, as it were, it's time to actually say the words. Don't pussyfoot around it. Speak the words they need to hear, but speak them kindly. It could be, "As you know, I've been unhappy in our marriage for a long time. I've been doing as much work as I can to determine if I can find happiness in our marriage, and I've come to the conclusion that I simply can't and I'm ready to move forward with a divorce." While *The D Word* may feel so hard to say, it's also the truth and hiding it won't help. Sometimes being absolutely clear in your intention is the kindest thing to do.

Remember, you're not *asking* for a divorce. You don't *want* a divorce. The words you use matter. You need to be firm and straightforward, but this doesn't mean you need to be aggressive; it simply means you are asserting your own rights as an individual to no longer be in a marriage that doesn't work for you. *And* you can do so while also being empathic and kind. Using words like, *I know this is hard for you*, or *I'm sorry this feels like a shock* (even if inside you're seething that it really shouldn't be a shock), will help ease them through.

Keep blame out of this conversation as much as possible. The more you keep your words about your own feelings and experiences, the better this will go. When you blame the other person for their failings, their actions, or their lack of commitment, you walk yourself right into a back-and-forth about what's true and what's not, and this is not the time for that. When you keep your words about your own experiences and feelings, you can reduce conflict by a large margin. After all, they can't argue with your feelings, but they can absolutely argue about their own actions or intentions. Keeping this entire conversation in *I* language will enable you to maintain much-needed control of the narrative.

You probably know all the things your partner will say in response to your declaration. After all, you know them best, and this is probably not the first time you've had this conversation. Will they rage? Will they beg and cry? You can expect all the stages of grief to show up really quickly, so be prepared for this so that you know how to respond. What do you imagine your partner will say? Craft responses that will guide the narrative back to your point. For example, *I'm sorry you're angry. I know this isn't what you want. Unfortunately, this is my final decision.* It's completely appropriate to bring notes to this conversation. You may write out your entire script and read it to them. That's perfectly okay.

If they bring up specific points, such as, *You're going to destroy our children,* you can address them by saying, *Divorce doesn't screw up kids. The research shows that children who go through a collaborative and healthy divorce with parents who are equally committed to putting them at the center of all their decisions go on to lead healthy and happy lives. I hope you'll agree to go through this process with me in a way that won't do any unnecessary damage to them.* This addresses their concern (or threat), but then immediately circles back to your objective: we are getting divorced.

Be sure not to get hooked into too many of their concerns, however, as they're often used as stalling tactics, and a way to wrestle the narrative back from you. For example, a common argument that's used is, *You can't make a unilateral decision like this!* The answer to which is, *Actually, I can. That's what divorce is.* Having consulted with an attorney so that you're armed with knowledge and information will help you combat some of the threats and assertions that may be flung at you.

Here are some additional scripts you can use:

I'm sorry you feel blindsided. We've talked about this many times; I'm sorry you didn't take me seriously, but I've reached the end of my rope.

I appreciate that you want to go to therapy now. Unfortunately, it's too late for me, and my decision is final. (Note: don't go back and forth about how many times you've asked to go to therapy, as this will end up in a circular conversation about therapy, not about your decision to end your marriage.)

I know this is really hard for you to process. We don't need to make any decisions right now; there's no rush. Why don't you take some time to process this with your therapist and we'll talk in a few days.

I know you're upset. We both have a lot of processing to do, and a lot of decisions to make. But for now, I just want to be sure you understand that my decision on this is final.

Please don't make threats about taking the kids away from me. That's not how the law works. I know you're angry, but what's best for our children is that we work together to make this process as col- laborative as possible. Let's talk more when you've had some time to process this.

I'm sorry you think it's all "your" money, but according to the law, I'm entitled to half of all of our marital assets. I suggest you con- sult with an attorney so you understand divorce laws in our state.

During the onslaught of their emotional response, your partner may make a lot of arguments against your decision. This is where the narrative can get lost really quickly. You may be tempted to counter every argument against divorce with your own argument *for* divorce, but again, this will lead to a cir- cular conversation. To avoid this, simply repeat what you've already said. *Rinse and repeat.* Each time they throw another argument at you, you simply repeat what you've already said, such as, *I know this is really hard for you. I hope you can find someone appropriate to process it with, like a friend or therapist. I am not that person, and this is my final decision.*

Surprisingly, no matter how many times you've told your partner that you're unhappy in your marriage, this will still be news to them. If you've had this conversation numerous times but each time they've managed to win you back, they're going to be completely gobsmacked that this time you actually mean it. They'll also pull out all the tactics that have worked in the past, which will make this even harder. You must stand your ground, or you'll be back to square one again and again and again.

I like to think about this like sleep training a baby. When my son was eleven months old, we hadn't slept more than two hours at a time in almost a year. He'd cry and cry and cry until it sounded like the walls were bleeding and the floorboards were rattling. I was absolutely sure he was in real distress, so I'd rush in to soothe him. Of course, he was fine, and as soon as I came in, he was happy as a clam. The sleep-training consultant we eventually hired explained that whether I go in after five, ten, or thirty minutes he knew I'd come in eventually, so he'd always cry. The only way he'd stop crying and sleep through the night was for us to *not go in.* That night, I moved into the living room, turned off the baby monitor, and turned the AC on high, while my husband slept in our room next to our son's room—just in case. It was a brutal night, but it was only one night. Two days later, we woke up after having slept eight hours straight and were completely disoriented. Our son was happily talking and playing in his crib, and he slept through the night from that day forth.

Similarly, if you've backed down before—one, two, or seven times—your partner will pull out all the stops that have worked before to get you to back down again. It may feel almost impossible to hold your ground, which is why you have to be as prepared as possible going into this conversation. Think of your notes and your script as your baby monitor turned off and your AC on high. These are your guardrails.

The best thing you can do is give your partner the grace and space they need to process your declaration. Don't file as soon as you've told them; if you try to move the process too quickly, they'll be reacting out of emotional shock rather than making decisions from a place of acceptance—which is really where you need them to be.

I know this is the hardest decision you've ever made, and the hardest conversation you've ever had to have. If you've been passive in your marriage, if your partner is controlling, or at all emotionally abusive, this will be even harder for you to get through. With proper preparation it will be exponentially easier, and can set your family up for a much smoother transition.

Exercise for How to Tell Your Spouse You Want a Divorce:

Using your journal, craft as much of this conversation as you can. Here are some prompts to help:

- When is the best time for you to have this conversation? Do you have a therapy appointment coming up? Do you need to have someone watch the kids for an evening? Do you need to have the conversation in public? Be as specific as you can when you plan for this.
- Write out exactly what you plan to say. Remember that the conversation has *one objective*, which is to tell your spouse you want a divorce. This is not the time to make any decisions. Use this framework in order to retain hold of the narrative:
  - Begin with empathy and appreciation.
  - State your decision clearly.

- Keep it in "I" language.
- Don't discuss any future plans.
- Knowing your spouse as you do, what's your best guess as to how they will respond?
- Knowing your spouse as you do, list three to five things you're sure they'll say.
- Come up with two to three statements that you'll return to over and over again, when they get scared and go off on tangents. (*Rinse and repeat.*)

How Your Spouse Will Likely React

I've coached countless women through having this conversation over the last decade, so at this point I have fairly good insight into how people, men in particular, usually respond. In an ideal world, someone who loves you would want you to be happy, and they'd accept your decision gracefully. But humans have fragile egos, so that's rarely how they react.

While the Swiss-American psychiatrist Elisabeth Kübler-Ross's stages of grief were created to help those diagnosed with terminal illness accept death, they are applicable to the stages your spouse will likely go through once you tell them you want a divorce. These stages aren't linear. They don't follow a predictable pattern. Your spouse may jump around from stage to stage, but here are some of the most common reactions I've seen:

The first stage is *denial*. In the denial phase, you'll find your spouse fixing everything in the house that you've been asking them to fix for years. They'll mow the lawn, start doing dishes, make you coffee, and scrub the bathtub. They'll act as if the conversation *never happened*. This may baffle you, but trust me; it's all part of the process. At this point, I recommend a follow-up conversation that goes something like this:

Thank you for all you've been doing in the house lately. I really appreciate everything you've done. It seems like you may be in denial about our conversation the other night. I just want to be sure you understand that my decision still stands.

At this point, they'll likely move into *anger*. Beware, this phase can be ugly. For victims of abuse, this stage can get violent and dangerous, and should, again, be accompanied by a clear safety plan, and your removal from the home. For victims of emotional abuse, this stage is loud and emotionally scarring. Take care of yourself during this phase and get out of the house as much as possible.

Once the anger subsides, the *bargaining* begins. This is when they start sobbing and telling you how sorry they are. They beg you to reconsider. They can see it all clearly now. They've been wrong. You've had to put up with so much. They regret how they've neglected you. They read books about abuse. They see the light. They beg you to go to therapy(!!) despite you having asked them to go to therapy for decades, despite them having scoffed at the notion for years, even going so far as to say that they'd rather get divorced than go to therapy, *now* they want to go. And because you've done all the really hard work to get to this point, including all the steps laid out earlier in this book, you have the tools to check in with yourself and decide if you're open to this at this point or not—and if you are, you also take my advice and separate for six months and *see what they do.*

The next stage of grief is *depression*. There's a lot of self-pity in this stage, which you're meant to have sympathy for. This is often when threats of suicide occur. If your partner threatens suicide when you tell them you want a divorce, or at any point in your marriage for that matter, you must call the Suicide & Crisis Lifeline (988), even if you think they're just being manipulative. Don't let a threat like this pass you by. I've seen more than my share of spouses follow through on this. Tell them that you're sorry they're suffering so much, but that you're not equipped to handle their mental health. Tell them you love and care about them, and that you need to call the lifeline so they can get the care and help they need. *Then do it.* If they're alone and in another location, especially if they have access to a firearm, you may also need to call a family member or the cops to do a welfare check. If they're at all serious about these threats, they'll get the help they need. If they're bluffing, they won't use this tactic again.

The last stage of grief is *acceptance*. Some people never get here. If you're divorcing a narcissist, abuser, or sociopath, acceptance isn't in the cards and you should know this. But that doesn't mean that you can't continue on your path. If you're divorcing an otherwise good human, they'll get there eventually. It may be a long, painful, winding road, but they will get there. Don't make any divorce plans or decisions until they do. Divorcing someone who has accepted your decision is far easier than divorcing someone who is in any of the other stages of grief that precede it.

How You Might React

Even if you're the one who wants a divorce, you too will go through a grieving process. For many women, this is shocking. *I wanted this! Why am I so sad?* Well for one thing, no one ever *wants* this. No one goes into marriage anticipating divorce, despite the statistics, so grieving is perfectly appropriate. When you got married, you had a dream of what your life would look like. Maybe this is a dream you've had since childhood. Now that your dream has been shattered, it's perfectly normal to grieve it.

You also never wanted this for your kids. No matter how much you know they'll end up okay on the other side, you will still worry about them. You'll still stay up nights wondering if they'll really be okay at your co-parent's house without you. You'll still miss them when they're not with you, and you probably can't even imagine what life will be like not being with your babies every single day.

You may already know that you'll have to leave your home. This is a lot to take in. If you're anything like me, you put your everything into creating the home you now share with your spouse and your children. The idea of leaving and starting over might be really painful, even if you know it's the right financial decision, or if you know that your only way out is for you to move because they never will.

There's a lot to grieve, even if this was your decision, and you are allowed to have all of these feelings. Grief isn't linear. Healing isn't linear. It's messy and confusing. Women often feel that they've already gone through their grieving process before making their final decision. It takes so much for us to come to this decision that once we're done, we're *done*. But that doesn't make us immune to the rollercoaster and confusion of human emotions.

When I first moved out of my house, I was *elated*. I felt finally free of so much oppression and negativity. I could breathe again. I could be myself without anyone bristling or criticizing me. I had parties in my new house, as run-down and tired it was. My friends remarked that my house had such *vibrant energy.*

A few months later, the dreams began. Dreams of my old life, dreams about still being married to my ex, except this time we were happy, dreams that had me wake up (next to a new man I thought I really loved) confused, angry, and sad. *What did these dreams mean?* It turned out that the dreams were letting me know that I still had some grieving to do. What I didn't realize, but would come to learn, is that there is grief in every transition, happy or sad. When we graduate high school, it's the most celebratory, exciting time in our lives, but there is also a grief that we rarely acknowledge. A transition from high school to college comes with loss: loss of family, loss of some of the oldest and closest friendships of your life, loss of a familiar bedroom, loss of daily snuggles with the family pet.

Even if a transition is happy, it's important to recognize and feel the grief that may accompany it. In my case, I was so happy and relieved to be out of my marriage that I didn't feel the grief until it seeped into my dreams and held me hostage in my sleep. I had to end the relationship I'd entered into way too quickly and focus on my own healing—which took many more years than I'd ever thought possible and in many ways is ongoing.

Living Together, Separated

It's very common for people, especially parents, to continue to live together for a period of time after having had *the conversation.* This can be awkward, at best. But if used intentionally, this time can also be healing and productive.

Often, this period of separation while living together can last around six months. Once the dust settles on some of the emotional upheaval, you'll have ample opportunity to get a head start on building a healthy co-parenting dynamic so you and your kids won't be dealing with every single change happening at once when one (or both) of you relocates. This is a great time to start implementing shared parenting time. Decide on a weekly schedule, who picks up the kids from school, and who helps with homework on what nights. Make arrangements between the two of you for after-school activities, and rotate evenings out. My ex and I used this time to really dive into our 12-Step programs. Making these transitions ahead of time will not only provide much-needed space between you and your soon-to-be ex, but it will give your kids a chance to adjust in smaller steps while they're still in a familiar and safe environment.

You can also use this time to reconfigure your roles in the family. If you know you're going to have an equal, shared parenting arrangement when you formally split up, both of you might have to learn about each other's past roles. For example, you may have always taken on the role of making breakfast and getting the kids to school. Use this time to walk your co-parent through your morning routine so you can keep the kids' routines as consistent as possible. Later, the consistency in routines at both houses will be a source of comfort for your children, and you'll have peace of mind knowing they'll always have what they need. Likewise, your co-parent has probably always handled specific tasks for your kids, too. Maybe they're the one who gives the kids a bath at night and tucks them in for bed. Get acquainted with the routine your kids are used to so they have less to adjust to in their new circumstances later on.

When you're separated while living together, it also gives both of you a chance to stand on your own two feet, financially. But first, you'll need to figure out how you'll split your current costs, which means you might want to start a new budget. Decide on the specific amount each of you will contribute toward household expenses during this separation time. If there's a big gap between your income levels, perhaps you'll split the costs equitably, rather than equally.

Doing this can help mitigate the stress for a stay-at-home parent. You might work out a temporary support arrangement to help ease this transition, and you might use this time to start looking for a job, or building a business, which will help you to enter the next phase of your life with autonomy and independence. Many people will advise you not to get a job until your divorce is final because it will impact support. I say, do what you need to do to feel good about yourself. If getting a job gives you a boost of self-esteem, and the income you generate will offset whatever you may lose in support, for the love of God, *get the job.*

Depending on the age of your children and how things have been in the home up until this point, you may want to let them know something different is happening in your home. You may want to say something like this:

Hey kids, you may have sensed that Mom and I haven't been getting along very well lately, and that things have been a bit tense around here. We've decided to give each other some space for a bit, so Mom is going to move into the guest room while we sort some things out. (At this point, older kids may ask if you're getting divorced. It's best to say, *That's one of the options we're considering right now, and if that's what we decide, you'll be the first to know.*)

Never lie to your children about a reality they can clearly see or fail to name what's going on for them. You don't have to tell them the whole truth, but you must address what they're experiencing and seeing with their own eyes or it can cause them to doubt their own reality. This is a form of gaslighting.

If you're in a more abusive situation in which there will be little collaboration while under the same roof, you may need to be the one to move out, and it might need to be done more quickly than you'd otherwise like. If this is necessary for your safety, then please consider it, but check with your attorney first.

Some people erroneously believe that if you leave your house, you give up all rights to it, citing *abandonment of property*. While every state has its own definition of abandonment (or *desertion*), generally speaking, abandonment refers to one person leaving the family or family home without communicating to the other spouse beforehand, and with no intention of returning. (It's more about abandoning the family, not the house.)

Since your home is considered marital property, if you own it, it will be part of the division of assets at the time of divorce, whether you leave it now or not. That being said, ownership is not the same as possession. If you want to live in your home later, it might be more difficult to regain possession of your house if your spouse refuses to move out down the line. In cases of domestic violence, however, safety is always the top priority. You can always find somewhere else to live. A house is just a house. *You* are your children's home.

It's common during this in-home separation for an abusive spouse, particularly an Entitled Misogynist, to try to make things very difficult for you. They'll take two hours to get ready in the morning, leaving you to do all the morning kid-chores. They'll refuse to spend any time with the children, since that's *your job.* If this is the case, keep a journal of everything that happens, how much time they actually spend with the kids, how much they contribute financially, and anything else that you can bring to your attorney to prove lack of participation during separation. It's common for these personality types to use court as the next stage of abuse. Sometimes they'll go so far as to file for full custody. Having proof that they spent little-to-no time with the children during separation could help you thwart their attempts.

However you end up using this time being separated under the same roof, use it intentionally and strategically, either by creating and implementing a shared parenting plan, or by documenting your co-parent's refusal to cooperate. Either way, you'll have used your time wisely.

CHAPTER THIRTEEN

How Do I Not Screw Up My Kids?

Everything You Need to Know to Protect Your Precious Babies

TELLING YOUR CHILDREN THAT you're getting divorced will likely be a difficult conversation. While parents may feel a lot of guilt about breaking up their family, avoiding having this conversation isn't the answer. According to Christina McGhee, author of *Parenting Apart: How Separated and Divorced Parents Can Raise Happy and Secure Kids* (Berkley, 2010), "Research shows that 95 percent of surveyed children reported feeling like their parents gave them little to no information about their separation or divorce." This can leave them feeling confused, frightened, and angry. Also, not telling your children what's happening can lead to them feeling personally responsible for the changes that are occurring in their lives and feeling that they can fix the rift between parents. Developmentally speaking, children are naturally self-centered. They can feel responsible for everything that happens around them, especially something as life-altering as divorce. If your children have a secure attachment to one or both parents, they naturally believe your world revolves around them, and that all your decisions are made in service of them. This is developmentally appropriate for a child. As such, it's important to talk very directly to your children about your divorce, giving them a clear and non-blaming explanation of your decision that centers around making sure they know that this is not their fault, and they're not responsible.

Preparing for the Conversation

If at all possible, work with your co-parent to craft a narrative that you can both agree on, keeping blame out of it entirely. When one parent insists that the other parent tells the kids it's their decision, or if one parent tells the kids that the other had an affair and that's why this is happening, it destabilizes the family at a time when as much unity as possible is key. If you can't agree on a narrative, and if one parent insists on blaming the other, it might be necessary to bring a co-parenting specialist or a therapist into the mix. If one parent can't keep their emotions in check, the other parent may need to have the conversation without them, but you should still try to agree on what's going to be said.

If you're able to co-parent through this conversation, script it as much as possible in advance. Be specific with the words you use. Don't beat around the bush or try to soften the blow by using euphemisms. Say *divorce* and *separation*. If you don't use the appropriate words, your children may be left confused about what's happening, or with false hope that you're not actually getting divorced.

Make as many decisions as possible before you tell the children. Decide on parenting schedules, who's going to move out, and if possible, have another place ready to go. The day we told my son, he wanted to see our new house, and I was able to bring him over that very day. I had his bedroom all set up, and he ran around the backyard, and ran circles through the kitchen and dining room. He was immediately able to envision his new life, which gave him a sense of security right away.

There's no perfect time to have this conversation, but, if possible, tell the children two to three weeks before the actual move-out date. This will give them time to adjust to the changes that are coming, without putting them in a position of feeling like they're in limbo. If you've been living together, while separated, the kids may already have a sense of what's happening, and if you've been naming things for them, as recommended in the previous chapter, they won't be as shocked as they might otherwise have been.

It's advisable to tell your children's teachers that this conversation is going to happen a day or so in advance. Ask them to be discreet and sensitive, and tell them that your children may have emotional reactions they should look out for and report back to you. Tell them not to initiate a conversation, and not to mention it unless the children do, but to be aware and sensitive to the changes occurring at home. In this way, your children will be supported in all environments, and won't be punished for any outbursts or inappropriate behavior.

It's a good idea to tell the children when you'll all be together for a period of time, and not before a period of separation, such as before bed, work, school, or karate class. Preferably tell them at the start of a weekend and then plan to spend as much of that weekend together as a family as possible, putting aside your differences in service of your children if you can.

Having the Conversation

If at all possible, tell the kids together—both parents and all children together—unless there's a significant age difference and the conversation may be different for each child. Because children think of themselves as half of each parent, keep blame out of the conversation entirely. If you say that their father is a liar and a cheat, for example, they may internalize this and wonder if they might become (or be) a liar and a cheat, too. Additionally, blaming one parent or the other will make your children feel as if they have to choose loyalty to one of you, and that's not a position any child should be put in, certainly not at this delicate time. Keep unnecessary details out of the conversation, opting instead to give them direct, clear, and plain facts.

Give the kids as much information as you have at this time: parenting arrangements, who will live where, who will take them to school and pick them up, etc. Be as specific and concrete as possible, but if you don't have an answer to something, don't make one up. Saying, *You know that's a good question, and we haven't made a decision about that yet. We'll let you know as soon as we know,* is entirely appropriate.

Your kids will naturally ask, *Why*? If they're anything like my kid, they'll ask it a million times in a million different ways. You don't need to answer that with any more information than you've already given them, as long as it clearly answers the question. When they repeatedly ask, *Why?* what they're really saying is, *Don't.* Return to your original conversation points and try to keep the conversation focused there. *Mommy and Daddy have had a hard time getting along, and we have decided it would be better for all of us for us to live in separate houses. We'll always be a family, and Mommy and Daddy love you so much, and we always will.* Never say that Mommy and Daddy don't love each other anymore, as your children may fear that you might stop loving them too someday.

Tell the children that this is an adult decision that you've both made together as a result of a lot of thinking and consideration, and tell them over and over again that it's not their fault. If true and appropriate, tell them that you'll always be a family, but the family will look different going forward. But you must be able to back that up. Don't spew bile and resentment in front of your children while also telling them that you'll always be a family. Honor and respect one another in front of the kids and save your spats for when they're way out of earshot.

It's okay to cry in front of your children. This may provide an opportunity for them to access their own emotions, and for you to tell them that this is hard for everyone. But don't become hysterical. Remember: You're the adult in this conversation, and if you lose control of your emotions, your children will feel the need to take care of you, turning them into the parent. Your children need you to be the parents in this conversation. They need to feel supported and safe.

Acknowledge and accept all your children's feelings. Let them be mad, or cry, or rage or shut down. Empathize and say that you know it's hard, and that it's hard on you too, and that you also feel angry, sad, etc. If they respond with *Then why are you doing this?* return to your first conversation and the script you worked out about what to say. You can also add, *Sometimes we have to make decisions that are the right thing to do, but that also make us sad.*

After the Conversation

It's likely that you will have several conversations about this with your children. You can even plan for a second conversation a couple of days after the first in order to check in and ask if they have any questions or feelings that have come up since the first conversation. If your child shuts down emotionally, keep checking in with them. Spend extra time, reading age-appropriate children's books about divorce, drawing pictures, and just being present for them. Many children do a lot of talking just before bed in the dark, or in the car. Make sure you're available to them during these times.

Be open to the fact that your kids may continue to have questions, try to convince you not to do this, or have a range of emotions for months after the first conversation. Try to answer all of their questions patiently, honestly, and fairly, without placing blame on the other parent.

When it's time to move, invite your children to pack up a box of belongings they want to bring to the new house. Children feel out of control in this process, so giving them agency in certain areas like this will help them feel more in control. If you have older children, allow them to pick out their new bedroom furniture, and decorate their rooms how they want to. Keep their routines intact and create even more routines if necessary. Try to communicate with your co-parent about routines at both houses so there's as much consistency as possible.

Don't take it personally if, when your child is with you, they say they miss the other parent. It's natural that they would. Allow them to call and keep in as much contact as they'd like. If a child says *I want to see Daddy*, assure them that they'll see Daddy in a couple of days, or after two sleeps, or whatever is appropriate, and that you know that Daddy misses them too. You may want to invite Daddy over for dinner, if that feels comfortable, and of course, tell your child they can call Daddy at any time.

Children should be allowed to contact the off-duty parent as much as they want, but forcing a daily call isn't in the children's best interest (unless there is a valid fear for their safety) as it pulls them out of settling into being with the on-duty parent. A mandated daily call is usually more for the parent than the children. Allow children to have their experiences with the other parent without interruption, and resist making them spies by asking them a lot of questions about what happens at the other parent's house.

While you can do a lot of research and be as prepared as possible, plan for not having all the answers, all the time. If your child asks a question that you're not sure how to answer, tell them you want to answer their question the best way possible, and that you're going to have to think about it. Be sure to get back to them in a timely fashion, and if you say something you later regret, go back and clean it up.

Deciding on Parenting Time

Parenting time, also known as *custody*, can be difficult to figure out and can lead to a lot of contention. As I mentioned in Chapter Eleven, many states tie the calculation of child support to parenting time, and this can lead to bitter custody battles—not necessarily because a parent wants to spend more time with their children, but because they don't want to pay support, or they want to receive more support.

There are many options for parenting schedules, and you'll need to figure out which works best for your children, and for you. CustodyXChange.com is a great website that has information on the best schedule for children at each stage of development, and examples of schedules based on how parenting time is shared. For example, if you have children under five, and have agreed to a seventy/thirty split, CustodyXChange will give you examples of what that might look like on a weekly basis. You can find their website at www.custodyxchange.com.

Even if you're feeling particularly collaborative with your ex, setting a parenting schedule is absolutely vital to both your sanity and your kids' security. Children need predictability, especially in times of upheaval, so having a clear plan will be very important. For younger children in particular, consider a schedule that's connected to specific days of the week, for example, *You're with Mommy on Mondays and Tuesdays, Daddy on Wednesday and Thursdays,* rather than one that alternates. Even color-coding a monthly calendar does little to soothe a confused small child, as they can barely track all the days in the month, let alone which day is an orange day or a green day, or even which one is today. For teenagers, alternating weeks might be best as it gives them more time to relax into each environment.

Many parents opt to *birdnest,* or *nest,* in which children stay in the home while parents rotate in and out, often sharing a studio apartment nearby. This is a great option for the early days of separation as it helps ease kids into the idea of being with one parent at a time, while giving parents needed space, but it's not advisable as a long-term arrangement as it can seriously impede parents' ability to move on with their lives. Nesting puts you in the position of sharing not one but two homes with the person you're divorcing. If you choose to nest, you must have a very strict agreement in place about things such as cleaning, laundry, grocery shopping, overnight guests, and more. Be very clear in your arrangement and expectations, or this could backfire very quickly.

Creating a Parenting Plan

A parenting plan, or shared parenting agreement, is the part of your divorce decree that covers how you transition from raising your children in one home, to raising them in two separate homes. Parenting plans can be extremely detailed and prepare for almost any eventuality, or they can be broad and loose. How you create your parenting plan will mostly be determined by how you communicate with your co-parent at the time of separation. For example, if you have trouble communicating or agreeing on parenting decisions, you should include as much detail as possible. If you get along fantastically, you can leave it loosey-goosey. That being said, I advise putting more into a parenting plan than might feel necessary at this time. Adding in more stringent protocols down the line may prove difficult. Then, if you and your co-parent collaborate well, you can be flexible with each other.

The most important thing to remember when creating a parenting plan is to *put your children at the center, not in the middle*, of all your decisions. This might mean crafting a plan that better suits your children's needs than your own, which is entirely appropriate. Parenting plans should not be about dividing hours and minutes, nor should they be about what's *fair* for each parent. In fact, what might feel fair to you, may not feel fair to your kids. For this reason, you must put your own feelings aside and look at this entire process through the eyes of your child. In cases in which coming to agreement may be more challenging, this may prove more difficult, so it may be helpful to work with a co-parenting specialist to help you craft a plan.

To create a child-centered parenting plan, begin with what your children's lives look like now and assess how you can minimize the amount of change they experience all at once. If your kids are used to being with one parent 90 percent of the time, does it really make sense (*is it fair to your children*) to suddenly have their time divided fifty-fifty because that's what's *fair* to the parents? It may be that an equal division of parenting time is the goal and there is a plan in place to get there—*eventually*. But changing the children's lives so abruptly, might be really disruptive. Thinking about this through the lens of the children makes these decisions a lot clearer. In a more high-conflict case, a co-parenting specialist can help you create a step-down plan that works toward equal parenting time.

Are there any routines or activities that you engage with as a family now? For example, if both parents always attend all soccer or baseball games, or attend church as a family, can you keep this in place for the sake of the kids? In a more high-conflict case, you may opt to alternate who attends games or church with the children. Sitting separately can make kids feel that they have to choose which parent to be loyal to. This can be confusing and scary for children.

What activities does each parent participate in now, and can those remain consistent? For example, if Mom always takes Sarah to ballet class, can you agree that that stays the same, regardless of whose day it is? If Dad takes the kids on an annual fishing trip, can you agree that that will stay in place for the sake of the children, no matter whose parenting time that may fall on? In a more high-conflict case, the annual fishing trip should be worked into the parenting plan, with dates selected as far in advance as possible, or set as *the second week of August each year*, for example

Exercise for Creating a Comprehensive Parenting Plan
(partially drawn from the Mosten Guthrie Academy's Co-parenting Specialist Certification Training with Christina McGhee):

Here is an extensive checklist for you to use as a guide to hammer out as many details as possible as you work through your plan. Use it as a guide to help you craft your parenting plan, but also be sure to consider any special circumstances of your situation. For example, if one parent has a history of alcohol abuse, the parenting plan should include the use of Soberlink or some form of alcohol monitoring system.

This is also available to download at kateanthony.com/book-resources

PARENTING TIME

While hours and minutes should never be counted, in

some cases it may not be enough to simply determine the days you'll each have the kids. You also want to define:

- Does the on-duty parent drop the kids off after their parenting time, or does the parent receiving the kids for their parenting time pick them up?
- If exchanges are done primarily at school (one parent drops off, the other picks them up), who is responsible for dropping off/picking up any belongings that go back and forth?
- What time does parenting time begin? For example, if there is no school, or a child is ill on an exchange day, who's responsible for parenting on that day, and at what time?
- If there is any emotional or physical danger, will you be exchanging at a neutral, safe place, such as a police station or McDonald's where there are often security cameras?
- How far in advance do changes to the schedule need to be made/submitted for approval?
- For younger children, is there a step-down custody plan? For example, infants and young toddlers may need to be with their primary caregiver full-time until it's developmentally appropriate for them to separate, at which time they may spend one or two overnights with the other parent, eventually moving into a more equal shared parenting plan.

In high-conflict cases these things need to be hammered out clearly, but in low-conflict cases affording each other flexibility can be key. Remember: whatever flexibility you offer, you will also receive—but keeping score will always shoot your children in their feet.

HOLIDAYS AND SPECIAL DAYS

Things to consider regarding holidays:

- When will exchanges take place? Will one of you have Christmas Eve/New Year's Eve, while the other has Christmas Day/New Year's Day? And what time, exactly, does that exchange take place?
- If you celebrate Hanukkah, how will you share the eight nights?
- Does that schedule alternate annually, or is it static? (Keeping it the same allows for traditions to be forged; rotating allows each parent to share special times.)
- Does the mother always get Mother's Day and the father Father's Day, regardless of whose parenting weekend it is? If parents are the same gender, how are those days shared? *In high-conflict cases, you may need to define the hours specifically.*
- Think through the calendar year and cover all special days or holidays that matter to your family.

Remember that this is about your kids, not you. Does waking up alone on Christmas morning suck? Yes, it does. But are your kids going to be showered with presents and love from your ex-in-laws when they spend the night at your ex's house on Christmas Eve? Yup! Will they be super happy and excited when they come to your house at 10 a.m. on Christmas Day? Also yup! And that's all that really matters.

TRAVEL AND VACATIONS

When planning travel and vacations with children, here are some things to consider:

- How far in advance does travel need to be planned?
- What kind of approval do you need from the other parent?
- Who is responsible for paying for the children's travel?
- Define the difference between domestic and international travel requirements. (Some international travel requires a notarized letter from the other parent if children are traveling with only one parent—even if you're married.)

Remember this is about your kids, not you! Don't hold your kids back from having an amazing time at Disneyland with your co-parent because you're jealous that you can't afford to do something this fun with them, or that your co-parent got to it first (even if it was deliberate).

RIGHT OF FIRST REFUSAL

Right of first refusal refers to the on-duty parent offering parenting time to the off-duty parent before calling in a babysitter or family member. Here are some things to consider when deciding to put a right of first refusal clause in your parenting plan:

- How much advance notice is required?

- Is there a minimum time for these requests? (for example, if you're going out for more than four hours.)
- How should these requests be communicated?

There are benefits and drawbacks to this kind of arrangement. On the upside, more time with your kids is great. On the downside, additional communication with your co-parent might be difficult. Additionally, do you really want to be told every time they go out on a date, or wonder if you're taking your kids on their parenting time so they can be with someone else? Eventually this will feel less difficult, but at first it might be very painful. Remember: Right of first refusal doesn't mean you have to accept; it just means you have to be offered first. My general advice is to skip this, unless your kids tell you they have babysitters a few times a week at your co-parent's house.

EXPENSES

It's not enough to say that you'll be splitting expenses. Here are some additional things to think about:

- Is this a fifty-fifty split, or is it *equitable*, meaning, if one party makes 75 percent more than the other, do they pay 75 percent of the expenses? And if so, how often is income disclosed or assessed?
- If one parent signs the kids up for an activity on their parenting time, does the other parent also share that fee?
- How far in advance, and what kind of agreement must there be before taking on an expense?

- How is accounting shared? Will you use a co-parenting app with a receipt tracker, such as FAYR or Our Family Wizard?

Don't drop a bomb on the other parent by sending a receipt for $250 for clothes when the other parent didn't know there was a shopping trip planned. Communicate the kids' needs in advance so you can agree on a budget.

ACTIVITIES

It's important to think through/discuss all eventualities when it comes to your kids' activities, such as:

- Who has decision-making authority, and what kind of agreement does there need to be from the other parent?
- Is one parent allowed to sign kids up for activities that fall on the other parent's parenting time?
- Who attends games/events, and how will you present for the kids? Will you sit together, stay apart, or alternate who attends?
- What are the rules/expectations about bringing new partners to games/events?

It's best for your kids if you can sit together at all games and events. This prevents kids from feeling torn about who they run to after a game or recital. If you can't sit together, consider attending on alternating weeks. Try not to bring new partners to games or events until well after they are an established part of your kids' life, and be considerate of your co-parent's feelings.

Remember, this event is about and for your kids and both parents should show up solely focused on them. Bringing a new partner to an event like this without the other parent knowing in advance is disrespectful and will cause a lot of stress and tension—not just for your co-parent, but for your kids.

BELONGINGS

Being on the same page about the kids' belongings is important. Here are some things to think about:

- What stuff goes back and forth, and what is duplicated at each house?
- Who is responsible for transporting important belongings back and forth?

Your kids' belongings belong to your kids. Don't hoard the new clothes or the good shoes. Kids should be returned to the other parent with the same kinds of things they arrived in. (For example, if they arrive in new clothes, don't send them back in clothes that no longer fit, or that have holes in them.) Each house should be fully appointed with diapers, wipes, underwear, socks, and enough clothes for their time at that house.

COMMUNICATION BETWEEN PARENTS

Here are some things to think about regarding communicating about kids:

- Will you be communicating via text, email, or through a co-parenting app?

- If using a co-parenting app, what is the emergency contingency? What constitutes an emergency?
- In high-conflict cases, is it necessary to set communication limits (for example, no more than three messages per day, no longer than one paragraph per message)?
- What is the expectation regarding responding to important communication? Twenty-four hours? Five hours?

In low-conflict cases, this shouldn't be an issue, although you still may want to set your own boundaries around this so you have time to adjust to being apart. In high-conflict cases, use of a parenting app, such as FAYR or Our Family Wizard, is imperative, as all communication is tracked, and can be read by attorneys, coaches, co-parenting coordinators, and judges, and abusers tend to be nicer when they think someone might be watching.

COMMUNICATION WITH KIDS

While your kids are with the other parent, you should always have access to communicating with them. Here's what should be decided:

- How often should communication be granted with the off-duty parent?
- Is this on the on-duty parent's phone/iPad/computer, or do the kids have their own?
- Is there a set time for these communications, or is it flexible?

It's not in the children's best interest to have to call the off-duty parent every day at a set time. It interrupts their flow with the on-duty parent, and can cause undue anxiety and stress. Usually, these calls are enforced not because the children want (or need) them, but because the parent does. That's not fair to the kids. Let your kids enjoy their time with their other parent when they're away from you. If they want to call, they should always be allowed and supported, but they should never be forced. The only exception to this is in cases in which the children may not be safe and in cases with a history of domestic violence. In this case, checking in on their safety is imperative, and a daily video call is advised.

COMMUNICATION BETWEEN PARENTS AND CHILDREN

- What are our expectations about ongoing communication?
- How will we talk to the children about our divorce? What is our common narrative?
- How will we refer to each home? (*Main Street House* and *Hill Avenue House,* rather than *Mom's house* and *Dad's house*)
- How will we support each other's ongoing relationship with our children?
- How will we ensure that our children still have meaningful relationships with their grandparents or other extended family members like aunts and uncles?

It's important to honor the relationship your children have with their other parent, as they feel that they are half you and half them. Disparaging the other parent should be avoided at all costs. In high-conflict cases, there may be some conflicting messaging, which should be addressed head-on.

MAKING IMPORTANT DECISIONS

It's important to hammer out how you'll make important decisions. Here are some topics to consider:

- **Healthcare:** Who's responsible for ensuring the children's health coverage? How will healthcare costs be shared? How will you make healthcare decisions? How will you handle the mental-health needs of your child? How will you handle vaccine recommendations?
- **Religion:** What are your thoughts on exposing children to religious or spiritual teachings? How will you handle religious or cultural differences? Are there religious or spiritual practices you want to support and maintain in both houses?
- **Education:** How will you decide what school your children attend? How will you handle day-to-day communication about homework and school activities? Will both parents be on all school email lists? How do you want to handle school tuition and college savings?
- **Discipline:** How have you handled discipline in the past? What consistency do you want in each home? How will you handle issues that come up right before your children goes to the other parent's home? (For example, can one parent take away screens at the other parent's house?)

- **Household rules:** What rules might differ between houses, and which rules will remain consistent? How will you communicate a change in rules to each other, and what is the expectation around the other parent following suit? How will you discuss with the children if there are different rules in each house?

- **Curfew:** What are the expectations around curfew? How will curfew change as the children age? What are the consequences of breaking curfew, and will this be consistent at both homes?

- **Potty-training:** Who decides when it's time to start potty-training, and can you agree on consistency in both homes? How will you potty-train? Is there a method you both agree on?

- **Food and diet:** What foods do your children already eat consistently, and do you both agree to provide healthy and nutritious food for the children at both houses? What are the current rules around fast-food, candy, and other *fun foods*?

- **Bedtime and morning routines:** What are the current routines that your children are used to? Will you work together to keep these routines consistent as the children grow up? How will you handle communicating changes in these routines?

- **Tobacco and alcohol use around children:** What agreements do you have in place about this already, and what do you agree to keep moving forward? If one parent has a history of drug or alcohol abuse, how will you communicate concerns in the future? Do you agree to the use of an alcohol monitoring system, such as Soberlink? If so, what is the blood alcohol limit at which parenting time will be canceled? Do members of your extended family smoke or have alcohol use disorder? What are the rules around having these people smoke or drink around your children?

- **Approved childcare providers:** What are your expectations around hiring and/or approving childcare providers? Do both parents need to approve all providers?

- **Dating and new relationships:** When and how will you notify the other parent before introducing a new partner to the children? Is there a time limit before which new partners shouldn't be introduced? (For example, I recommend that you should be dating for at least six months and have been fully separated for at least a year so the children have had ample time to adjust. Note that in some states it's considered adultery to date before your divorce is final, so check your state laws.) What are our individual perspectives about a new partner spending the night when the children are with us? What are our individual expectations around how new partners are incorporated into our kids' lives, for example, birthday parties, or sporting events? Is there an expectation that the other parent should also be able to meet the new partner? (I don't recommend this unless there is significant reason to distrust the new person and/or your co-parent's decision-making. Usually, you're not really ready to meet your co-parent's new partner, and it can be really painful to do so. Trust that any new person in your children's lives will likely be a benefit to them.)

- **Remarriage:** How will you notify one another if you decide to remarry? What role might a stepparent play in the kids' lives? What role might they have in decision-making, caretaking, and discipline?
- **Moving:** If one of you chooses to move or relocate, how will you work together to manage the change for your kids, and how might that impact your parenting time?

It's best for everyone to be on the same page on important decisions; otherwise kids get confused. If a major change occurs in one house (such as potty-training or elimination of a pacifier), it must be backed up at the other house; as such, these decisions need to be agreed upon before being implemented by one parent.

This may seem like a lot, but the more detailed you make your plan, the less stressful the future will be. The more child-centered the plan, the healthier and happier your children will be in the long run.

CHAPTER FOURTEEN

What's on the Other Side?

Moving Forward with Integrity and Grace

A S YOU MOVE FORWARD INTO your new life, you'll be faced with obstacles you can see and anticipate, as well as land-mines that will take you by complete surprise. In the following pages, I try to account for many of these obstacles and land-mines so you're not as surprised by them as I was when I first got divorced. While I can't account for every eventuality, I try to address the many questions that women ask me every day as they move forward into their new lives.

Who to Tell, What, and When

One common question I get asked is *What do I tell the people in my life about my divorce?* And my answer is this: you get to tell who you want, what you want, when you want. The trouble so many people run into is that they don't want to badmouth their ex, or say anything they won't agree with or approve of. But here's the thing: you get to own your narrative. You and your ex are unlikely to agree on the narrative of your divorce just as you're unlikely to agree on the narrative of your marriage. Part of getting divorced is that you get to own your truth and speak it freely. This might be challenging for someone who's been in a controlling or abusive relationship, or who has never been able to fully own their truth in other aspects of their lives. After all, you may have been told to keep quiet about the state of your marriage, or you may have suppressed your own feelings for so long that accessing and making sense of them may be really difficult. This is the time for you to dig deeply into your own truth by connecting with your Inner Guide. Sit quietly with her and ask her *What is my truth?* And then listen. Grab a pen and paper and write it all down. *Identifying your truth is the first step in owning it.*

When Maria and her husband, Phil, were divorcing, Phil wanted them to tell everyone together. When Maria told her family, Phil was upset she'd done it without him. When she spoke to her sister-in-law without Phil, he spun a yarn about how disappointed he was because it was so important that they *present a unified front* to friends and family. Maria was really confused about this because what Phil was saying sounded somewhat reasonable, but she also didn't feel that they needed to tell everyone together; after all, they were getting *divorced*. When she brought this to our coaching session, I posited that perhaps Phil wanted to be sure he could control the narrative to friends and family and didn't trust Maria to not out him as an abuser to those close to them. When she heard this, it all made sense to Maria, and she was enraged that, even in divorce, Phil was trying to control her. I let Maria know that she got to own her truth and share it with whomever she pleased.

Once you've identified your truth for yourself, you'll want to decide who you share it with. Not everyone is safe to be let in, so you'll want to be discerning about this. I suggest dividing the people in your life into three camps that correspond to the garden metaphor I laid out in the section on boundaries in Chapter Two: your *friends*, who are free to enter your garden, and to whom you can tell your entire truth; your *bunnies*, who are allowed into most of your garden, but from whom you protect your more vulnerable vegetables, and to whom you may tell a version of the truth that lets them know what's happening but doesn't reveal too much; and your *deer*, from whom you're very protective, and to whom you tell very little.

Your *friends* are those you know you can trust. These are your best friends who have been with you along the way, or the coworker who has picked you up off the floor and covered for you when you've been barely functional. This could be certain members of your family, although, by all means, not all. The people in this camp need to have earned access to your garden; they have your back, and you know it. And if you choose not to tell them something, these folks don't take it personally, but simply lend support or give you space because they know that this period of time is about you and your needs, not them and theirs!

Your *bunnies* are those to whom you feel safe enough to say, *Yeah, we're getting divorced and it sucks. Let's just say, it's been a long time coming,* or, *We're getting divorced, and it's the best decision I've ever made!* If they ask for more information, you get to gauge how you feel. Do you feel that they're asking because they're genuinely concerned for you? If so, feel free to give them as much or as little information as you feel like divulging. Or do you feel that they're asking because they want the dirt? Consider that anyone who asks for more information than you're willing to initially offer up is likely digging for dirt, because if they were genuinely concerned about you, they'd say, *I'm so sorry; let me know if I can help in any way. I'm here for you.*

Your *deer* are the people you work with, the parents you see at school drop-off, and nosy neighbors who see the moving truck and want to know what's going on. Some of them will be respectful of your boundaries, and others will be working you hard for access to your garden. To these people you owe absolutely nothing. Do you hear me? You. Owe. These. People. Nothing. This is *your* divorce. To these people you might say, *Yes, we're getting divorced. It's a very difficult time for all of us, but we have very good support systems in place and really just request privacy at this time.* If they push for more information, you simply repeat what you've already said. Rinse and repeat as many times as it takes.

In cases of abuse, you want to be even more careful who you tell, and what you tell them. This is for your own protection. Most people who haven't experienced some form of domestic violence have no idea what to say to victims or survivors. They may ask why, if it was so bad, you stayed as long as you did, which is the least helpful thing to say to a survivor, even if well-intentioned. They may say, *Gosh, he was always so nice to me!* which may make you feel like they don't believe you. They may go on a rampage about your ex, which could compound any trauma you're already working through. Even the most well-intentioned of friends, if not trauma- or domestic violence-informed, may make you feel worse than you already do. In case of abuse, you want to protect your garden gate fiercely.

This period of your life is going to be a hard-won lesson in boundaries, and the more conscious awareness you can bring to categorizing these people in advance and deciding who you feel safe to tell what, the more prepared you'll be for the onslaught of looky-loos who aren't in it for you, but for their own egos and satisfying their need to be in-the-know.

Exercise for Deciding Whom to Tell and What You'll Say:

- Make a list of everyone in your life you'll need to tell you're divorcing.
- Put an F, B or D next to each person, depending on your relationship with them.
- Write a script for each category (*friends, bunnies, and deer*) tailoring your narrative for each person if necessary.
- Keep your scripts short and to the point, only sharing what makes you comfortable.

Co-parents for Life

For better or worse, if you're divorcing a person with whom you have children, you will be in a co-parenting relationship with this person for the rest of your life. It doesn't end when they're eighteen; there may be graduations, marriages, babies, and any number of things you'll need to be communicating about and collaborating on for as long as your children grace this earth.

My ex and I separated when my son was three-and-a-half. I had no idea the number of school meetings, doctors' appointments, medical decisions, back-and-forths of medications and stuffed animals, or serious life changes we'd have to navigate over the next fourteen years. We have vastly different parenting styles, which has led to enormous, often nasty, conflict over the years, and, despite the many boundaries we've both set, we've had to tread some extremely difficult waters, both separately and together. I don't tell you this to scare you, but just to impress upon you that divorce doesn't end the relationship you have with your spouse; it does, however, force you to expand your capacity for being in a long-term relationship with someone with whom you have a difficult history.

If you're divorcing an abuser, you may end up suffering *post-separation abuse*, in which the abuser uses the courts, children, finances, stalking, and other harassing techniques to continue to maintain power and control after the separation has taken place. In these cases, it's important to enter into a *parallel parenting* relationship, rather than a *co-parenting* one.

As I stated in Chapter Eight, in cases of abuse, learn to communicate using Bill Eddy's BIFF Method for Communication (*brief, informative, friendly,* and *firm*) and if at all possible insist on communicating through a co-parenting app, such as Our Family Wizard, or FAYR, when you draw up your parenting plan. The key to effective communication with a high-conflict personality is to not take their jabs personally. If you take everything they say or do personally, you'll perpetuate your toxic dynamic and keep responding as if you're being attacked. If, instead, you can sidestep their lobbed grenades and let them fizzle into the ether, you'll be able to respond in an emotionally detached, transactional way that simply focuses on what's absolutely necessary, addresses what's important, and ignores everything that's not.

For example, if you receive an email that says, *Lindsey, you forgot to send Aidan's lunch box this weekend, so now I have nothing to pack his lunch in on Monday morning. I can't believe you'd be so irresponsible and disrespectful. How hard is it to pack a fucking lunch box, Lindsey? I don't have time to go to your house to pick it up, so you'd better be prepared to drop it off before Sunday evening. Honestly, you call yourself a mother. SMH,* a BIFF response would be, *Hi, thanks for your email and the reminder. I'll drop it off tomorrow morning. Going forward it would be best if we each have one on hand in case of mishaps. Have a great rest of your day.*

This response is brief (it's half the length of their diatribe), informative (it gives necessary information only), friendly (you aren't picking up or responding to their nastiness), and firm (it's not asking for agreement).

Now, if your blood just started boiling, because *oh my God, they were such an asshole, how can I not respond to that?* you certainly *could* respond to it, but where would it get you? Right back into the same twisted toxic relationship you worked hard to leave. So, if you don't want them to continue to abuse you, don't give their abuse a runway to land on. Abusers abuse because they're abusers. They have an innate need to be abusive. But the more you sidestep the grenades, the less satisfying lobbing them will be. The less satisfying the impact, the fewer abuses they'll hurl, and in time they'll have to find someone else to abuse. (This is often called a *new supply.*)

Frankly, I believe all co-parents should begin their divorces with more of a parallel parenting arrangement than a co-parenting one. For many, the relief of getting out of an unhappy re-lationship is enough to be able to put negative feelings aside and move forward as friends. It's really easy to dive into being best friends, spending holidays together, even traveling to-gether after your divorce. However, this creates a number of pitfalls that are best avoided, and since I fell into every one of them, let me save you some misery.

Becoming best friends with your ex fast on the heels of your divorce can lead to the perpetuation of some of the dy-namics that led to your divorce in the first place. While people focus on getting legally divorced from their partners, they often forget to get emotionally divorced as well, which is, frankly, far more difficult. We often take (strange) comfort in the toxic dynamics of our relationships; after all, this is what a trauma bond is based on. Fighting with your ex may feel *good* to you, in that it's familiar and keeps you connected, even if negatively so. While you may be friendly a lot of the time, you're also leaving yourself vulnerable to abuse that may flare up from time to time.

When I first got divorced, my ex and I were *best friends*, and while the toxic cycles weren't as frequent as they'd been during our marriage, they still cropped up often enough for me to put an end to our friendship for a few years, about five years into our divorce. While the abuse and conflict spiked multiple times a day when we were married, it still spiked multiple times a month when we got divorced. The longer we were divorced, however, the less tolerant I became of any such conflict, so one day, after a particularly heinous incident, I put a stop to it all. I realized that I was still occupying the role of victim of his abuse, and that the only way for me to protect myself was to remove myself from any unnecessary interaction with him. What followed were about three years of parallel parenting—conversing only about our son and only when necessary—until I had firmly established my boundaries and significantly healed from the trauma of my marriage and divorce. It was only then that my ex and I were able to slowly begin to communicate more often, and in friendlier tones. The boundary I set was messy, but effective, and while we still have arguments from time to time, my ex has never abused me again.

Being close with your ex immediately after the divorce can also be super confusing for your kids. If, like I did, you've told your younger children that you're divorcing because you have a hard time getting along *and then you spend time together getting along*, this sends a mixed message, and will likely end in your kids yelling at you to get back together, as mine did over our first Thanksgiving dinner together, which was heartbreaking for everyone involved.

In the interest of the long game you're playing as co-parents, don't dive into your new dynamic blindly, or headfirst. Take some time to separate, and then ease into the relationship you want to have once you're fully separated and individualized. Doing some grief work around the loss of your relationship, and more importantly, the loss of the dream of what you thought your relationship might be, will be important here.

You may have heard that somewhere around 50 percent of first marriages end in divorce. What you may not know is that 68 percent of second marriages also end in divorce, and 74 percent of third marriages do too. This is due to what Freud called *repetition compulsion*, which is when we unconsciously repeat painful or traumatic events from our past, even when we consciously try to avoid them. In other words, we don't do the work necessary to heal the trauma we experienced, so we re-

peat patterns over and over again. Grief work is a necessary antidote to these horrifying statistics, and the unconsciously
re-traumatizing behaviors that undergird them. Unfortunately,
there's no sidestepping grief. The only way to the other side is
to go through it. When you try to sidestep it, you run the risk
of acting out in unhealthy ways, either by drinking too much,
doing drugs, overeating, or developing anxiety or depression,
or all of the above. Grief work is hard and long and painful, but
oh so necessary.

Exercise for Processing Relationship Grief:

(Partially inspired by Susan J. Elliott's Relationship Inventory
in her book *Getting Past your Breakup: How to Turn a Devastating Loss into the Best Thing that Ever Happened to You* (De Capo
Books, 2009.)

Take your time with this process. It's long, and emotionally
taxing, but it's important. Use your journal, as the questions
may elicit a lot of feelings that will be helped by journaling.

1. Make a list of everything you resent about your
    spouse. Everything. It could go on for pages. Get it
    all out until there's nothing left.
2. What were some red flags that you totally missed?
    Think back to the beginning of the relationship and
    make a list of all the early warning signs. Did you
    have an argument early on, or was there some be-
    havior that gave you a clue that this was not the
    relationship you thought it was? Maybe something
    that gave you a clue that they were capable of hurting

you deeply? What warning signs were flashing loud and clear? What did you do about it? What did you not do about it? How did you manage to rationalize it to yourself, or did you just ignore it completely? What could you have done about it way back when? Why didn't you? What compromises or bargains did you make with yourself? What price did you pay for those compromises?

3. Write down the five most hurtful incidents that have happened to you in the relationship. What was done? What was said? Was there an apology or reassurance that it would never happen again? Did it happen again? Were there apologies and promises made and not kept?

4. What did you like about your spouse that you later realized kinda sucked? For example, at first you liked that they were neat, but later realized they had a serious case of OCD; at first you loved how emotionally open they were, until later you realized that they were needy and narcissistic; maybe you thought they were really confident, but then later realized they were actually seriously controlling.

5. Now, make a list of *your* worst qualities that may have contributed to some issues in the relationship. Maybe you were easily triggered and flew off the handle. Maybe you weren't all that committed yourself. Maybe you put up walls that kept your spouse at a distance. Maybe you were controlling. In other words, look deeply at how you may have contributed to some of the problems you're having now. (Be completely honest. This is just for you.)

6. Can you identify your key childhood wounds that might have been triggered by this relationship? How does this relationship mirror your relationship with your mother? How does it mirror your relationship with your father?

7. Write the story of how you met, fell in love, and your early time together. Answer some of these questions: How did you meet? What attracted you in the first moments? What did you first feel? What fantasies did you have for the relationship? What fears did you have at first?

8. Make a list of everything you like (or have liked) about being in a relationship with your spouse. Try to view the relationship as an "other," and identify key things you really liked about the relationship itself.

9. Make a list of all your spouse's positive qualities, the things you genuinely liked about them. Perhaps they had a great sense of humor. Maybe they always brought you flowers when you were down. Maybe they were really great at organizational thinking and helped you with your business ideas. Whatever was/is good, write it down.

10. Using the information from the previous two questions, make a gratitude list for the relationship. What do you deeply appreciate about the time you had together? What gifts can you honestly say the relationship—and your spouse—have given you?

11. Make a list of everything you forgive your spouse for. Forgiveness doesn't mean the other person is no longer responsible for their behavior; it means that you're no longer going to carry a resentment about

it. Forgiveness doesn't let someone off the hook, but it does release you from the resentment that binds you to them.

12. Make a list of everything you forgive *yourself* for.

13. Make a list of everything you would ask your spouse to forgive you for if they were here right now.

14. Write your spouse a letter (that you will never give them, like, literally, *never*, under any circumstance). In it, tell them everything you forgive them for, everything you are still pissed about, everything you wish to be forgiven for, and anything else you feel is still unsaid between you. Sit with this letter. Read it over a few times to make sure it is complete. Notice how it feels in your body to have said everything you've needed to say.

15. Now go take a walk and allow this process of having said what you need to say wash over you. When you return, you may want to add a few things to your letter. Do that.

16. Sit with the letter again. Ask yourself if there is anything else you want to say.

17. When you are fully complete with this process, burn the letter. Make it a ritual. Light candles and incense, dim the lights, chant something about letting go if you want. Do a cord-cutting meditation (there are many available on YouTube). The full moon is a particularly powerful time to do this. This is your outward manifestation of your inner letting go, so make it count.

18. Now go out and do something really nice for yourself. Get a massage, go to the spa and get a scrub, go for a walk in nature. Allow the letting go to settle

into you and congratulate yourself on this momentous shift in your being.

Congratulations! This is a huge step towards healing and forgiveness. You should be very proud of yourself for completing this exercise.

Spending Time Without Your Kids

One thing I hear a lot from women who are contemplating divorce, especially those who've been stay-at-home moms, is that they can't fathom being away from their children for a day, let alone three-to-four days a week! My answer to this is, *Yes, it's hard, but it shouldn't be that hard.* When women say to me, *But my children are my life!* my inner alarm bells immediately go off, and I know they have a problem with Self-identity.

If this is you, and you can feel yourself getting defensive right now, I hear you, I really do. Believe me, I felt the same way when I was facing divorce. But that was because I had so completely lost my sense of Self in my marriage that my only identity was *Mother*. I honestly had no clue what I'd do with myself in the time I wasn't with my son. On the one hand, this makes perfect sense: being a stay-at-home mom is basically a 24/7 job. You don't get weekends off (in fact, weekends are even more hands-on), and you've trained yourself to be ever vigilant about the whereabouts, safety, happiness, and health of your children *at all times*. Even sending a child to preschool for the first time can feel really frightening. This is the first time that other people are going to have input and influence over your child. So, of course the idea of being away from them is unnerving.

But on the other hand, at least in my case, and in the cases of the thousands of women I've counseled on this, it was more than just habitual focus; it was a loss of Self that was being highlighted in the empty spaces. While married, I could busy myself with motherhood, and mask the ways in which I'd lost myself, but when I was on my own for half the week, the emptiness was inescapable. Before I went back to school and built my business, I had no idea how to fill my time. I would go for walks, shop, see friends, shop, date, shop... It took years for me to fill the void that was left in the wake of my divorce.

The time away from your children can also be important to your future, if used wisely. In fact, equal shared parenting, if safe for the children, is best for moms who are starting out on their own, especially those who've been stay-at-home moms (using the step-down plan discussed in Chapter Thirteen). It's common for stay-at-home moms to want to fight for more custody in a divorce. However, this does them a grave disservice by keeping them tethered to their exes for financial support, and extending the time it will take to restart a career and become self-supporting. If you have your children half the time, the other half can be spent healing in therapy, going back to school or taking some continuing education courses to brush up on important skills, and learning who you are at this point in your life. If, however, you fight for, and win, full custody, you may end up a full-time single working parent, or not working at all, neither of which will be healthy for your self-esteem, financial future, or stress levels.

If equal shared parenting isn't safe for your children, you should, by any and all means, work to keep them safe. It is a sad fact of the family law system in America that most judges have no training in domestic violence, and that they favor equal shared parenting to the degree that they even force children to go through dangerous *reunification* programs with abusive parents, rather than simply give the safe parent full custody. In fact, many abusive parents will accuse the safe parent of *parental alienation* when the safe parent tries to protect their children from an abuser. Parental Alienation Syndrome is a term coined by the late Richard Gardner, "based on his personal [not scientific] observations and work as an expert witness, often on behalf of fathers accused of molesting children," which has been dangerously adopted by the Father's Rights Movement today, and widely debunked by domestic violence advocates and experts (*Overview on Dr. Richard Gardner's Opinions on Pedophilia and Child Sex Abuse,* The Leadership Council on Child Abuse and Interpersonal Violence). Let me be clear, Parental Alienation Syndrome is pseudoscience, and the term should never be used.

Unfortunately, claims of parental alienation have led to the death of many children throughout the United States, including seven-year-old Kayden Mancuso. According to the California Protective Parent's website, Kayden's "protective parent, Kathy Sherlock, fought to protect her from her abusive father with a documented history of violence and mental instability. The courts refused to protect Kayden with full protective orders. On an unsupervised visit with her father, Kayden, only seven years old, was violently murdered by him on August 5, 2018."

Kayden's Law was added into the Violence Against Women's Act, passed by Congress, and signed into law by President Biden in March of 2022. Kayden's Law "incentivizes states to ensure that their child custody laws adequately protect at-risk children by:

1. Restricting expert testimony to only those who are appropriately qualified to provide it. Evidence from court-appointed or outside professionals regarding alleged abuse may be admitted only when the professional possesses demonstrated expertise and experience in working with victims of domestic violence or child abuse, including child sexual abuse.

2. Limiting the use of reunification camps and therapies which cannot be proven to be safe and effective. No 'reunification treatment' may be ordered by the court without scientifically valid and generally accepted proof of the safety, effectiveness, and therapeutic value of the particular treatment.

3. Providing evidence-based ongoing training to judges and court personnel on family violence subject matter, including: (i) child sexual abuse; (ii) physical abuse; (iii) emotional abuse; (iv) coercive control; (v) implicit and explicit bias; (vi) trauma; (vii) long- and short-term impacts of domestic violence and child abuse on children; and (viii) victim and perpetrator behaviors." (*What is Keeping Children Safe from Family Violence, or "Kayden's Law"* California Protective Parents Association)

While Kayden's Law has been adopted into the Violence Against Women's Act (VAWA), it doesn't mean it's now the law of the land. All it really means is that US state legislatures will receive financial incentives to increase child safety in custody cases. This means that each state will have to pass its own bill to protect abused children from an unsafe parent, based on the model of Kayden's Law. Many states are bringing such measures up for a vote, each sadly named for a murdered child, but we have a long way to go before all fifty states adopt these laws, and there is significant pushback from some fathers' rights groups, which are, in effect, full of domestic abusers.

Fathers' rights groups like to assert that the family law system is skewed against fathers in favor of mothers, but that's been found to be untrue. In 2017, George Washington University Professor, Joan Meier, published a study entitled "Mapping Gender: Shedding Empirical Light on Family Courts' Treatment of Cases Involving Abuse and Alienation" in which she found, among other things, that when mothers make claims of domestic violence, they are credited by the court only 41 percent of the time—meaning that 59 percent of the time, women are not believed by the court. Only 27 percent of women who accuse men of child abuse are believed by the court, and accusations of child sexual abuse are credited by the court only 15 percent of the time (unfortunately, child sexual abuse is very difficult to prove). When abusive fathers make claims of *parental alienation*, however, the court credits mothers' claims of abuse even less (from 27 percent to 18 percent in cases of child physical abuse, and 15 percent to 2 percent for child sexual abuse). Consistent with these findings, Meier also found that mothers reporting fathers' abuse actually *lost* custody of their children 26 percent of the time. This is clearly not a system that favors mothers.

Even if a judge believes a mother's claim of domestic violence, because judges aren't required to be trained in recognizing the signs of domestic violence, they often erroneously believe that if a parent has abused their spouse but never abused their children, the children will be safe with that parent. Nothing could be further from the truth. First of all, anyone who has abused their co-parent has automatically abused their children. It is child abuse to bring violence of any kind into a home. Period. Secondly, since abusers need to abuse, once the parent who's been the target of the abuse has left the house, it's very common for an abuser to turn their sights onto their children. One only has to look at Kayden's Law to see that children are not safe from domestic abusers.

If you are concerned for your children's safety, you must educate yourself on these laws and the many horrifying statistics on the danger to children when forced into custody with an unsafe parent. You can learn more about this at the National Safe Parents Organization's website (nationalsafeparents.org), at Custody Peace's Medium page, (custodypeace.medium.com) and by following Tina Swithin (onemomsbattle.com), Kaitlyn Jorgensen (kaitlynjorgensen.com), and the work of Dr. Christine Cocchiola (coercivecontrolconsulting.com), who has wonderful programs for protective parents. Unfortunately, in these cases you must become your own advocate. You cannot rely on your attorney or judge to be the experts in this as they simply are not; *you* must become the expert—which is really hard to do when you're also recovering from abuse, but your inner Mama Bear *will* find a way, and there is support out there from the advocacy groups and experts I just mentioned, as well as your local domestic violence shelter.

Spending time without your children can be hard, there's no denying it, but it's important to determine why you're uncomfortable with it. Are your children in actual danger, are you unsure how you'll spend your time without them, or are you so deeply identified as a mother that you can't fathom being anything else? In each of these cases, there's an answer. In the former, it's all about education and advocacy. In the case of the latter two, it's all about the Self work laid out for you earlier in this book.

Friendship Shift and the Loss of Family

Two things happen when you get divorced that you never count on: one is that the people around you have very surprising and personal reactions to it, and the second is that it becomes contagious. These things are actually not unrelated.

When I first separated from my ex, my two best friends of more than twenty years, both of whom had purported being in very happy, nurturing marriages I often admired and was jealous of, had extreme emotional reactions. Now, these two women had been trying to convince me to leave my marriage in some subtle and not-so-subtle ways for years. One of them even sat me down before my wedding to try to convince me not to get married. She also, apparently, had to go through a "very difficult" therapy session to process how she was going to stand up as maid of honor at my wedding. They knew I was unhappy. They knew the marriage wasn't right. And yet, when I finally separated from my husband, they both lost their ever-loving minds.

When I first separated from my husband, I reconnected with an old flame who lived 3,000 miles away (so common, it's practically cliché). iPhones were pretty new back then, and he and I were texting—a lot. I was probably more distracted than normal, and definitely not in my right mind (no one is when they go through divorce), but there was nothing dangerous going on, and I was still the loving, caring, attentive mother I'd always been. My friends, however, became extremely fearful of how this new relationship was affecting my son. (With the benefit of hindsight, I can honestly say that yes, I was on my phone a lot more, but I was also happier and more vibrant than I'd ever been, partly because of the freedom I'd just afforded myself, and partly because of the flirty attention I was getting, so if anything, my son was getting a much better version of me than he had been.)

Apparently, I wasn't going through my divorce in what my best friends considered the *right* way, so they took me out to lunch for an intervention. What ensued was one of them (the much less emotional and more controlled of the three of us) screaming bloody murder at the top of her lungs about the damage I was doing to my son in the middle of a crowded restaurant in our neighborhood. It was clear that my friend was being triggered back into her parent's ugly and violent marriage and divorce from which she had never emotionally recovered, but in that moment what I needed was my best friends' loving arms around me, not screaming bloody murder at me. As I fled the restaurant, the other friend ran after me, saying, "I'm so sorry; this wasn't the design of this lunch," to which I responded, "I can't believe you guys had a *design* at all," and walked away, shaking with rage and grief. Funnily enough, the person I turned to in my sorrow was my ex-husband, who was having similar experiences with his friends.

After that lunch, I realized that when you get divorced, you don't just drop a bomb on your own life, you drop a bomb on all of the relationships around you as well. Every friendship I had changed in the months and years following my divorce.

You don't count on that. You think your *relationship* is changing but that your *friends* (especially those who've been by your side through thick and thin for over 20 years) will still be there for you. Being abandoned by your closest friends in the middle of your divorce can be the most devastating part of the whole process, but it's also very common. By getting divorced, you are, in effect, holding a mirror up to everyone around you and making them look at their own relationships. When my ex and I announced our separation to the couples therapy group we'd been with for two years, we had an entire three-hour session of processing *for the group*. Three other couples had to process our separation and we showed up for it. It was therapeutic, healthy, and devastating for us all. They all talked about how seeing us fall was making them feel more fragile. (I'm happy to report, all of these couples are still married.)

The rest of my friends didn't have this kind of venue to process their feelings, so they just projected their own fears onto me when I needed them most. Predictably, both of my friends' marriages ended within the year following my divorce, which is what they were really afraid of when they were yelling at me. Trust me when I say that those who have the biggest reactions to your divorce will be the next to fall.

The other relationships that shift dramatically during and after divorce are the relationships with your extended family. Losing contact with your extended family can be one of the hardest side effects of divorce, and cause a whole additional layer of unexpected grief. Your in-laws may turn their backs on you, not because they don't love you, but because they believe *someone* has to be the bad guy and their loyalty will naturally be with their family member. If your divorce is contentious, parents will side with their child, as would you. That being said, I've heard a number of stories in which the parents of an abuser try to remain as neutral as possible for the sake of their grandchildren, or take the victim's side if they've witnessed the abuse.

In-laws often feel sad and confused about how they're supposed to act. If they're like my in-laws, they may have no experience of an amicable divorce, and believe they need to take sides. If your divorce is amicable, you may want to reach out to your in-laws to let them know how much you love them and that you hope your relationship will remain unchanged. If you extend this olive branch and they don't respond in kind, you'll have to take a step back for a bit. They may come around in time, especially as they witness your relationship with your ex-partner grow and flourish over time.

While we've gone through our ups and downs over the years, my in-laws and I remain extremely close to this day. My sister-in-law is one of my closest friends, and she and I text daily; my brother-in-law and I connect on some deep family issues, and my mother-in-law and I speak on the phone for hours at a time and always have at least one dinner alone together when she visits, along with all the family time we spend together. As I mentioned earlier, before his death, my father-in-law and I were very close as well.

These things are never black-and-white, nor are they set in stone. If your friends or your in-laws seem to shift away from you during your divorce, try not to take it personally, and give it some time. Sometimes people need to watch how your life unfolds before they know how they're supposed to act, or where they fit in. And sometimes their preconceived notions or past traumas will get in the way of them ever being able to support you. What's most important is that you use this time to surround yourself with people who *do* support you—and this might end up being a whole new group of friends and chosen family.

Is the Grass Really Greener on the Other Side?

When my son was about nine, we went to Disneyland for the umpteenth time, but this time he wanted to go on some of the scarier rides. We started with the Matterhorn. The line was long, as they tend to be, and my son was a bundle of nerves, excitement, and fear. Never shy, he latched on to the group of twenty-something-year-old annual passholders covered in lanyards and buttons and asked them a million questions about the ride until we finally got to the front of the line.

In order to squelch his anxiety, my son wanted to know *exactly* what to expect from the ride: how many big drops, how many jump-scares, how much darkness. While the extreme Disney fanatics ahead of us did their best to patiently walk him through it all, when we got on the ride my son was just as nervous because, of course, how do you describe a roller coaster? You have to experience it. (My son's new friends cheered him on as we boarded the ride behind them, and waited to see how he'd liked it at the end. He exited the ride flushed and amped, declaring that he wanted to do it again because it was *soooo fun!*)

Divorce is much like a roller coaster. Your life on the other side can't be determined by anyone but yourself, and, while no one has a crystal ball, there are some common experiences worth mentioning. Two questions I hear over and over again are *Will I be alone forever?* and *What if he meets someone before I do?* Let me address the second question first: he will. If you're divorcing a cis-hetero male, the odds are that he will partner again very quickly. Why? Because most men can't actually live without the free labor provided by women. Think of everything you've provided your partner: emotional labor, carrying the mental load, working the second shift, invisible labor… Now imagine taking all that away. How will he function? All of the work that you do to support his life, whether it's taking care of his emotional needs, taking care of the children, the home, what-have-you, all of that contributes to supporting *his* life and *his* success. Take that away, and he'll likely spiral into an abyss, which he'll soon need to fill.

Add to this the fact that under the patriarchy women have been taught that caretaking is our relationship currency. In much the same way a male peacock will fan its vibrant feathers in an effort to win the affections of a female, women fan our nurturing feathers when we begin a new relationship. We look around their dirty house and think, *I can help with this.* We organize their sock drawers and are endlessly patient and supportive of their emotional needs (admit it). Little by little we make the depth and richness of our currency known, and a man who's been recently deprived of his wife's emotional and physical labor will soak up all a new woman has to offer.

Meanwhile, when we get divorced, we're exhausted. We've been shelling out our labor for so long that when we're finally on our own, we don't want to have to support anyone other than ourselves and our children. When I moved out, I didn't even take the dog, that's how exhausted I was. I'd spent the previous few years taking care of two dying cats, a dying dog, a toddler, and a man-child. I just wanted to learn how to take care of myself for the first time in my life, while also taking care of my son and *no one else*. I was very excited to start dating again, and I had dreams of falling in love and remarrying, but I was in no way ready for such a thing, as I'd soon find out.

A man who abused you will re-partner even more quickly, and he'll treat his new partner better than you ever remember him treating you. He may buy her all the gifts you never got because you met him while he was just starting out, and he built his success on the back of your labor. You'll be pissed because it feels like someone else is reaping your rewards! He'll tell his new partner how toxic you were, driving a wedge between you so you'll never talk or compare stories. He'll lavish her with trips and gifts, all while dragging you through the mud or the court system. Don't be fooled into feeling jealous or angry. The likelihood is that he used some version of this tactic to lure you in too, it's just long forgotten at this point, and whether it's in two months or ten years, he *will* reveal himself to her and she might even end up on your doorstep in tears, seeking answers to some confusing questions. Let her in, make her some tea, and open your heart. After all, she is you, and she needs validation, compassion, and understanding. (Please don't reach out to his new supply to try to warn her in advance. She'll never believe you, and you'll look like the vindictive monster he's already making you out to be.)

To the question, *Will I be alone forever?* I say, *Probably not, but what if you are?* which usually gives rise to panic. The truth is, if you really want to re-partner, you'll work to make that happen for yourself someday. But again, I say, *What if you are alone forever?* because I want to impress upon you that becoming someone who doesn't need a relationship to fulfill them must be the first order of business. I've been divorced since

2009. As of writing this book, fourteen years later, I am single. I've dated a bunch, and I've had a few meaningful relationships in that time, but I've been single by choice for the last six years. Why? Because I wanted to focus on my business, myself, and my son; and I haven't yet met anyone who is a *benefit* to my life in this season, rather than a detraction from it. Since marriage benefits men and depletes women, many divorced women think twice about re-entering that imbalanced alliance. (In fact, almost 77 percent of women who divorce over fifty do not remarry.) I've spent the last fourteen years working on myself so that I am now deeply discerning about who I let into my life, and my emotional labor is no longer available without significant return. I would rather be alone than in an unhealthy, unhappy, or imbalanced relationship.

It's often said that you need to love yourself before you can love another, and I think that's bullshit. Self-love exists on a continuum and is ever evolving. But more than that, we live in a culture that consistently tells women there's something wrong with us (we're too fat, we're too wrinkled, we're too gray, we're too nerdy, we're too sexy, our eyelashes aren't long enough, our jaws aren't chiseled enough, our boobs are too big or too small, our hips too wide or too straight), and then sells us all the products, programs, and procedures to help us fix ourselves. Talk about abuse! While we are our own harshest critics, our self-criticism often stems from patriarchal and capitalist structures that present an image of inner and outer beauty almost impossible to attain—all for their more than sixty-billion-dollar gain. Additionally, self-love is not easily manifested by those of us who've had a lifetime of trauma. If you don't love yourself, it doesn't mean you don't deserve to love or be loved. It just means you've been the victim of trauma and cultural abuse. Often the love of another who can see and accept our full selves can be dramatically healing in itself.

While I don't believe self-love is the goal, I do think we should have healthy *self-esteem* in order to be in a healthy relationship, and that comes from *self-knowledge,* as discussed earlier in the book. If I don't have healthy self-esteem, I will choose partners who mirror my sense of self, and that will undoubtedly bring unhealthy partnerships into my life. Healthy self-esteem doesn't mean I'm perfect, but it means that I am aware of my full Self—wonderful qualities and flaws—and am able to express my faults to my partner and take full responsibility for how they make me show up in a relationship.

For example, when newly divorced and dating, Colleen used to get unreasonably angry if a date was even ten minutes late. We began discussing this on our coaching calls. She was indignant and would sometimes go on a tirade. I asked her what made her so upset, and she told me that it was disrespectful, and that if someone wanted to go on a date with her, he should show up on time, and if he couldn't be bothered to do that, then screw him! I kept questioning her, knowing that this was deeper than Colleen was even aware of. It turned out that when Colleen was a little girl, her father was an addict and was in and out of her life at various intervals. There were many times when Colleen would be waiting for her father to pick her up for her weekend with him and he wouldn't show up. As a child, Colleen learned to stuff her emotions. She didn't want her mom to see her upset because she knew her mom would just yell and rage at her dad. She didn't want her dad to see her upset because she didn't want him not to come the next time.

But now Colleen's suppressed rage found a new outlet: the unsuspecting man who had trouble finding parking and showed up a few minutes late to a date. As we dug into Colleen's rage, what we found was a wounded, scared little girl who felt unloved, unworthy, and unwanted. These feelings could not have been more valid for Little Girl Colleen, but because they weren't addressed in the proper time and place (either with her dad, or in therapy later), they were leaking out the edges in ways that got in the way of the one thing Colleen really wanted: love.

When Colleen was able to understand that her response to these men was not right-sized for the occurring event, and was able to tie it to her past trauma, she was able to remain in her adult brain and communicate her needs to the men she dated. Her new-found self-knowledge allowed her to learn to say to the men she dated, "I have some historical issues around lateness. It would really help me if you'd call or text if you're going to be late; that way I won't get into a story in my head and I'll be happy to see you when you arrive." She didn't have to get into detail until they got to know each other better, which would create greater intimacy down the line. This self-knowledge helped Colleen have higher self-esteem because she wasn't acting in ways that ultimately made her feel ashamed and really bad about herself.

Another question I get asked about the other side is, *When can I start dating?* and my answer is, *Whenever you want! But you must know the difference between dating and relationships, and not dive into a relationship with the first person you date who gives you goosebumps.* (The only exception to this is if you live in a state in which dating before you're fully divorced can be considered adultery. Check the laws in your state—and the penalties.)

At the time of my separation, my therapist told me that I could consider myself *certifiably insane* for the next two years. *Certifiably insane.* She actually said those words. "But I'm going to find the love of my life within the next six months!!" I protested. "Certifiably insane," she repeated.

Truer words were never spoken.

When I look back at the choices I made as I stepped out into the brand-new world of singlehood, I'm embarrassed, ashamed, and often amused. I think about the men I dated and I cringe. One would *have* to be certifiably insane to think she was in love with a stoner who lived three thousand miles away, who would turn off all the lights to video-chat so she couldn't quite see what he looked like and who ended up having a complete mental breakdown that resulted in him putting tinfoil on the ceiling because *they* were watching. Or the manly, buff, bear-like millionaire inventor who carried around a tiny Maltese all day every day and rented out his Malibu mansion for porn shoots. (To be fair, I only found this out later.)

Certifiably insane? Likely. But ultimately harmless to my family and myself because there always came a point when my thrice weekly therapy sessions paid off and I came to my senses. The insanity lessened marginally over time, and eventually I was making smarter, more informed, *sane* choices. These more informed choices came about when my therapist urged me to stop fixating on whether or not these men liked *me*, but to take my own temperature to gauge whether or not *I* liked *them*. The idea was absolutely radical to my codependent brain, and it took many years, and a lot of work, for it to take root.

So, to you I say, go forth and date! But keep taking your own temperature, and consider early dating to be some of the greatest exploration of Self imaginable. Know that you likely won't be ready to enter into a healthy relationship for at least a year and a half post-separation because, as my therapist advised, you'll be certifiably insane. (Side note: I had another therapist use the words *certifiably insane* a couple of years ago about a friend of mine who'd just gotten divorced. They must teach this in therapy school.)

Women will often tell me about the dates they go on post-divorce, and they'll tell me how *amazing* the new guy is. I remind them that anyone can be amazing for a few hours at a time. Everyone is on their best behavior for the first handful of dates. You don't know who someone really is until you've known them through a full cycle of seasons, at increasing levels of intimacy. Go slowly. Take your time. And keep the focus on how you feel while you're with them—and when you're apart. If, when you're apart, they bombard you with texts, gifts, and flowers, and you're in a constant state of *swoon,* you're being *love-bombed* and the red flags are waving. The reason dating experts recommend no more than one or two dates per week in the beginning, and to date multiple people at once, is that you need the time between dates to truly reflect on how you feel about the other person. The purpose of love-bombing is to keep you destabilized so you can't think with your discerning, adult brain. Additionally, if, when you're with the person, you feel butterflies and your heart races, and you get that *crazy feeling,* please understand that your central nervous system is reacting to something unconsciously, and that what you're feeling is actually *anxiety*. This is usually brought about when the unconscious recognizes toxic behaviors that it's seen before, and this is your cue to *run*. The more intense an initial connection, the more likely it is to be unhealthy.

If, when you're with this new person, and apart from them, you feel calm, rational, interested, curious, attracted, and intrigued, congratulations, keep going... *slowly.*

In answer to the general question, *Is the grass greener on the other side?* I say, *It absolutely can be, but you must do the work on yourself to make it so.* As they say, the grass is greener where you water it. But if you've spent years watering dead grass that won't grow, you've done your part. If you've done all you can to heal your relationship, if you've kept your side of the street as clean as you possibly can, and if your relationship is still not working, it could truly be unworkable. If that's the case, then yes, the grass will be greener, as long as you water and fertilize it. After all, it's your grass.

I once met a man who had been separated for about two years. He and his ex-wife had no children and one day she up and left him with, according to him, no warning and no explanation. Two years later, when I asked why he thought she'd left, he said, "My best guess is that she had a psychotic break." I was dumbfounded. He hadn't taken the two years after his separation to figure out what might have been missing in his marriage, and to examine what his part might have been. He'd simply decided that she had had a psychotic break, and while that may have been true, I highly doubt it.

Divorce is fertile ground for self-realization and growth, as long as you take the opportunity that's been given to you. If you don't, you'll end up standing on a different patch of dry, dead grass wondering how the hell you ended up here once again. If you do, you'll be out there watering your lush, green lawn, and one day you'll look over and see someone standing nearby watering their own lush, green lawn, and then you just might choose to water closer and closer to one another until you merge your lawns into one big patch of vibrantly green grass large enough for you and all your kids.

Or, you'll just keep watering your own lawn and feel fully content to sit on your chaise with a book and some iced tea, enjoying the fruits of your own damn labor.

Acknowledgments

I FIRST WANT TO ACKNOWLEDGE you, dear reader, along with my podcast listeners, social media followers, Facebook community members, and my amazing clients for opening your hearts to me and for sharing some of your darkest and most difficult secrets. I truly, deeply love each and every one of you, and I thank you from the bottom of my heart for reading this book, and for being its main source of inspiration. I quite literally couldn't do what I do without you.

This book is dedicated to my son, Emmett, who kept pushing me to write it. All kids think their moms are the bee's knees, but Emmett's belief that I could—and *should*—write this book kept me going at some of my lowest and most difficult points. When your kid looks at you and says, "Mom, when are you writing your book?" you write your book! The idea of disappointing him was too much to bear. I love you, bud. You are my everything.

To my parents, thank you for being relentless champions of anything that I do. I'm so grateful for the sacrifices and hard work you put in to shaping me into the woman I am today. And thank you for getting divorced so I could become the world's youngest divorce coach to all my friends in kindergarten and beyond.

Thank you to my agents, Holly Root and Alyssa Maltese at Root Literary, for taking a chance on me and my book, and for getting it into the perfect hands. You have been an incredible support during this entire process, and I'm so grateful for you both. (Shoutout to C.J.

Redwine, who I hired as a book coach, but who made me stop writing and submit my proposal to Holly.)

Thank you to my amazing editor, Denise Silvestro, and everyone at Kensington who had a hand in bringing this book to life. From our first conversation, I knew Denise shared my vision, not just for this book, but for what I want for all women. I immediately felt confident that my book would be in the right hands with her, and I was absolutely right.

Thank you to Emily Kristofferson who keeps my business running and my sanity in check. There's no way I'd be able to write a book or run my business without you at the helm. You've changed my life. You're the best business manager in the universe, and I'm beyond lucky I get to work with you.

Thank you to Darlene Victoria for keeping my podcast on the air for the last six years. You're the sweetest and the best podcast editor and producer a girl could hope for. I swear I'd have stopped podcasting years ago were it not for your professional, magic touch.

Thank you to Mark A. Merriman, my attorney, for looking out for me, and also for being a wonderful friend who brings hilarity to my Facebook feed every day. #resist

Thank you to Martina Martinez who not only keeps my house clean, but is a valued member of our entire family, and an inspiration as a single mom of three doing it all her own.

Huge thanks to Laura Belgray and Zoë Kors who helped me through writing my proposal, choosing an editor, and writing my book. I am so incredibly grateful for your friendship, your inspiration, and the fires you kept lighting under my ass.

Enormous thanks to Susan Guthrie, Esq., Dr. Christine Cocchiola, and Stacy de la Rosa for the read-throughs, notes, and confidence boosts.

I couldn't do any of what I do without the support and camaraderie of my colleagues, most of whom I consider dear friends. Susan Guthrie, Esq., Michelle Dempsey-Multack, Christina McGhee, Dr. Christine Cocchiola, Gabrielle Hartley, Zawn Villines, Leslie Morgan

Steiner, Annette Oltmans, Tina Swithin, and so many more—there are not enough words to express how grateful I am to be in this field with you. I learn from each of you every day, and you make me a better coach and advocate.

Huge shoutout to Bea, Victoria, Katie, Liz, Jarius, Erica, Alyson, and Beth who have dedicated countless hours to keeping my Facebook group running and safe for all members. Your selfless dedication to my work and our group humbles me. Thank you from the bottom of my heart.

I am blessed with so many amazing and wonderful friends, all of whom have contributed to bringing this book to life in one way or another: Peggy Woo, Kate Movius, Mindy LeMoine, Lisa Gilford, Tracey Howard Heckel, Robert Bahedry, Michelle Dozois, Miry Whitehill, Beavers, Bitches, B-Used-to-Bes and Breakthru Babes, thank you. Seriously. I'd be lost without you.

Thank you, Ray Ford, for being the best best friend, and *older brother* a girl could have. Thank you for being a guiding light in Emmett's life and for the psychic ability to know when to call your sister Baby, we a stah!! Hookah loves you. NMRK.

My ex-husband once wrote to me, "Our relationship is vast and it can't always stay in narrow lanes. The twenty-five years of closeness has twists and turns and can't be categorized simply." We have one of the most complex relationships in the world: People who have loved each other, created a life together, broken up, and still remain connected for life. To do that successfully takes more work than most can imagine, and I'm beyond grateful for the work we've both put in to keep this strange, vast machine running. For all our twists and turns, I think we've done an amazing job raising our beautiful, talented, phenomenal kid together and I am forever grateful for your partnership and friendship, and for your support of my work and this book.

A final note of gratitude to Jeff Stubblefield, who was the very first person to say, "Your blog posts really helped me through my divorce; have you thought of writing a book?" I hadn't. But then I did. And now I have.

Bibliography

"Financial Abuse." Pennsylvania Coalition Against Domestic Violence. Accessed June 23, 2023. https://www.pcadv.org/financial-abuse/.

"FreeFrom." 2023. https://www.freefrom.org/.

"Justice Ruth Bader Ginsburg's 1992 Commencement Speech." Lewis & Clark Law School. September 24, 2020. https://law.lclark.edu/live/news/44348 -justice-ruth-bader-ginsburgs-1992-commencement.

"Livable Wage by State." Wise Voter. March 5, 2020. https://wisevoter.com/state -rankings/livable-wage-by-state/.

"Overview of Dr. Richard Gardner's Opinions on Pedophilia and Child Sexual Abuse." The Leadership Council on Child Abuse and Interpersonal Violence. http://www.leadershipcouncil.org/1/pas/RAG.html.

"The Allstate Foundation." 2023. https://allstatefoundation.org/.

"The Duluth Model." Domestic Abuse Intervention Programs. https://www.the duluthmodel.org/.

"The Male Emotional Suppression Cycle in 50 Seconds. Just the Brutal Facts." Remaking Manhood. April 23, 2017. Video, https://www.youtube.com/watch? v=CBMFmLVMGoY&ab_channel=RemakingManhood.

"What Is Keeping Children Safe from Family Violence or "Kayden's Law"." California Protective Parent's Association. 2022. https://www.caprotectivepar ents.org/federal-laws-to-state-laws.

"Abigail Adams to John Adams, 31 March 1776," Founders Online, National Archives, https://founders.archives.gov/documents/Adams/04-01-02 -0241. [Original source: The Adams Papers, Adams Family Correspondence, vol. 1, December 1761–May 1776, ed. Lyman H. Butterfield. Cambridge, MA: Harvard University Press, 1963, pp. 369–371.]

Adams, Adrienne E. "Measuring the Effects of Domestic Violence on Women's Financial WellBeing." *Center for Financial Security, University of Wisconsin-Madison,* (2011). Accessed June 23, 2023.

Anonymous. 2022. *Cheatingland: The Secret Confessions of Men Who Stray.* New York: Atria.

Arkowitz, Hal, and Scott O. Lilienfeld. "Is Divorce Bad for Children." Scientific American, March 1, 2013. https://www.scientificamerican.com/article/is-divorce-bad-for-children/.

Bancroft, Lundy. "Narcissists Vs Abusers." Lundy Bancroft. November 30, 2021. https://lundybancroft.com/narcissists-vs-abusers/.

Bancroft, Lundy. 2003. *Why Does He Do That: Inside the Minds of Angry and Controlling Men.* London: Berkley.

Beattie, Melody. 2022. *Codependent No More: How to Stop Controlling Others and Start Caring for Yourself.* New York: Spiegel & Grau.

Belkin, Lisa. "The Opt-Out Revolution." *The New York Times Magazine,* October 26, 2003.

Bennetts, Leslie. 2007. *The Feminine Mistake: Are We Giving Up Too Much?* 2nd ed. New York: Hyperion.

Bergen, Raquel K., and Elizabeth Barnhill. "Marital Rape: New Research and Directions." VAWnet. National Resource Center on Domestic Violence (NRCDV), February 1, 2006. https://vawnet.org/material/marital-rape-new-research-and-directions.

Berman, Jillian. "Women's Unpaid Work Is the Backbone of the American Economy." MarketWatch. April 18, 2018. https://www.marketwatch.com/story/this-is-how-much-more-unpaid-work-women-do-than-men-2017-03-07.

Breslau, J et al. "A multinational study of mental disorders, marriage, and divorce." *Acta psychiatrica Scandinavica* vol. 124,6 (2011): 474-86. doi:10.1111/j.1600-0447.2011.01712.x

Byrd, Alita. "Fighting Abuse in the Faith Community." *Spectrum Magazine,* July 23, 2021. https://spectrummagazine.org/interviews/2021/fighting-abuse-faith-community.

Chapman, Gary. 1992. *The Five Love Languages: How to Express Heartfelt Commitment to Your Mate.* Chicago: Northfield.

Carson, Daniel L., Amanda J. Miller, Sharon Sassler, and Sarah Hanson. "The Gendered Division of Housework and Couples' Sexual Relationships: A Reexamination." *Journal of Marriage and Family,* (2016). Accessed June 25, 2023. https://doi.org/10.1111/jomf.12313.

Cocchiola, Dr. Christine. "Coercive Control Consulting." Dr. Christine Marie Cocchiola. https://coercivecontrolconsulting.com/.

Cunha, Darlena. "The Divorce Gap." *The Atlantic*, April 18, 2016.

Custody Peace: https://custodypeace.medium.com/

Diagnostic and Statistical Manual of Mental Disorders. 2013. 5th ed. American Psychiatric Association.

Doyle, Glennon. 2020. *Untamed*. New York: The Dial Press.

Eddy, Bill LCSW, Esq. 2011. *BIFF: Quick Responses to High-conflict People, Their Personal Attacks, Hostile Emails and Social Media Meltdowns*. Scottsdale: Unhooked Books.

Eddy, Bill LCSW, Esq. 2020. *BIFF for Coparent Communication: Your Guide to Difficult Coparent Texts, Emails, and Social Media Posts*. Scottsdale: Unhooked Books.

Elliott, Susan J. 2009. *Getting Past Your Breakup: How to Turn a Devastating Loss into the Best Thing that Ever Happened to You*. Cambridge: De Capo.

Emma. "You Should've Asked." Emma. May 20, 2017. https://english.emmaclit.com/2017/05/20/you-shouldve-asked/.

Flannery, Shelley. "A Guide to Coercive Control How to Recognize This Subtle yet Dangerous Form of Domestic Abuse." DomesticShelters.Org. August 4, 2021. https://www.domesticshelters.org/articles/identifying-abuse/a-guide-to-coercive-control.

Frank, Britt. 2022. *The Science of Stuck: Breaking through Inertia to Find Your Path Forward*. London: TarcherPerigee.

Green, Mark. 2016. *Remaking Manhood, Stories from the Front Lines of Change*. Create Space Independent Publishing Platform.

Helliwell, J. F., Layard, R., Sachs, J. D., De Neve, J.-E., Aknin, L. B., & Wang, S. (Eds.). (2022). World Happiness Report 2022. New York: Sustainable Development Solutions Network.

Herman, Judith L. 2022. *Trauma and Recovery: The Aftermath of Violence—From Domestic Abuse to Political Terror*. New York: Basic Books.

Hull, Megan, and Dr. Anna Pickering Ph.D. "Sex Addiction Facts and Statistics." The Recovery Village. August 22, 2022. https://www.therecoveryvillage.com/process-addiction/sex-addiction/sexual-addiction-statistics/.

Jorgensen, Kaitlyn. "Creating Stronger Strategies in Response to Intimate Partner Violence & Post-Separation Abuse." Kaitlyn Jorgensen. The Family Court Strategist, https://www.kaitlynjorgensen.com/.

Karakurt, Günnur, and Kristin E Silver. "Emotional abuse in intimate relationships: the role of gender and age." Violence and victims vol. 28,5 (2013): 804-21. doi:10.1891/0886-6708.vv-d-12-00041

Kirshenbaum, Mira. 1997. *Too Good to Leave, Too Bad to Stay*. New York: Plume.

Lambert, Carol A. MSW. "Marital Rape Is Criminalized But Not Upheld: Legal Loopholes Protect the Rapist in These Cases." Psychology Today. March 10, 2022. https://www.psychologytoday.com/us/blog/mind-games/202203/marital-rape-is-criminalized-not-upheld.

Marriage Recovery Center. https://marriagerecoverycenter.com/.

McDugal, Sarah. 2019. *Myths We Believe, Predators We Trust: 37 Things You Don't Want to Know About Abuse in Church (But You Really Should)*. Wilder Journey Press.

McGhee, Christina. "Coparenting Specialist Certification Training." Mosten Guthrie Academy. March 16, 2022.

McGhee, Christina. *Parenting Apart: How Separated and Divorced Parents Can Raise Happy and Secure Kids*. New York: Berkley, 2010.

Meier, Joan S. and Dickson, Sean, "Mapping Gender: Shedding Empirical Light on Family Courts' Treatment of Cases Involving Abuse and Alienation" (2017), GWU Legal Studies Research Paper No. 2017-43. Available at SSRN: https://ssrn.com/abstract=2999906

Mellody, Pia, Andrea W. Miller, and J. Keith Miller. 2003. *Facing Codependence: What It Is, Where It Comes from, how It Sabotages Our Lives*. 2nd ed. New York: Harper & Row.

Mills, Lindsey. "The Science Behind Women's Intuition." Executive Matchmakers, March 8, 2021. https://www.executivematchmakers.com/the-science-behind-womens-intuition/.

National Coalition Against Domestic Violence (2020). Domestic violence. Retrieved from https://assets.speakcdn.com/assets/2497/domestic_violence-2020080709350855 pdf?1596811079991.

National Domestic Violence Hotline. National Domestic Violence Hotline, Accessed June 23, 2023. https://www.thehotline.org/.

National Safe Parent's Organization: https://www.nationalsafeparents.org/

Peck, M. Scott. 1978. *The Road Less Traveled: A New Psychology of Love, Values, and Spiritual Growth*. New York: Simon & Schuster.

Pew Research Center, April, 2018, "The Changing Profile of Unmarried Parents"

Rodsky, Eve. 2019. *Fair Play: A Game Changing Solution for when You Have Too Much to Do (and More Life to Live)*. New York: Putnam.

Sohn, Heeju. "Health Insurance and Risk of Divorce: Does Having Your Own Insurance Matter?." *Journal of marriage and the family* vol. 77,4 (2015): 982-995. doi:10.1111/jomf.12195

Steinberg, Amanda. 2017. *Worth It: Your Life, Your Money, Your Terms*. New York: Gallery Books.

Stokes, Kyle. "Here's How Much Money LA Parents Are Fundraising For Schools, And What It Buys." LAist. January 10, 2022. https://laist.com/news/edu cation/los-angeles-unified-parent-fundraising.

Swithin, Tina. One Mom's Battle. https://www.onemomsbattle.com/

Tessler, Bari. 2016. *The Art of Money: A Life-Changing Guide to Financial Happiness*. Berkeley: Parallax Press.

W., Bill, and Dr. Bob. 2002. *The Big Book of Alcoholics Anonymous*. 4th ed. New York: Alcoholics Anonymous World Services.

W., Bill. 1952. *Twelve Steps and Twelve Traditions: The "Twelve and Twelve" —Essential Alcoholics Anonymous Reading*. 1st ed. Alcoholics Anonymous World Services, Inc.

Wallerstein, Judith. 2001. *The Unexpected Legacy of Divorce: A 25 Year Landmark Study*. New York: Hyperion.

Wezerek, Gus, and Kristen R. Ghodsee. "Women's Unpaid Labor Is Worth $10,900,000,000,000." New York Times. March 5, 2020. https://www.ny times.com/interactive/2020/03/04/opinion/women-unpaid-labor.html.

Whitworth, Laura, Karen Kimsey-House, and Henry Kimsey-House. 2011. *Co-Active Coaching: Changing Business, Transforming Lives*. Nicholas Brealey Publishing.